MIRACLES OF THE GODS

By Erich von Däniken

MIRACLES
OF THE GODS

A Hard look at
The Supernatural

by

ERICH VON DÄNIKEN

Translated from the German

by

MICHAEL HERON

SOUVENIR PRESS

Originally published in German by Econ-Verlag under the title
ERSCHEINUNGEN: Phänomene die die Welt erregen.
Copyright © 1974 by Econ-Verlag, Düsseldorf und Wien.

Translation copyright © 1975 by Dell Publishing Co., Inc.
and Souvenir Press, Ltd

First British Edition published 1975 by Souvenir Press Ltd,
43 Great Russell Street, London WC1B 3PA
and simultaneously in Canada by
J. M. Dent & Sons (Canada) Ltd,
Ontario, Canada

ISBN 0 285 62174 2

Printed in Great Britain by
Bristol Typesetting Co. Ltd,
Barton Manor, St Philips, Bristol

CONTENTS

FOREWORD

This is a book I had to write from the heart. I've been carrying it around inside me for ten years, ever since my first visit to Lourdes, that vast caravanserai where hope, despair and commercialism thrive side by side. I was haunted by the images and dirges I had seen and heard there.

While I was following the trail of my astronaut gods through the five continents, I made a point of visiting every accessible visionary shrine. How alike they all were in essence! It became increasingly clear to me that the phenomenon of visions is something that concerns us all. I did not forget my space-travelling gods, but there are some books that ripen like autumn fruit.

What are the people who seem to be predisposed to have visions really like?

Are they psychologically unbalanced religious fanatics?

Are their 'miracles' simply an attempt to ingratiate themselves with the Christian churches, especially the Roman Catholic Church, that accept their wonders as 'genuine'?

Did the dogmas of the Catholic Church, which also play a vital role in visions, originate by divine inspiration?

Are we really supposed to believe that God's word, the last Court of Appeal when authoritative Christian judgments are delivered, is inspired by the Holy Ghost?

Are the multifarious miracles which undoubtedly happen at places of pilgrimage delusions or self-delusions?

Is there a broad basis of medical and scientific fact behind these miracles which makes them credible and explicable?

While mountains of documentary material were piling up, while I was making special journeys to places of pilgrimage, while I was rummaging in many of the world's great libraries, a deluge of questions assailed me. As I am not by nature the sort of person who can *believe*, in the good old-fashioned way, but want to *know* what can be explained by our god-given reason without appealing to an anonymous and much-abused Holy Ghost, I set to work. I set to work as a curious labourer in God's vineyard, as someone who considers God too exalted an arbiter to be constantly invoking him in support of his arguments.

After studying visions for years, I think I can say fairly safely that this is the first compendium of its kind. Consequently some questions remain open to discussion, but I hope that in the future competent scholars and ecclesiastical courts, too, will accept my researches into the cause and effect of the vast and complicated field of miracles and visions to rectify frankly and honestly the false conceptions that are still in circulation.

I should like to thank Dr Robert Kehl, Zurich, most sincerely for many suggestions and for his special help when he acted as guest author for one section. Dr Kehl first studied theology, but later switched to law and political science. His legal commentaries are in daily use by Swiss lawyers and he has made a name for himself with two important works on moral theology, among many others.

At the same time I should like to express my thanks to the thirty-two publishers who are going to arrange for the world-wide publication of this book.

Visions are real, they do exist.
Visions arise in intelligent brains.
Every intelligent brain has the prerequisites for creating visions.
The impulse for producing visions is of extraterrestrial origin.

* * *

To establish my hypothesis of the visit of extraterrestrial beings to our globe I drew a great deal of information from mythology. This store of knowledge from the old chronicles is fascinating because it preserved for mankind *Facts* with implications whose meaning and significance the writer could not recognize in his time. As far as contacts between terrestrial and extraterrestrial beings are concerned, mythology is a treasure trove with more than a little importance.

* * *

Extraterrestrials visited this and other solar systems, and on the planets that seemed suitable, they left behind scions 'in their own image'. Certain groups of these descendants have an advantage over us: they tamed, developed, and trained the 'brain, the monster' better than we have done. These preferred students or overripe intelligences are sending energetic thought impulses to us, their brothers and sisters of the same heritage. These impulses are intended to stimulate and enlarge our consciousness.

* * *

A few 'chosen people' – I do not mean religious personalities – have always found access to the wonderful unconscious, from which they evoked *visionary* great discoveries.

Chapter 1

VISIONS – DO THEY EXIST?

UNFORTUNATELY I have never witnessed a vision. Not one of the 12,000 saints has ever said so much as 'Good day' to me, but since I was first at Lourdes ten years ago I have realized that the phenomenon of visions is something that concerns us all. I saw people in ecstasy, I heard their doleful plaints, and observed endless suffering. I was disgusted by the exploitation of credulous creatures. I saw no miracles. 125 years ago a fourteen-year-old girl saw visions at Lourdes: today five million pilgrims visit her shrine year after year. 'Lourdes' stands as an example for hundreds and thousands of places of pilgrimage where miracles are 'performed' under much the same conditions.

How can we explain this mystery, the 'perception of divine grace in man', to use the Catholic vocabulary?

It always begins with individuals or small groups of people having a vision of members of the Holy Family – in the Christian west mainly Mary, mother of Jesus, one of the archangels, or even Jesus Christ or God the Father in person. The apparitions seen in visions are not neutral. Those who appear do not come as mere observers, all smiles and blessings – they tell men what they may and what they must do and what they are strictly forbidden to do. All personified visions assert that they are envoys from heaven and divine messengers with the power to save, redeem and even to destroy mankind. They interfere with religious and political affairs, they infiltrate and dominate the brains of mass assemblies.

I went on pursuing my astronaut gods, but I could not forget the deep impression Lourdes made on me. I collected 'official' publications and pamphlets about visions of the sort offered for sale at the pilgrimage shrines which spring up wherever visions have been seen. In *every* case and in *every* place individual visionaries or small groups of them unleash an unending sequence of processions, whether the Church has already recognized the 'miracle', forbidden it or merely tolerated it in silence. 'The Church gives its blessing to what it cannot prevent' (Kurt

Tucholsky). The human longing to *believe* in miracles is always stronger than any prohibition.

A few years ago a representative public opinion poll was held in West Germany and Berlin. 53 per cent of the people questioned believed in miracles and visions, 36 per cent did not and 11 per cent did not know. I assume that those results were not solely representative of Western Germany and the inhabitants who were questioned. There are countries, especially Catholic ones, where the percentage of those who believe in miracles is much higher.

In what primitive soil does this belief flourish? What obviously timeless force makes it thrive? Independently of space and time and culture? Untouched by the kind and quality of the different religions?

In order to understand the phenomenon at all, you have to get to know the 'visionaries', places and circumstances involved. So at the beginning of this account I am giving detailed sketches of some astonishing cases of visions which have all the essential characteristics of such miracles.

*   *   *

The event which made Montichiari, five miles south of Brescia, Italy, an attraction took place in the spring of 1947.

A young nurse called Pierina Gilli saw a beautiful lady in a violet dress floating in the air in the hospital chapel. The stranger was weeping. Three swords stuck out of her breast but not a drop of blood flowed. The mysterious apparition said in a mournful voice: 'Prayer, sacrifice, penance.'

The pious Miss Pierina was perplexed. Was it a ghost? Were her eyes and her reason deceiving her? Or had she, the simple Pierina, had a 'genuine' vision? At first she kept the extraordinary experience to herself.

On 13 July 1947, the miracle was repeated. This time the beautiful unknown was dressed in white and there were no horrible swords, but she was adorned with three roses, one white, one red and one yellow, which again protruded from her breast. Pierina was frightened and asked: 'Who are you?' The lady smiled and answered: 'I am the mother of Jesus and the mother of all. . . . Every year I want 13 July to be observed in honour of the "mysterious rose" *(Rosa Mystica)*. . . .'[1] Slowly the vision faded.

The miraculous apparition was repeated on 22 October, and on 16 and 22 November 1947, in the village church. On these occasions the strange lady answered a number of Pierina's questions. The last of these encounters was especially dramatic because the stranger solemnly promised to reappear at noon on 8 December in the village church.

The news of Pierina's strange experiences had long ago spread beyond Montichiari until the whole of Lombardy knew about them. So it was not really surprising that on 8 December several thousand people travelled there, filling the church to bursting point and blocking the streets. It took quite an effort to drag the main character in the drama, Pierina Gilli, through the wall of humanity into the church. She knelt down in the middle of the nave on the spot where she had on three occasions met the beautiful lady, whom the people had long since christened the 'Blessed Virgin'. She began to say the rosary together with the crowded congregation of believers and curiosity-seekers. Suddenly she cried out: 'Oh, the Madonna!'

There was dead silence. No one could see anything, or rather, some people were not quite sure whether they could make something out or not. At all events, everyone fixed their eyes on Pierina so as not to miss the conversation between their countrywoman and the Blessed Virgin. Information was passed on to the expectant crowd outside the church in brief hasty whispers.

Pierina saw the Blessed Virgin, so the story goes, on a high snow-white staircase, once again adorned with white, yellow and red roses. With an otherworldly smile the lady proclaimed: 'I am the Immaculate Conception. I am Mary of Grace, mother of my divine son Jesus Christ.'

As she descended the white staircase, she said to Pierina: 'Now that I have come to Montichiari I wish to be called "the mysterious rose".' When she reached the bottom step, she promised: 'Whoever prays on this tile and weeps tears of repentance will find a sure ladder to heaven and receive grace and protection through my maternal heart.'

For nineteen long years nothing happened.

As so often happens, Pierina was mocked by some and also referred to as a saint by others. After 8 December 194 church of the vision was the goal of believers in mirac people in search of a cure, for a series of miracles took place here in Montichiari, there is no doubt about that.

*　*　*

Pierina spent 'white Sunday' of 17 April 1966, in the neighbouring village of Fontanelle, which is only about two miles from Montichiari. While Pierina was sitting on the steps that led to a small spring, to her complete surprise the 'mysterious rose' hovered over the surface of the water. She ordered Pierina to kiss the steps three times from top to bottom and told her to set up a crucifix to the left of the bottom step. The vision said that anyone who was sick should pray to the Lord Jesus for their sins to be forgiven and kiss the crucifix before taking water from the spring to drink.

Pierina carried out her orders.

At about 11.40 on 13 May 1966, when about twenty people were praying with her near the spring, the 'mysterious rose' appeared again and voiced this specific wish: 'I wish a spacious basin to be made here so that the sick can immerse themselves in it.' Pierina, now on intimate terms, asked the rose-bedizened lady: 'What shall we call the spring?' The lady answered: 'The spring of grace.' Pierina continued: 'What do you want to happen here at Fontanelle?' 'Works of charity for sick people who come here.'[2] With that the Blessed Virgin vanished.

The sick can be cured at this spring at Fontanelle! The message went round the countryside like wildfire: bring the sick here! Miraculous cures actually took place.

*　*　*

The afternoon of 8 June 1966. More than 100 people knelt in prayer at the spring. Pierina arrived soon after three o'clock. She told the visitors to say the rosary with her. A few moments later she interrupted the prayer and cried: 'Look up at the sky!'

In addition to Pierina, some of the faithful also saw the Blessed Virgin floating over a cornfield, six metres above the spring.

Once again the lady was wearing her three roses and requested them to make hosts from the ears of corn. She instructed them that these hosts should be taken to Rome and on 13 October to

Fatima. When she had given this instruction, the lady was about to depart when Pierina entreated her to stay a little longer. The Blessed Virgin turned round to her chosen vessel, Pierina, who relayed to her the wishes and questions of believers, priests and sick people.

The afternoon of 6 August 1966. Over 200 people were praying at the spring. Pierina arrived at 14.30 and once again asked everyone to say the rosary. During the fourth mystery of the rosary Pierina cried: 'Our dear lady is here!'

Prayers and conversation died away. Everyone listened as Pierina conversed with a being who was invisible to them. Asked for more detailed instructions about the home-made hosts, the 'mysterious rose' said that some of the corn should be sent to her 'beloved son, Pope Paul', so that it should be blessed in his presence. Bread rolls were to be baked with the remaining corn and distributed in Fontanelle in memory of her coming.

Since then people have hoped and prayed in Fontanelle and Montichiari. Every day and every night. As in many places where visions have taken place.

*　　*　　*

Taken by and large, that is a classical example of a vision. A person unknown before the miraculous event sees 'something'. Confused and perplexed by the experience, he or she spreads the news and summons the faithful to the spot. Are they specially qualified people? Are they more devout than the average? Are they religious bigots? Are they extroverts? Do they want to get into the limelight?

In an attempt to answer these questions, I collected 'visions' for ten whole years. When I began I had no idea what an incredible mass of printed matter would accumulate. I have been selective, choosing characteristic cases to stand for countless others, so that I can offer explanations of the phenomena on the basis of this extensive sample.

When I say that the estimated number of visions in the Christian world alone is over 40,000 (!) you can imagine how varied the material is. Riding a bold steeplechase through history down to the present day I am going to present the reader with documented cases of visions. Not until the vast terrain has been cleared of undergrowth will it be possible to show what conclusions can be drawn, and what explanations can be offered or are theoretically conceivable.

*   *   *

Every year on 16 August in Iborra, Spain, the faithful pray to a blood-soaked cloth. This relic* has been the object of religious veneration since the year 1010.

At that time the Right Reverend Bernard Olivier is supposed to have been assailed by doubts when during the mass the tintinnabulum (bell used in the mass) rang to transform the red wine into Christ's blood. From that moment, so the story goes, the blood mysteriously increased in volume, and it seemed to the faithful as if it flowed from the cloth of the Lord over the altar steps down to the floor of the chapel. Imagination went so far that some determined women mopped up the blood from the stone floor with cloths, the annals record. The Bishop of Solsona, St Ermengol, heard of the happening and told the Pope. Pope Sergius IV (1009-1012) allowed public veneration of the strange relic, the bloodstained cloth of Iborra.

It is not always holy figures that provoke visions, their trappings can do it, too. Iborra is not an exceptional case.

*   *   *

The pious Monsieur Thierry, Rector of Paris University, was murdered in Pirlemont, Brabant, in 1073. The brutal murderers threw his corpse into a muddy pond. For a long time the inhabitants vainly searched all over the village for the victim, when suddenly a 'wonderful light', which radiated from the body, shone from the pond. In gratitude for this miraculous discovery an artist painted a wooden panel of the Blessed Virgin floating over the water. In 1297 the picture was transferred to a recently built chapel. During the consecration ceremonies, so it says in the records, the picture was suddenly enveloped in an 'inexplicable

---

* A relic may be the remains of a saint or a saint's possessions, also one of the instruments of martyrdom.

blaze of light'.[3] Even though it was not officially recorded, I suspect that here too the Blessed Virgin, tirelessly active everywhere, performed some other strange feats. Perhaps she smiled at the congregation; perhaps she waved her hand in blessing from the frame.

* * *

On 23 February 1239, a small army of Christian warriors fought against a vastly superior force of Mohammedans on the hill of Codol, three miles from Jativa, near Valencia, Spain.

Before the battle six of the Christian leaders were praying before taking Holy Communion. They had just had time to confess their sins, but not to receive the host, because at that very moment the enemy's battle-cry reached the church from nearby Mount Chio. The leaders grabbed their weapons, since prayer would no longer serve. Terrified that the Moslems might destroy the church, the priests hid the altar cloth and host under a pile of stones. The Christian knights were victorious. When the priests took the altar cloth from its hiding place, six *bloody* hosts were stuck to it. But there was more to come! The next day the Moslems attacked with heavy reinforcements. The situation seemed hopeless and the Christians had to withdraw to the Castle of Chio, which they had captured the day before. The priests had a brilliant idea. They tied the altar cloth, made sacred by the apparition of the hosts, to a pole and waved it at the enemy from the battlements of the castle. Tradition relates that the altar cloth sent out rays of light far and wide and that they were so luminous that the enemy were blinded and fled.

Is that a proof of the primitive power of visions? They can sway whole armies and even the battle-cry 'Great is Allah!' is no help against the blood of Christ. No, visions are not always peaceful. If necessary, they can also spread fear and panic.

Any visitor to Spain can see that altar cloth with six red spots in the church at Daroca.[4]

* * *

At some time in the fourteenth century, the exact date is unknown, a mower gave himself a fatal wound with his scythe near Trois-Épis in Upper Alsace, France. In memory of his tragic death the local farmers nailed a crucifix to an oak tree and called the scene of the accident 'A l'homme mort'. On 3 May 1491, the blacksmith, Dieter Schöre, a sturdy man with no nonsense about him, was riding past it when the figure of a lady in a white robe and wearing a veil appeared to him. In one hand she held an icicle, in the other three ears of corn. She told the bewildered smith that because of the sins and vices of the local people Almighty God would send terrible diseases, heavy rain and frost to punish them if they did not repent and do penance. But the lady said that the ears of corn were a symbol of blessing and good harvests which God would grant through her intercession.

The blacksmith did not attach much importance to the phantom: he wasn't going to breathe a word of it to the villagers of Niedermorschweiher. But then it happened! He bought a sack of corn in the market, but although he was helped by some stalwart labourers he could not lift it on to his horse's back, for the sack got heavier and heavier. Then blacksmith Schöre, as we can understand, bowed to God's power and told the people about his vision. The priests understood at once and summoned the faithful to form a procession to the spot known as 'A l'homme mort'. The fine lady usually had a firm hand on the pulse of her flock. Anyone who promises farmers a good harvest has won the battle already.

Trois-Épis is a well-known place of pilgrimage in Alsace.[5]

*   *   *

The Convent of Concepción, Chile, belongs to the Trinitarians. In it stands a lifesize gilded cedarwood statue of the Blessed Virgin, whose hands are not folded in prayer – they look as if they were throwing something! There is a good reason for this.

When the city of Concepción and the chapel in which the cedarwood statue then stood were attacked by the enemy in 1600, the statue of the Virgin is supposed to have left the chapel in a mysterious way and appeared to the hostile Indians in a tree. She scooped up earth and showered the attackers with bog clods. It seems quite credible in the chronicles of the event that even valiant Indians fled in panic at the sight of such a martial wooden lady. Today we cannot prove whether this is fact or charming legend, but it is true that the 'clod-throwing statue' of Concepción is devoutly honoured to this day.[6]

I find it worthy of note that frequently visions are far from 'ethereal' that they will even throw mud if they can ensure an effect on their flock. The end justifies the means.

*　　*　　*

Tradition tells of 'a terrifying occurrence', dated 3 December 1712, in Besançon, a town in the French Jura, today the seat of an archbishopric. Magopholis describes this vision in his book *Neue Galerie des Übernatürlichen, Wunderbaren und Geheimnisvollen,* published in Weimar in 1860.

The sun was shining brightly in a cloudless sky when, about nine o'clock in the morning, people saw the figure of a man floating in the air at a height of 'nine lances'. He cried out thrice in a loud voice: 'People! People! People! mend your ways or your end is nigh!' This happened on a market day and Magopholis says that it took place 'in the presence of' more than 10,000 people'. After these harsh warnings the figure disappeared into a cloud as if it was ascending directly into heaven. An hour later the air had grown so dark that it was impossible to make out heaven or earth from a radius of twenty miles. In Magopholis's words:

Alarm and terror seized all souls; many people died a sudden death. The population held processions and uttered fervent prayers to heaven. At last, when three days had elapsed the air cleared again; but a terrible wind storm arose, much worse than any of the oldest men in the town could remember, and lasted for about an hour and a half. Then came a fearful cloudburst so that water poured down from heaven as if great barrels were being emptied, and simultaneously there was a tremendous earthquake that destroyed the whole city. Over an area fourteen miles long and six miles wide only one castle, a church tower and in the middle of the area three houses had been left standing. You can see them standing there on a round hill; you can also see some parts of the city walls and you can see flags and standards fluttering in the tower and the castle from the side where the village of Quetz lies. No one can approach them. In the same way no one can say what all this means and no one can behold the scene without the hair of their head standing up, for this is a miraculous and terrifying occurrence.

The unidentified man from heaven — obviously of Christian origin because of his threat (Mend your ways or your end is nigh!) — caused great confusion by his appearance at Besançon. Those who are to be kept in fear of the Lord need an unequivocal sign from time to time. Besançon must have had an exemplary effect on the whole countryside.

* * *

Since the story of human intelligence has been told there have been visions in all religions and civilizations. They have taken place up to the present day and will always do so.

Belonging as I do to the Christian West, brought up in the Roman Catholic doctrine of deliverance and salvation, knowing that this book will be read mainly by readers from the Western world, I am primarily concerned with Christian visions. But it is also true, and I would like to say so explicitly, that similar data giving rise to similar questions could be reported from Asiatic, African, Indian and South American regions. If I were to go into all these phenomena (which would be entirely possible!) the result would be a volume the size of the Manhattan phone book. However, in order that the reader may have some idea of the ubiquity of visions, I have added a VISION ALMANAC, at the end of the book. It records facts only, but it makes clear to anyone familiar with such phenomena in the Christian sphere that visions are by no means solely a Christian, and are certainly not an exclusively Catholic, privilege.

* * *

The Jews did not recognize Jesus as the Redeemer and so His Holy Family did not concern them in the least. Why then does the Old Testament literally teem with visions? Two angels appeared to Abraham, and also to Lot before the destruction of Sodom and Gomorrha. Jacob, son of Isaac, who defrauded his brother Esau of his birthright with a mess of potage', had to wrestle with an angel near the ford at Jabbok. Moses witnessed vision after vision. The best known was on Mount Sinai where he was commanded by Yahweh to free the people from their captivity in Egypt. The story is that for forty years the Israelites followed a vision that shone like a pillar of fire by night and a pillar of cloud by day.[7] Even Bileam, who has the reputation of being a false prophet and a heretic, experienced a vision of God, and Nebuchadnezzar, who certainly has not gone down in history as one of the elect, was surprised by the vision of a 'writing hand' during a banquet in Babylon. The archangel Raphael (today patron saint of chemists) appeared to the heroic Tobiases, father and son, in the apocryphal Book of Tobit. In addition to other visions, the Son of Man appeared to the pious David on a cloud in heaven — i.e. at a time when the 'Christian' Son of Man did not even exist! Solomon, King of Israel and Judah, to whom we are indebted for the 'Judgments of Solomon', which are unfortunately so seldom recognized as such, saw the 'Lord' several times, according to his own account. And we must not forget that visions already occurred in Paradise. God and various angels appeared to our disobedient ancestors Adam and Eve.[8]

This list of biblical visions lays absolutely no claim to being complete.

*   *   *

According to legend Rome was founded by Romulus and Remus, the twin sons of Mars. Exposed as new-born babies, they were suckled by a she-wolf and brought up by the shepherd Faustulus. One day Romulus, who is reputed to have reigned in Rome from 753-716 BC, had a vision of Servius Tullius, son of Vulcan, who appeared in 'gleaming flames above his head'.[9] Herodotus, who lived in the fourth century BC, was a widely travelled historian, one of whose major works was an account of the Persian wars. He relates that the Persians heard such terrible screams in the Temple of Athena Pronoia at Delphi that they fled. There are many stories about voices heard without the persons who caused them being present, 'acoustic' visions, in other words. In the temple of Aesculapius, God of healing, the god made a daily personal appearance to those seeking cures — as naturally as a medical superintendent at the beds in a modern clinic.

The famous lawgiver Numa Pompilius, second king of Rome

according to legend, Minos, king of Knossos, son of Zeus and Europa, and Lycurgus, legendary lawgiver of Sparta, all received most of their creative ideas through direct visions of the gods. Aeneas, hero of the Trojan epic cycle, appeared after his death to his son Ascanius in full armour, together with his attendants. Caius Julius Caesar, born 13 July 100 BC, assassinated on 15 March, AD 44, appeared to a Thessalonian, whom he commissioned to inform his adoptive son Caius Octavianus of the imminent victory of Philippi. Zoroaster, founder of the ancient Iranian religion, who emerged as a prophet in 600 BC, received crucial passages of the Avesta (the religious text of his followers) in several visions. Mohammed, circa 570-623 AD, founder of Islam and prophet of Allah, the one and only god, felt himself called to higher things about 610. In Mecca he preached the revelations which are recorded in the Koran and partly came to him in visions.

Obviously the founders of religions would never have managed without visions: they used them as positive authorization from the supernatural. In that way their doctrines became more effective and attractive. Their wise and clever ideas would have been sublime without calling on visions – yet the nimbus, the halo, released powerful impulses.

*   *   *

The holy characters in visions are generally only observed and heard by male and female 'visionaries'. The urge to pass on their experiences turns them into heralds of the vision and symbols of the miracles that occur *nolens volens* soon afterwards. Like a snowball the miraculous news rapidly reaches a large number of people who seem to have been waiting for exactly this.

That was how things began in the village of Fatima in the province of Estremadura in Portugal. From 13 May to October 1917, three shepherd children had visions of Mary as the 'Divine Mother of the Rosary', who constantly urged the children to erect a chapel on the scene of the apparition. The children related the story of their visions excitedly and enthusiastically. In the summer and autumn of 1917 they were *the* main news item in Portugal and further afield.

At first the three children alone received communications on the 13th of every month, but it did not take long before an endless caravan of pilgrims came to Fatima. On 13 October 1917, according to reliable reports, there were between 70,000 and 80,000 people waiting at the scene of the vision for a miracle to happen. And it was worth their while, for an event which was not confined to the shepherd children awaited them.

It was raining cats and dogs: the conditions for a vision of Mary were wretched. But suddenly the clouds split open, revealing a patch of clear blue sky. The sun shone brilliantly, but was not blinding. The 'solar miracle' of Fatima had begun and everything that follows can be found in the records of the great day. The sun started to quiver and oscillate. It made movements to right and left and finally began to rotate on its axis with tremendous speed like a gigantic Catherine-wheel. Cascades of green, red and violet shot out of the star and bathed the landscape in an unreal unearthly light. Ten thousand people saw it and eye-witnesses claimed that the sun stood still for a few minutes as if it wanted to give them a rest. Immediately afterwards the fantastic movement began again and so did the giant firework display of glowing lights. Observers reported that the spectacle could not be described in words. After another pause the sun dance began a third time, with the same magnificent display. The solar miracle lasted for twelve minutes altogether and was visible over a radius of twenty-five miles.

In spite of *government* opposition at first, Fatima became the goal of pilgrims. Today it is one of the most important places of pilgrimage in the world. On the first and last day of the visions, 13 May and 13 October, Fatima is one great garden of expectation. Thousands and thousands of people hope for a vision, a miracle: but most of all they would like to experience the solar miracle again.

* * *

Examination of the total of recorded visions shows that in ninety cases out of a hundred children are the receivers and transmitters of transcendental phenomena.

Should this objective statement be taken as an indication that young people before and during puberty develop special cerebral currents that facilitate their access to another sphere of consciousness (or infraconsciousness)? Or does native curiosity, combined with unbounded childish fantasy, open up special contacts with the astral world?

Is it possible that visions are 'projected' into a child's brain and then transferred to the brains of other children of the same age by telepathy, a medium that is no longer disputed by science? Is there any doubt that although visions cannot be photographed or objectively registered by any other apparatus, they take place subjectively in the 'limbic system'[10] of our brain, in the archaic brain tissue?

If objective control of visions by outsiders is impossible, where do the words, orders, wishes and concrete instructions come from, over and above the images that appear?

How can the absurd idea that a strange lady wants to be called the 'mysterious rose' get into a child's head? Are the children singled out by visions psychologically disposed or psychically susceptible to them? I do not think so, because the children who see visions are always described as normal healthy creatures with all the usual attributes of their age. So we are going to investigate visions seen by children, children of our time.

*   *   *

As an overture to this part of my 'vision' opera I have chosen a case which in my opinion resolves itself into three questions. It needs describing in full detail.

Sixty-two miles south-west of the Spanish town of Santander in Old Castille lies San Sebastian de Carabandal, Carabandal for short, a hamlet with narrow stone streets and about forty houses.

Sunday, 18 June 1961, 16.30 hrs. Four little girls were playing in the market place. They were Conchita and Jacinta, both aged twelve, and Marie Cruz, aged eleven. Their surname was Gonzalez, but they were not related, for the name Gonzalez is as common in Spain as Smith, Dupont and Müller are in other countries. The fourth little girl was called Mari Loli Mazon, aged twelve. These children decided to steal apples from their teacher's garden.

About eight o'clock at night they were walking down the stony road called Calleja back to the village, with heavily laden skirts and very bad consciences. To fight the uneasy feeling they had in the pit of the stomach they picked up stones which they threw at an imaginary 'bad angel' whom they thought they could make out on the left-hand side of the road.[11]

Suddenly Conchita stopped and stared up at the sky. She told the others that she could see 'a very beautiful figure in a bright light'. The other three thought it was a new game, but Conchita insisted: 'No, no! Look over there!'

The little girls gazed at the clouds and cried: 'The angel!' They were quiet as mice and gaped at the sky for several minutes, as motionless as the angel who had appeared. Then the phenomenon vanished as quickly as it had appeared.

The little girls ran home and told their story. The news spread like the wind in the superstitious village.

Could four healthy, sensible little girls have seen the same 'face' at the same time, people asked themselves. Why should children lie for no reason, how could they each give exactly the same description of the event, as they were not expecting anything worse than being punished for stealing apples? Why did they stubbornly repeat their statements without a mistake, and continue to do so in the future? Their account was received with barely suppressed doubt.

Children always want to make quite certain. So the four of them ran up the Calleja on the next day, with the rosary tightly held in their fingers. The angel did not show himself.

On 20 June they repeated their walk accompanied by a few curious villagers. As they were returning in disappointment, the children suddenly saw a 'radiant light' in the firmament. No one else observed the phenomenon except them.

The next day a larger group was with them in the Calleja. This time the angel showed himself spontaneously. Once more the villagers did not notice anything, though some of them photographed the transfigured faces of the children.

The mocking ceased. A certain awe of the supernatural and inconceivable seized the people. 'Their' angel showed himself to the children on 22, 23, 24 and 25 June at the same spot. According to the children it was always the same angel, though he never spoke.

The little girls were accompanied by a crowd of sensationalists at the evening rendezvous on 1 July. The angel appeared and

stayed for two whole hours. Once again the spectacle was confined
to the children, but those present heard the conversation with the
angel. To put it more precisely: they heard the little girls' questions and answers. On this occasion the angel spoke for the first
time, introducing himself as the Archangel Michael. The audience
were unanimous in describing the children's strange unnatural
attitude. They knelt for the whole two hours, their heads bent
far back, frozen in a rigid posture.

On 2 July, a Sunday, the whole of Carabandal was afoot:
swarms of people from neighbouring villages had hastened there.
From 15.00 hrs onwards the rosary was recited in the church.
Towards 18.00 hrs, the procession, including doctors and priests,
with the girls at its head, got under way. On the scene of the
vision four posts had been driven into the ground and connected
with ropes to form a fence to stop the children from being
crushed to death by the crowd.

The miracle happened again.

Scarcely had the children reached the 'ring' when the Blessed
Virgin showed herself to them, flanked by two angels. One of
them, Michael, was familiar to the girls, and they said of the
other that he might have been Michael's twin. The children
made quite independent statements in which all the facts tally
completely. They also contain a description of the Virgin which
varied little on other occasions. She had long dark brown hair
parted in the middle, a longish face with a narrow nose and soft
lips, a snow-white dress with a light blue cloak over it and she
wore a crown with gold stars on it. Her age was between seventeen and eighteen. As in other cases, the girls noticed that the
figure did not move her feet when she changed position – she
floated through the air. To the right of the Blessed Virgin they
could make out a 'reddish flickering image', from which rose a
triangle with an inscription which they could not decipher. The
angels wore smooth blue robes. They too had narrow faces and
dark ('black') eyes. Their fingernails were cut short – the
children's observation was as accurate as that! – and large pink-
ish-red wings grew from their backs.

The village priest Don Valentin questioned the little girls. Four
statements made quite separately from each other agreed down
to the last detail.

Peter Ramon Andreu drafted a report of the spectacular vision on 2 July for Bishop Aldazal in Santander. The following is a literal quotation:

It was not possible to bring the children to their senses even with painful cuts, brutal blows and burns. They perceived nothing of the external world. One could convince oneself of this by suddenly passing a light or other object in front of their eyes. There was absolutely no movement of the eyelids or pupils.[12]

There were two visions on 27 July. Early in the morning the angel announced a second appearance for eight o'clock sharp in the evening. This news spread like wildfire. According to official estimations over 600 people assembled, among them priests and doctors and even a 'spy' from the Workers' University of Cordoba, a Dominican father.

Archangel Michael arrived punctually and stayed for eighty-five minutes. Eyewitnesses claimed that the children became so rigid that two men could only lift their small bodies with the greatest difficulty. Various attempts to move the heads or arms of the visionaries were unsuccessful.

Naturally there were sceptics. Even the church had its reservations. People spoke of hypnosis, hallucinations, prefabricated lies and deceit, even of promoting business for the benefit of the isolated farming village.

Conchita, it seemed obvious, had the strongest personality of the four. So it was suspected that she might have influenced her friends suggestively. To avert this she was taken to Santander to join other children and went swimming on the beach with them to cure her cramps.

After a week had passed the family came to take Conchita home. Then things really began to happen! One vision after another, visions by the dozen. The interest of much wider circles was aroused. The avalanche of spectators that poured into the village acquired frightening proportions. According to an official estimate there were more than 5,000 people on 18 October.

The weather was most unseasonable for the time of year with rainstorms and violent squalls. The field on which the crowd waited patiently was turned into a quagmire. They stuck it out, because they were expecting a miracle. Nothing happened.

At about 22.00 hrs a message signed by one of the children and ostensibly dictated by the Mother of God was read out. It called on everyone to bring sacrifices and do penance, because otherwise – as always in such messages! – mankind would be punished.

I do not intend to give a detailed record of the many visions at Carabandal. The literature is available for those who are interested.[13]

*   *   *

What became of the four little girls? After the one great journey of her life – she visited the Pope in Rome – Conchita returned to her village, but soon entered the Order of the 'Calced Carmelites' at Pamplona. Mari Loli and Jacinta were received into a convent near Saragossa. Only Mari Cruz stayed with her parents, whom she helped in the home and on the farm.

I find three important points in the logbook of the stormy events at Carabandal:

1. The miracle of the host. It happened on the night of 18 July 1962. About two a.m. the Archangel Michael is supposed to have appeared in Conchita's room, in which some relatives were also staying. It says in the records that the girl suddenly rushed down the stairs with face transfigured, and ran through the streets before throwing herself to the ground. She lay there rigid, with her tongue sticking far out of her mouth. Eyewitnesses on the night declared that a snow-white fairly thick host suddenly appeared on the girl's tongue and remained visible for about two minutes. Then Conchita swallowed it.

This materialization was filmed by one of the spectators! About forty photos actually show a round white 'object', somewhat resembling a host. Witnesses swore that Conchita had made no movement with her hands or even touched her tongue. During this 'communion' she had neither withdrawn her tongue into her mouth or under her gums: it was also inconceivable that she had concealed something so white in her mouth. Incidentally I find the amateur film taken by a Mr Daminas and developed in Barcelona a little miracle in itself. It was night and the only light came from some pocket torches. Isn't it a miracle that the film exposed at all?

2. During the last vision, on 13 November 1965, the girl received a message for the Pope from the Mother of God. In

January 1966, Conchita actually travelled to Rome, where she was questioned for more than two hours by the right reverend gentlemen of the Congregation of the Faith, formerly the Holy Office, and *then* by the Pope. (From Rome Conchita went to San Giovanni Rotondo to visit the wonder-working Father Pio.)

3.   The really absurd thing about the events at Carabandal is this: Mari Cruz, the girl, who works in her parents' home, suddenly denied that she had ever had a vision!

What was the reason for this retraction?

Under the headline 'No visions have taken place in Carabandal' I read the following text in the 17 March 1967 edition of the Catholic newspaper *Vaterland*, which is published in Lucerne:

In an official note dated 17 March 1967 Bishop Puchol Montis of Santander established the following three points. 1.   There has not been a single vision either of the Most Blessed Virgin, the blessed Archangel Michael or any other heavenly figure. 2.   No message was transmitted. 3.   All the events that took place at Carabandal have a natural explanation.

One is dumbfounded.

There are photographs and tape recordings from Carabandal. All kinds of investigations were carried out, including a hearing by the Congregation of the Faith. All the examiners confirmed that the girls' statements coincided down to the smallest detail. Conchita was received by the Pope.

It is not denied that 'events' took place, but a natural explanation has been found for them. It would be desirable if official Church statements laid down not only what is not allowed to have happened, but also what *is* allowed to have happened. Not least for the sake of the faithful.

Nevertheless, it would not surprise me if the status of 'Major miracle' were not attributed to the events at Carabandal in a decade or so.

The Church is crafty and does not mind waiting. Should that happen one day, Mari Cruz could say (or leave a deposition in her will) that she had to lie and retract on direct orders from heaven in order to 'test the faithful'. The other three maidens would be prepared as quasi-saints in their convents; they would pronounce the right words at the desired time.

Incidentally, inexplicable miraculous cures continue to take place at Carabandal as they did before.

*   *   *

It has occurred to me that there is a contradiction even in the visions examined and checked by the Congregation of the Faith. The Blessed Virgin continually refers to the power conferred on her by God the Father or her son Jesus Christ. If she has this power and the pressing wish to be more widely worshipped by the faithful all over the world, why does she always show herself in isolated places and mostly to poor little creatures who can do so little to carry out her wishes?

Without the help of supernatural inspiration, I can think of a better occasion on which to satisfy her wish for publicity.

When on important church holidays the Pope pronounces the blessing *urbi et orbi* (the city [Rome] and the world) to a crowd of several hundred thousand in St Peter's square, television stations transmit this highest act of ecclesiastical grace to all five continents. The Pope speaks from the church which was built over St Peter's tomb. Could there possibly be a more effective scene for visions, if they really come from heaven and always seek out the elect? Is there not an excellent opportunity for granting the fulfilment of Mary's dearest wish?

I cannot savour the kernel of the sweet fruit of visions. It is bitter. I cannot accept the idea of the Blessed Virgin, of all people, going cap in hand for more people to revere and pray to her. Is it 'divine' for her to threaten bluntly that her almighty son will destroy mankind if her wishes remain unfulfilled? Does this kind of behaviour tally with the generally held ideas of God and his son, of their almighty power and goodness?

What goes on here? Do visions need mystery, in the sense of its original meaning, namely, a secret cult that is only accessible to the initiate and gives them a personal relationship to the godhead who is worshipped? H. U. von Balthasar has some pertinent words to say on the subject:

Wherever man honours the rare, precious and holy, he removes it and sets it apart: he takes the sacred object away from the gaze of the public; he hides it in the cell of a sanctuary, in the half-light of a sacred room; he makes use of a fabulous legend to snatch it from the humdrum course of normal history; he surrounds it with mystery. . . .[14]

Mystery is always good value, that much is certain. The most harmless document becomes worth reading as soon as it is stamped Top Secret. The simple man wants to share in the 'secret', he is driven to belong to a circle of initiates, he wants to be 'in'. Mystery religions, secret societies, secret agents etc. have something uncommonly exciting and alluring about them. Sacred secrets are a brilliant invention. The 'mysteries' I am going to mention here can be tracked down.

*   *   *

The events at Heroldsbach are a classical example of the dictatorial behaviour of the Roman Church. This story could have been invented by Agatha Christie or Georges Simenon.

The village of Heroldsbach is situated in Mittelfranken, Bavaria. 9 October 1949.

The children Marie Hellman, aged 10, Kuni Schleicher, aged 11, Grete Gugel, aged 11, and Erika Muller, aged 11, were collecting autumn leaves of different trees for their school botany lesson. On their way home they saw above the treetops radiant handwriting, 'like the sun shining through a green beer bottle', forming the three letters IHS. The writing disappeared. Then 'a white lady who looked like a white nun' appeared, floating above the birch wood.[15] The vision moved slowly hither and thither.

The sensible children did not lose their heads. To make sure they were not dreaming, they began to count, told each other about noises they could hear and ran to the pond on which seven ducks were swimming as usual. No, they were not dreaming. The figure of the lady was still floating 'up there' on the hill, higher and higher, until she vanished into the blue sky. The vision lasted for a quarter of an hour.

At home no one believed a word of the children's story. Their mothers set out to put an end to the phantom by going to see for themselves. On the hill they observed how the children — 'suddenly' of course — looked fixedly at the wood. They could perceive the vision again. The mothers could only confirm that the children were strangely and deeply moved in a way that communicated itself to them, too. The records, prepared separately, gave identical descriptions of the phenomenon by the children.

10 October.

Kuni Schleicher went to the hill with a girl friend. They were followed by four boys who were teasing them: Andreas Büttner, aged 13, Michael Lindenberger, Adolf Messbacher and Heinz Muscha, all aged 12. Then *all* the children saw the lady only thirty feet away above the treetops and moving slowly earthwards.

12 October.

The little girls saw only a 'white gleam', whereas Michael Lindenberger and his brother Martin claimed to have seen 'a white lady'.

13 October.

Antonia Saam (the circle of visionary children was growing) asked the vision: 'What is your wish?' *All* the children heard the answer: 'The people must pray hard!'

The children asked the village priest Gailer to accompany them to the hill. The priest refused and informed his religious superiors, the episcopal administration at Bamberg.

16 October.

Herr Kummelmann, sent by the cathedral chapter, was able to observe the children in their visionary ecstasy.

In the months and years to come the visions were repeated and the number of those who claimed to have seen them also multiplied. The recorded dates are: 13 January 1950, 5, 9, 17 and 18 February, 4, 16 and 25 May, 15, 16, 24, 25 and 26 June, 10 July, 7 and 8 October. Visions took place with considerable frequency right down to the last phenomenon on 31 October. Then peace came to Heroldsbach.

Did it really? We shall see.

The figures in the visions were not always the same. Sometimes the Blessed Virgin, with or without the infant Jesus, sometimes prominent angels, sometimes the Trinity and sometimes even father Joseph were sighted. At Christmas 1949 the story of Christ's birth is supposed to have unfolded before the children's eyes like a film.

What have the representatives of the Holy Ghost made out of Heroldsbach? A modern Inquisition.

30.10.1949. The faithful received a warning not to go to the scene of the vision from the episcopal administration at Bamberg.

10.1.1950. An announcement from the pulpit said that the episcopal examination had produced nothing to justify the assumption of visions of supernatural origin. Processions and pilgrimages were forbidden.

2.3.1950. By episcopal decree all ecclesiastics were forbidden to participate or collaborate in religious events if they were connected with visions.

6.3.1950. Archbishop Dr Kolb summoned the village priest Gailer and forbade him to visit the scene of the vision in the future.

2.10.1950. The Archbishop received a letter from the Holy Office dated 28 September. It said:

Furthermore the Holy Office approved the steps your Excellency (Archbishop of Bamberg) has taken in this matter, and praises the clergy and the members of Catholic Action, who have conscientiously observed the Archbishop's instructions. The remainder of the faithful who have opposed the decision of the ecclesiastical authorities up to the present, are exhorted to comply with them . . . . We also ordain that praying on the hill is tantamount to recognizing the authenticity of the visions and therefore must cease. . . .

12.10.1950. The ecclesiastical authorities requested that devotions on the hill, which had been taking place for some time without priests being present, should cease.

4.8.1951. Gailer, the grey-haired parish priest, who had looked after the parish of Heroldsbach for thirty-eight years and was loved by his parishioners, was transferred with immediate effect because he supported the authenticity of the visions. Eight years later he returned to his parish as a corpse.

15.8.1951. A new decree by the Holy Office was published.

On Wednesday 18 July 1951, Their Eminences, the Right Reverend Cardinals, who are entrusted with the highest guardianship in matters of faith and morals, have decided as follows after examination of the records and documents at a plenary session of the Highest Congregation of the Holy Office: It is established that the visions under consideration are not supernatural. Therefore the cult connected with them is forbidden in the above-mentioned place and elsewhere. Priests who take part in this forbidden cult in future, will be immediately suspended from carrying out their priestly duties. On the following Thursday, the 19th of the same month and year, His Holiness of divine providence, Pope Pius XII, approved,

B

ratified and ordered the publication of the decree of Your Eminences presented to him at the customary audience granted to His Eminence, the Assessor of the Sanctum Officium.

Given at Rome, at the Palace of the Holy Office, on 25 July 1951.

22.8.1951. After examining them like an inquisitor the acting priest Dr Schmitt excluded the visionary children from receiving the Holy Sacraments and ordered them not only to stay away from the hill, but also to assert in future that they had never seen the Blessed Virgin. Out of fear of the Curia the children stayed away from the hill for five months, but in spite of that they did not receive the Sacraments.

15.5.1955. The judgment in a case brought by the episcopal administration ordered the compulsory clearance of the hill (statue of Mary, small altars etc.).

4 – 6.2.1957. A case was held in the county court of Forchheim in which Paul Schneider, a retired government servant, was the defendant. In 1954 he had published a treatise on the subject of Heroldsbach.[16] The episcopal administration again appeared as plaintiff in this action. Among the witnesses were some of the visionary children, who were seventeen and eighteen years old by then – 1957. They confirmed the visions they had seen in the years 1949-1952.

I should mention that on 8 December 1949 Heroldsbach was the scene of a solar miracle that was observed by 10,000 people. The parish priest Gailer stated in evidence:

The sun came towards us, making a loud crackling noise. I saw a crown of roses five inches wide inside it. Antonia Saam saw the Blessed Virgin and child inside the sun. There were five of us priests up on the hill. I shall testify to this as long as I live.

Dr J. B. Walz, Professor of Theology, gave this description[17]:

It grew lighter and lighter and more dazzling. The sun seemed to become more blinding and bigger and to be coming nearer us. I felt blinded. I had the overwhelming impression of something quite abnormal and also felt that something awful was going to happen at any minute. I was terrified. . . . Then the sun began to turn very quickly on its own axis and the rotations were so clearly visible that it seemed as if a motor was turning the sun's disc at a regular speed. During this process it took on the most wonderful colours.

* * *

I can give the Holy Office a helping hand with dozens of cases of visions which are less documented than the one at Heroldsbach and were observed by fewer spectators, but have long been recognized as 'genuine'.

It obviously depends on the type of report made by the competent ecclesiastical authorities, and such reports are not free of errors, in spite of the charisma of the people composing them. What did the authorities in Bamberg say when they wrote to Rome? Were the visionary children insubordinate because they did not always describe the same vision? Because they had the whole of the Holy Family parading above the treetops? Or were there messages which did not synchronize with the holy doctrine at the end of the secret record? As secrets are traditionally better kept in the Sanctum Officium than in the worldly ministries and chanceries, even without a 'top secret' stamp, we shall *never* know.

Rome is right. Although in other cases a tiny back door is always left open so that the verdict can be revised for the good of the Church, the door was slammed tight in the case of Heroldsbach after Pope Pius XII was sanctified. *Cuius regio, ejus religio!* (A man must profess the religion of the prince in whose state he lives!) A well tried Roman maxim. . . .

* * *

After studying hundreds of official records of visions it becomes quite clear that the Catholic Church claims the exclusive right to recognize or reject these phenomena, regardless of the fact that the visions have been and still are seen by people of all races and religions. But according to its decree neither the Blessed Virgin, nor the Lord Jesus Christ, nor the archangels are free to appear to anyone they want. Even the visionaries themselves are not allowed to judge of the authenticity of what they have observed. (It is rather like when the Church joins in the discussion about birth control. It is not concerned personally!)

The Catholic Church derives its claim to be the sole authority which can recognize the 'authenticity' of the phenomena, from its teaching mission. For example, if the Blessed Virgin gives a message in a vision that does not correspond to the official doctrine the vision is classified and rejected as 'not authentic', and hushed up or forbidden, as if it had never taken place.

But if someone who does not believe in the only true faith has a vision, the poor haunted character can only submit to psychiatric treatment . . . or he must become a Catholic as quickly as possible.

*   *   *

Rudolf Krämer-Badoni, writer and Catholic, asks: 'Should the Church behave like a club and issue statutes that must be accepted by every member when he joins?'

The arrogance of the ecclesiastical authorities is painful to behold. Thou art not allowed to have seen anything that is not ordained and approved — thou art not allowed to have heard messages whose content is not officially blessed. And then there is the perpetual enlightenment of the charismatic gentlemen by the Holy Ghost, the unassailable chief witness for everything! Here is another quotation from Krämer-Badoni's book *Die Last, katholisch zu sein* (the Burden of Being a Catholic):

Has the Church the right to call on the Holy Ghost as witness for every legal decision? How then does traditional rubbish continue to accumulate that must constantly be cleared away (to make room for fresh nonsense)?

It would be a terrible omission in a summary of historical and present-day visions if two world-famous ladies, Katherine of Siena and the Maid of Orleans, were left out.

The visions of these maidens occupy a special position over and above the relevant religious phenomena, because both ladies had a profound effect on politics that was directly connected with their visions. The maxim of the Jesuit Father Hermann Busenbaum (1600-1668) from his book *Medulla theologiae moralis* (Of moral theology) was already valid: '*Cum finis est licitus, etiam media sunt licita*' ('When the end is allowed, the means are allowed, too'). The Church's strategy is admirable: it is especially impressive in retrospect.

*   *   *

In the thirteenth century, Siena, a city in Tuscany, Italy, was at the height of its political power and in the fourteenth century, when Katherine was born, at the peak of its artistic flowering. Siena was the rival of Florence, until it was conquered in 1559 and reduced to the provincial centre of the rich farming country around.

Katherine was born circa 1347, the twenty-third or twenty-fourth child (she had a twin sister) of the master-dyer Benincasa. At the age of seventeen she entered the Tertiary Order of the Dominicans, who did not live a communal conventual life but followed their own rules of Caritas. She lived, so it was said, 'entirely in her mystical contemplations'.

In the book *Katharina von Siena — Politische Briefe*[18], which received the imprimatur of the Bishop of Chur on 6.12.1943, it says:

Circa 1370 she experienced the 'mystical death' in order to receive from her beloved master her mission to the new life of the apostolate.

In 1357 Katherine prided herself on immediate association with her 'fiancé' Jesus Christ with whom she had exchanged hearts and whose stigmata she had received. The story goes that even as a child she was different from other girls.

Scarcely had she come to the age of reason when the Lord appeared to her, wearing the papal robes and crowned with a tiara. He stretched out his hand towards her in blessing. This image stamped the unity of Christ and Church indelibly on her heart, from then on she saw in the Pope the epiphany of 'Christ on earth. . . .'

When I hear of such a useful start on her pilgrimage through life, Psalm 4 (German version), occurs to me: 'God leads his saints in a wonderful way', but I should like to change the text to 'The Church leads its saints in a wonderful way!'

It was the purely mystical period of her youth, culminating in the mystical death, the great turning point of her life. For four whole hours people thought she was dead. During this time the Lord showed her the holiness of the saints. . . .

Katherine hastened through Siena in a white wool robe with a black cloak draped round it. Her visions and ecstasies had been bruited abroad. She was well known in the town. She had an irresistible influence with her 'compelling eyes'. Miracle after miracle took place in her presence. The people made pilgrimages to her.

From 1374 people testified to 'her coming universal mission', which at first consisted of dictating fiery committed letters – 'political letters' – to kings and queens, popes and bishops (she only learnt to write in the last years of her life). She was a passionate advocate of participation in the Crusades:

'God wants it and I want it.'

As we can see, Katherine was no model of Christian humility and modesty. Her activities, which were ostensibly inspired by religious motives, had political effects in reality.

Pope Gregory XI (1370-1378) lived in exile with the papal government in Avignon. Urged on by the mission given her in a vision, Katherine wanted to bring the Pope back so that he could maintain the unified power of the Church and rule it once again from its spiritual home, i.e. Rome. She enlisted sympathy for her ecclesiastical-cum-political mission in the castles of powerful nobles and among everyone she credited with worldly power. She also travelled 'to the brilliant worldly court of the Popes at Avignon . . . Katherine was first and always the favoured mystic. . . . Only from that starting point is it possible to understand her political missions. . . .'

A dubious bit of whitewashing!

For one long year Katherine fought bitterly for the return of the Pope. In 1377 she achieved her goal. Rome was Rome again, the church at the seat of its power.

While people constantly and all too clearly emphasize her credulous naïvety and quote her visions as first-class references for her political commitment, they wrap the political tool Katherine of Siena in so much cottonwool that we completely lose sight of her. It may be that visions cannot be proved; but ecclesiastical and political power achieved by them can. That is something we should understand, if we are not 'smitten with blindness' (Genesis 19, 11).

*   *   *

Then there was the no less politically active peasant girl Joan of Arc, who became a world star among visionaries. She was born between 1410 and 1412 in the village of Domrémy on the Maas in eastern France. Today Domrémy is called 'Domrémy-la Pucelle' (*la pucelle* = the virgin), and has about 280 inhabitants, all eager to show tourists the house in which their famous saint was born.

The peasant girl from Domrémy – known in literature as Jeanne d'Arc, St Joan or the Maid of Orléans, the central figure of many great dramas – intervened in major European politics, claiming that she was instructed to do so by visions.

At the age of thirteen Joan had her first visions and heard voices. Statements by the martial maid at her trial are preserved in the 'Manuscripts of the Royal Library'.[19]

'At the age of thirteen I heard a voice in the garden of my father at Domrémy. It came from the right, from the side near the church and was accompanied by a great brightness. At first I was afraid, but I soon realized that it was the voice of an angel, who has accompanied and instructed me ever since. It was St Michael. I also saw St Katherine (of Siena!) and St Margaret, who spoke to me, exhorting me and guiding all my actions. I can easily tell by the voice whether a saint or an angel is talking to me. Usually but not always it is accompanied by a bright light. Their voices are soft and friendly. The angels appeared to me with natural heads. I have seen them and I still see them with my own eyes. . . .'

After five years when Joan was looking after the cattle, a certain voice said: 'God has pity on the French people and you must go forth to save them.' When she began to cry, the voice ordered her to go to Vaucouleurs where she would find a captain who would lead her to the king without hindrance. . . .

'Since that time I have done nothing that was not a consequence of the revelations and visions I have had, and even throughout my actual trial, I am only saying what I have been inspired to say. . . .'

At the siege of Orléans Joan predicted the capture of the town and also that she would shed blood from her breast. On the following day she was wounded by an arrow that went 'six inches deep' into her shoulder.

In constant communication with her voices, Joan was summoned to political activities two or three times a week. Towards the end of 1428 the orders were so specific that they charged the young girl to bring help to her countrymen immediately: she was to end the siege of Orléans by the English.

It was all right for the voices to give orders, but it was a difficult political task for a peasant girl, for France was split into two parties. There was the Orléans party under the feeble Dauphin (title of the heir to the French throne), whom Joan crowned King Charles VII in 1422 at Rheims. There was also the Burgundian party under Henry V which was allied with the English.

The maid was driven by her permanent visions as if by the Furies. In her peasant rags she easily overcame the courtiers with her ready wit and forced her way into the presence of the infantile Dauphin, whom she harangued at such length that he appointed her 'Chef de Guerre'.

At the head of 40,000 warriors Joan forced the English to withdraw from Orléans. This victory brought the turning point in the Hundred Years' War between France and England. Joan's remaining political wish, a reunited France, Orléans *and* Burgundy, could have destroyed England, but it was frustrated by the weak king.

Once again the valiant maid set forth to do battle, but she was taken prisoner by the Burgundians near Compiègne. 'Her' simpleton of a king left her to her fate. The Burgundians sold their prisoner to the English for a great deal of money. (Saints have their price, too!) They had had such unpleasant experiences with the maid that they wanted her in their power on pragmatic political grounds, regardless of the cost. They knew that France would no longer have a force to drive her to unity without Joan (and her visions!). The English regarded their prisoner of war as a magician. For safety's sake they put the maid in an iron cage!

The trial began on 21 February 1431, under the Bishop of Beauvais. The records[20] show that Joan's visions and voices were an essential part of the evidence.

22 February 1431 – a castle at Rouen.

The cross-examiner:	When did you first hear voices?
Joan:	I was thirteen years old when a voice from God rang out to help me to live righteously.
The cross-examiner:	Did the voices often haunt you?
Joan:	Two or three times a week they said to

	me: 'Thou shalt leave your village and go to France.'
The cross-examiner:	What else was revealed to you?
Joan:	I was told that I should raise the siege of Orléans. . . .

The vision gave Joan what was clearly a political task! When they threatened her with torture on 28 March in order to sentence her as a heretic, she abjured her visions.

Joan:	Since the Church asserts that my visions and revelations are unbelievable and cannot be supported, I do not wish to insist on them.

On 2 April she retracted the recantation that had been wrung from her.

The Bishop:	Have you heard the voices of St Katherine and St Margaret since Thursday?
Joan:	God told me through the blessed ladies what miserable treason I had committed when I abjured and recanted in order to save my life.

On 30 May 1431, lay executioners set fire to the stake with the tacit approval of the Christian judges. Joan died crying 'Jesus! Jesus!'

Twenty years later a court usher stated in evidence that Joan's heart had remained undamaged, although the rest of her body was completely destroyed.

It is no use puzzling or making far-fetched interpretations, the figures in Joan's visions wanted to achieve political goals. What kind of interest could the 'blessed in heaven' have in them?

In 1456 the Church saw its chance to lead both a saint and a national heroine back into the fold. The Church set aside the verdict that had brought their co-religionist to the stake. She was beatified in 1894 and canonized in 1920.

In the Epilogue to Bernard Shaw's *St Joan* it says:

The Gentleman:	On every thirtieth day of May, being the anniversary of the death of the said most blessed daughter of God, there shall be in every Catholic church to the end of time celebrated a special office in commemoration

of her; and it shall be lawful to dedicate a
special chapel to her, and to place her image
on its altar in every such church. And it
shall be lawful and laudable for the faithful
to kneel and address their prayers through
her to the Mercy Seat.

Shaw used the official text literally. That is the kind of basic
revision the Church subjects itself to, when saints are not only
saints, but also active political power factors with whom they
can advantageously identify themselves.

*   *   *

I have already mentioned that the Roman Catholic Church
claims for itself all the visions designated 'genuine' by its courts.
This is usurpatory, for there are other large Christian communities
and sects who *also* base themselves on the Old and New Testaments. These millions of adherents of different Christian religions
do not consider themselves a lesser breed of Christians, as second-
or third-raters. They, too, champion the 'authenticity' of visions
in *their* religious world.

Once again, this obstinacy is contrary to all logic. The messages
in visions received by Methodists, Baptists, Jehovah's Witnesses,
the New Apostles, members of the Greek Orthodox Church etc.
work the very same religious miracles and proclaim the same
values – such as faith, prayer, good behaviour, loving one's neighbour, respecting one's fellow-men, the proscription of criminal
acts – that the Roman Catholic doctrine requires. Why then in
the devil's name does the devil, if only Lucifer can appear to
them, achieve such typically Christian aims among the 'others'?

*   *   *

The prophet Joseph Smith (1805-1844) founded the Church
of Jesus Christ of Latter-day Saints. During the night of 21
September 1823, he had a vision[21]:

While I was so engrossed in prayer to God, I perceived a
light shining in my room that increased in power until the
room was lighter than at noon, upon which an angel appeared
beside my bed, standing in the air, for his feet did not touch

the ground. He was clad in a loose robe of extraordinary white-ness. He was whiter than anything else I have ever seen; nor do I believe that anything terrestrial could be so exceptionally white and brilliant. His hands were bare and so were his arms until just above the wrist. His feet were also unshod, and his legs until just above the ankles. His head and throat were also bare. I could see that he wore nothing else besides this robe, for it was open and I could see his breast. . . . He named me by name and told me he had been sent to me as a messenger from God and that he was called Maroni; God had work for me to do. . . . He said that a book was preserved written on gold plates which gave an account of the earlier inhabitants of this continent and their origin; it also contained the fullness of the eternal gospel as proclaimed to those former inhabitants by the Saviour. . . . After these pronouncements I saw the light in the room slowly shrinking around the man who had spoken to me, and this continued until the room was dark again, except around him. Then I could suddenly see into heaven as if through a shaft of light and the visitor rose up until he disappeared entirely and the room was once more as dark as before the vision of heavenly light. . . .

How does the vision in this report differ from the visions ap-proved by the Roman Catholic Church? Joseph Smith had more visions, in which he was shown the gold plates, the text of which he transcribed. In this way the Mormon Bible *The Book of Mormon* came into being in 1830. In 1848 the Christian Mormon community settled by the Salt Lake of Utah, USA, after lengthy wanderings in the desert, and founded the Mormon State of Utah with the flourishing settlement of Salt Lake City as its centre. Today the Mormon Church has over a million and a half members, who are scattered all over the world. Mormons really do live ac-cording to their Christian laws: they are more than a sect that could be dismissed as a *quantité négligeable*.

Who on earth can credibly explain the 'miracle' experienced by Joseph Smith except as an 'inspiration', i.e. a vision? Neither the FBI nor a smart private eye knew the place on the unknown hill where Smith was to find the gold plates containing the Book of Mormon. No archaeologist had ever dug there. The vision led Smith to the hidden treasure, on the contents of which he was to base his religion. *No one* knew about it, no one had been there before him so no one could have led the seventeen-year-old there telepathically. However it is logical that someone somewhere *did know* about this hiding place, indeed *must have put* the plates there. As this great unknown was not a contemporary of Smith, the impulse to search in this spot must inevitably — how else? — have come from people in the know outside our planet, people who at some point in time unknown to us had sojourned on the earth. For those who emitted the energy for the Smith vision must also have been on the hill at some time. Even they can only induce what they *know*, and they know more about our race and hidden knowledge than we have been able to discover so far. Smith was an instrument of the extraterrestrials. I should be genuinely grateful for any other convincing explanation of this phenomenon.

The *Book of Mormon*, which originated from these visions, contains such a wealth of historical events, with facts, names and geographical data, that it could not have formed part of the knowledge of a seventeen-year-old boy.

As with all visions, there was 'something' here. This 'something' needs investigating. It was definitely not a demonstration by the powers of hell, because the results were positive. That would be, to follow the Church Fathers, a *contraria contrariis* (fighting opposites with opposites).

*   *   *

The Coptic Church is the Christian national Church of Egypt, with over a million believers. It is led by the Patriarch of Alexandria, who has had his seat at Cairo since the eleventh century.

On 2 April 1968 passers-by observed figures like white doves, which had fluid outlines and slowly met in a mist, above the domes of the old Coptic church in the Cairo suburb of Zeitun. In a ghostlike metamorphosis the mist assumed the aspect of a human figure. It was so radiant that the spectators were blinded and could only follow the phenomenon with their eyes screwed up. The vision showed itself at the same place in the same way on other evenings.

The Coptic Patriarch Kyrillos VI at once convened a commission of priests, scholars and lay members of the Coptic community. This commission, along with thousands of Cairo citizens – Copts, Moslems, Hindus, Christians of all shades, members of sects – declared that they had seen a 'beautiful lady' radiating light above the domes of the church. That was six years ago. On the evening of 12 April the Egyptian photographer Wagih Rizk Matta, on the hunt for a sensation, took the first snapshot of a vision of Mary in the sky. On 14 April the Patriarch produced the photograph at a press conference. It showed a dazzlingly white shape with an unidentifiable figure against the background of the three domes near the lower edge of the picture above the church roof. Numerous witnesses confirmed having seen a 'beautiful female figure', by signing a document to that effect.[22]

* * *

I had been to Lourdes and Fatima. On my journeys across the continents, there was not a single place of pilgrimage in which I had not observed the environment and history of the 'miracle' with critical attention. But I had never had the privilege of being the neutral spectator of a 'sudden' vision or of talking to an active male or female visionary. Then reports of the works of 'Mama Rosa' began to arrive regularly on my desk. 'Mama Rosa' is considered to be a visionary. Was this a chance to fill in a gap in my knowledge?

On 22 March 1974 I visited the godforsaken hole of San Damiano. It was not easy to find, for there is no signpost to show the way. I soon realized that signposts are unnecessary here, as everyone you ask knows the farm of the Quattrini family on which 'Mama Rosa' lives and works. (San Damiano lies south of Piacenza and Piacenza south of Milan.) Pilgrims from every country under the sun find their way here, as a park full of cars of every make, with number plates of every nationality, proves.

The monotonous sound of the rosary being recited came from a window of the farmhouse: 'Hail Mary, full of grace, the Lord is with thee, blessed art thou among women. . . .' The pilgrims muttered the responses rhythmically.

The south wall of the farmstead was covered with votive tablets (offerings dedicated to a saint at a pilgrimage shrine): Maria has helped! Cured of severe illness! Thanks for all eternity! I am healthy again! Passed my examination! None of the languages

I know are missing from these *ex votos*. 'Mama Rosa' must indeed be able to work miracles. I had come to the right address.

In one part of the yard long rows of red oil lamps flickered on iron shelves. Behind them on a table stood the large plastic bottles with 'miraculous water' from San Damiano. It is given away free: nothing is sold at Mama Rosa's. Devotional objects and souvenirs are on sale in the few shops in the village.

A white statue of the Blessed Virgin sat with inviting demeanour, a rose in each hand, framed with flowers, behind an iron grille on a stone plinth, locked up like a rare animal in the zoo. To the right was a pew, behind it a 'cloister'. Figures in a plastic tunnel represented the Stations of the Cross. Here and in front of the statue pilgrims knelt on the cement floor, their faces turned to the grille.

A farm woman in a shapeless dress met me. She was about fifty years old. Judging by the photographs I have seen, she could be Mama Rosa's sister.

I addressed her: 'Excusa, signora. . . . I have come all the way from Switzerland to ask Mama Rosa a few questions.' 'No, no! That's not possible. Mama Rosa has to pray now.' 'It doesn't matter, I'll wait an hour or two or come back in the morning. I'm a writer and I'm interested in visions of the kind Mama Rosa. . . .' In a fury she literally spouted at me: 'Mama Rosa cannot talk to you, she's ill, she's really ill. . . .' I was persistent. For a fraction of a second the idea flashed into my head of trying a few lira notes, which open the thickest doors elsewhere in Italy. I did not do so; after all I am at a miraculous spot. But – I am getting no further.

Before I went there, I knew from publications[23] what was supposed to happen at San Damiano and what made Mama Rosa a magnet for believers in miracles.

On 29 September 1961 Mrs Rosa Quattrini was doubled up with pain in her bed. She was due to have a hernia operation on the following day. She had already had three children by Caesarean operations. The eldest was studying at the seminary at Piacenza, the little ones were looked after by Aunt Adele.

Money was always scarce in the house. On that particular day they had scraped together 1,000 lire to take to the hospital. Aunt Adele was cooking a meagre repast in the kitchen when a young lady knocked at the door. She asked for a generous gift for the

Church of Santa Maria della Grazia in San Giovanni Rotondo where miracle-working Father Pio was active. Aunt Adele, to whom money was as 'sacred' as it is to all poor people, asked Rosa what she should say to the suppliant. Rosa spontaneously handed over half the money. The stranger approached the sick woman to thank her and encouraged her to stand up. Finally she pulled Mrs Quattrini gently out of bed: 'My daughter, you are cured!' The pain seemed to vanish as if by magic. The operation did not take place.

The young lady recommended Mrs Rosa to visit Father Pio. Having recovered in this miraculous way, she travelled to San Giovanni Rotondo where Father Pio, to whom long-distance cures were also attributed, advised her to start caring for the sick, as far as her family duties allowed her.

For three years life on the farm at San Damiano followed its usual course.

On 16 October 1964 Mrs Quattrini was talking to a neighbour in the orchard. Both ladies 'suddenly' — how could it be otherwise? — noticed a strange little cloud, like a veil of mist, enveloping the branches of the plum tree. Then the remarkable shape floated over to the pear tree and there a radiantly bright female figure with the two obligatory roses in her hand and a crown on her head showed herself in the cloud, which seemed to solidify. The lady threatened: 'I have come to admonish the world to pray, for the Day of Judgment is at hand!' The crafty Rosa asked: 'How will anybody believe a poor woman like me?' The Madonna answered distinctly: 'Fear not, I shall give a sign. I shall make the pear tree blossom!' The vision faded.

In October the tree still bore a basketful of ripe pears, but — as far as anyone could see — not a single flower bud. And yet the tree blossomed: not slowly, but — as eyewitnesses claimed to have seen — from one minute to the next. The miracle was repeated on the following day on the damson tree.

Since the trees flowered in that autumn, visions have never ceased for Rosa Quattrini. Nearly every Thursday Mama Rosa speaks to the Blessed Virgin and receives instructions and messages, communications for specific persons and threats for those who are not of the right faith.

I strolled through the orchard and the courtyard. From a window of the farmhouse came the noise of prayer: 'Blessed

art thou among women and blessed is the fruit of thy womb!'
Two French priests in full ceremonials knelt in front of the grille
guarding the statue of Mary.

Mama Rosa does not make things easy for Rome. The messages
ostensibly received from Mary are contradictory, naïve, often
tyrannical and sometimes larded with harsh threats. The records
prove that all her loquacious chatter could scarcely arise from
contact with any kind of divine inspiration. Nevertheless, miraculous cures take place at San Damiano, so it is said. Hundreds
of witnesses have experienced two solar miracles there.

The Church still remains aloof. On 16/17 November 1970 the
Osservatore Romano published an announcement by the Bishop
of Piacenza:

> The ostensible messages, visions and miracles have no con-
> nection with the supernatural . . . Rosa Quattrini has daily
> and publicly refused to obey her bishop. We hereby formally
> advise Rosa Quattrini that we are forced to deny her the
> sacraments, as well as access to the church. . . . The Priest
> Edgardo Pellacini, former Parish priest of San Damiano, re-
> ceived in his decree of removal from office approved by the
> Holy See the formal charge not to concern himself further
> with the so-called 'happenings at San Damiano'. . . . In addition
> we warn all other members of the church and responsible
> persons . . . both priests and laymen . . . against spreading
> reports of ostensible visions of the Blessed Virgin and messages
> from her and organizing journeys to the spot . . . otherwise we
> are forced to forbid them access to the Church and the sacra-
> ments. Disobedient priests are further threatened with sus-
> pension *a divinis*.

A slim young Capuchin monk in a brown soutane with a white
cord round his waist was strolling round the yard. I had been
watching him for hours and he smiled at me.

The hypnotic sound of *Ave Maria* being recited was everywhere: 'Holy Mary, Mother of God, pray for us sinners now and
at the hour of our death.'

I spoke to the Capuchin. I was still hoping to have an interview
with Mama Rosa. Perhaps the pious man could help me: he
behaved as if he was at home here. 'No, you cannot see Mrs
Quattrini, she has to pray. What paper do you write for? What
did you say your name was? . . . No, no one can visit her, she

doesn't receive anyone, she is talking to the Madonna.' 'Rome,' I said, 'is very obviously keeping its distance from San Damiano.' The Capuchin shrugged his shoulders, as if to say: 'Of course, but. . . .' He meant that that was the normal attitude the church would adopt; when all is said and done they would have to wait – for years or decades.

In that case what was the ecclesiastical observer doing here? I had been watching him for hours. From whom or what was he supposed to be protecting the old lady, who he said was talking to Mary? She was closely guarded. . . . When I finally gave up, I heard again the monotonous praying which hung over the courtyard like an enervating curtain of noise. Without a break. 'Who arose from the dead – who ascended into heaven – who sent us the Holy Ghost. . . .'

For six whole hours it ground out as if unreeled by a prayer wheel. Suddenly I had rather an unkind thought. Was someone in the house playing a tape over and over again?

The Capuchin was quite right. People would wait. For years. For decades. For a century. Only then would 'Mama Rosa' from San Damiano do her bit in confirming the one true church by joining the army of the saints.

I should love to be able to thumb through the list of saints, if there still is such a thing, in one or two hundred years' time. I would probably find 'Mama Rosa's' name perpetuated in it.

*   *   *

Ecclesiastical scholars such as the historian and hagiographer Walter Nigg[24] are cultivating the ground in which saints can grow and miracles flourish:

Saints personify the Christian existence, they are the best teachers of intercourse with God, and they led us directly to the burning bush. There is nothing more vivid and alive than the saints; they are exemplary men who have God before their eyes as if they could see him.

I have made a summary of characteristic cases of visions with the spectrum of their potentialities. Should we agree with Franz Werfel, author of the novel about Lourdes *The Song of Bernadette*? 'For the believer an explanation is unnecessary, for the non-believer an explanation is impossible.' Is it really?

So many visions have been confirmed in Christian countries alone and so many documented in our century that the reactions and judgments of many scholars merely bewilder me. That which is at first incomprehensible and indefinable, that which is not measurable or physically recordable, does not exist. Rationally it can only be a question of mumbo-jumbo and that is something no one talks about. People should not make it *so* easy for themselves. After studying mountains of documents, it is absolutely clear to *me* that subjectively perceived visions have taken place. At the very moment I am writing on 17 April 1974 someone is probably having a vision somewhere in the world.

The part played by imagination due to religious 'enthusiasm', the effect on what is subjectively experienced of environment, upbringing and outside influences, these are things that call for inevstigation. The negative point of view of those who deny everything that is not measurable is no longer consonant with present-day research.

It may be attractive to be witty about phenomena which one does not understand or even try to understand in order to provide small talk at parties. The task of proposing new themes, phenomena and problems for research is left to bolder spirits than mine.

Enquiry and rationalization can suggest *hypothetical* explanations of the phenonema of visions, but one thing we can definitely prove is which causes of visions can be *excluded*. Let us begin with the 'Holy Scriptures'.

Chapter 2

WHO REALLY
SPEAKS THROUGH THE BIBLE? –
ARE THE ORIGINAL TEXTS
'GOD'S WORD'?

MORE THAN a hundred thousand million people in this world call themselves Christians. What is it that ties them to their creed? A common basis is necessary for the purpose. That basis was and is the Bible.

The word Bible comes from the Greek: *ta biblia*, books. Under the entry 'bible' in the dictionary it says: 'Book of books, Holy Scriptures, the collection of writings which are regarded by the Christian Church as *documents* of the divine revelation, *God's word*, and as binding in faith and life. . . .'

Against their better judgment, the churches proclaim that the Bible is 'God's word'.

To the ears and simple heart of the humble Christian this proclamation from the anointed tongues of theologians sounds as if God in person had inspired the Book of Books and/or dictated it, and as far as the New Testament is concerned he is left to believe that the companions of Jesus of Nazareth took down his speeches, rules of life and 'prophecies' in shorthand, observed his miracles at first hand and soon afterwards noted the miraculous events down in a chronicle. The Christian then is supposed to accept the Book of Books as a collection of authentic reports. Professor Hans Conzelmann, Professor of New Testament Studies, Göttingen, admitted that the Christian community really continues to exist because the conclusions of critical examinations of the Bible are largely unknown to them. That is not the proper Christian way, but it is true.

The Bible is not what it is represented to be and even the Holy Ghost is no longer what it was originally supposed to be. I know that my theological critics will raise their eye-brows and say: 'But we know that perfectly well, you can read it in our theological literature.'

They are right. But: the churches, large and small, live among and by the public. They accompany the simple man from the cradle to the grave, at important stages of life they make themselves 'indispensable' by their ceremonies, they exercise their power and fill the church coffers in public. So it is quite unfair to say that all the errors (publicly diffused as the ultimate truth) of religious biblical dogma are available (and admitted) in the books of remote theological libraries. How many of the more than one hundred thousand million Christians ever crosses the threshold of one of those libraries?

*   *   *

Joachim Kahl[1], graduate in theology of Phillips University, Marburg, states: 'The ignorance of most Christians is largely due to the scanty information provided by theologians and ecclesiastical historians, who know two ways of concealing the scandalous facts of their books. They either twist reality into its exact opposite or conceal it.' *I* call both methods cheating the faithful.

The layman has a right to be liberated from erroneous Christian dogmas that have long since been superseded; he can, since it happens in the name of the Lord, demand that he be told the truth in an intelligible way in language without complicated and impossible theological gymnastics.

In the Constitution of the Council on the Church on 21 November 1964, in the statement of 28 November 1965 on the relationship with non-Christian religions, as well as in the solemn credo of Pope Paul VI of 30 June 1968, it was once more expressly laid down:

that the Catholic Church alone proclaims the infallible truth,

that the Catholic Church is necessary for salvation,

that the Catholic Church alone is the true heir of the divine promise,

that the Catholic Church alone is in possession of the spirit of Christ,

that the Catholic Church alone is entrusted with the infallible teaching office,

that the Catholic Church alone is in possession of the absolute truth.

On 18 November 1965 the Catholic Church proclaimed solemnly and most officially in the dogmatic constitution:

that *God was the originator* of the Bible,

that *all parts* of the Bible are sacred,

that *all parts* of the Bible were composed under the influence of the Holy Ghost,

that *everything* that the inspired composers of the Bible say must be considered to be written by the Holy Ghost and that what is taught in the Bible is *accurate, true and without error.*

So that they can defend this exclusive property to the vast community of believers, theologists, unaffected by the results of their biblical research, base themselves on the evangelists, the epistles of the apostles and the miraculous 'original text' of the Holy Scriptures.

But none of the evangelists was a contemporary of Jesus and no contemporary wrote an eyewitness account. Nothing was written down about Jesus and his followers until after the destruction of Jerusalem by the Roman Emperor Titus (AD 39-81) in the year 70. And if the year 30 is accepted for the death of the Son of God, then Mark, the first author of the Bible, wrote his gospel at least forty years after the crucifixion of Jesus. Dr Johannes Lehmann[2], co-translator of a modern edition of the Bible, says on this point: 'The evangelists are interpreters, not biographers; they have not illuminated what had grown dark with the passage of generations, but obscured what was still light. They have not written history, but made history. They did not want to report, but to justify.'

The 'original texts', so frequently consulted and so abundant in theological hairsplitting, do not exist at all. What do we possess? Transcripts that without exception originated between the fourth and tenth centuries AD. And these transcripts, some 1,500 of them, are transcripts of transcripts, and not a single transcript agrees with another. Over 80,000 (!) variations have been counted. There is not a single page of the 'original texts' without contradictions. From copy to copy the verses were understood differently by sympathetic authors and their functions transformed to suit contemporary needs.

The biblical 'original texts' teem with thousands and thousands of easily provable and well-known errors. The most prominent of them, the *Codex Sinaiticus* – written in the fourth century AD, like the *Codex Vaticanus* – was found in the Sinai Convent in 1844. It contains 16,000 corrections, which are supposed to go back to seven correctors. Many passages were altered three times and replaced by a fourth 'original text'. Friedrich Delitzsch[3], author of a Hebrew dictionary and a first-rate scholar, established about 3,000 copying mistakes in the 'original text'.

This business of the 'original text' is a symptom of the sublime art of theological description. Every normal mortal connects the concept 'original text' with the very first version, an undisputed and undisputable document. What would the Christian layman say if he was told openly from the pulpit that an original text in this sense did not exist?

It is staggering that the fairy tale of the Bible as 'God's word' has endured so long – there is no comparison in the 7,000 years of human history. But the fact that the 'original texts,' which teem with contradictions and falsifications, are still publicized as 'God's word' borders on schizophrenia. I know that falsification is a harsh description, for falsification means nothing more or less than being intentionally misleading. But even the Fathers of the Church of the first centuries AD agreed that, though they might quarrel about the culprits, the 'original texts' were falsified; they still spoke openly of 'interpolations, profanation, destruction, improvement, corruption, erasing' – but that is long ago and then as now the hair-splitting does not alter the objective fact of falsification.

Christian theologians, naturally enough, do not like to hear anyone talk about falsifications. They take the forgers under their black wings and whisper about 'conscious alterations', they wrap the correctors in verbal cotton wool and claim that they acted in the interests of the true word of God – to which they must have had access long after Christ.

Dr Robert Kehl[4], Zurich, writes in connection with the falsifications: 'Frequently the same passage has been "corrected" by one corrector in one sense and immediately "recorrected" in the opposite sense by another, depending entirely on which dogmatic view had to be defended in the relevant school. At all events, a completely chaotic text and irremediable confusion has already arisen owing to individual "corrections", but even more so to deliberate ones.' And the priest Jean Schorrer[5], for many years spiritual adviser to the Cathedral of Saint-Pierre, Geneva, came to the conclusion that the theory of the total inspiration of the Bible and the idea that God was its author were untenable: this idea clashed so fiercely with the most elementary knowledge of healthy human reason and is refuted so clearly by the Bible itself, that it could only be defended by ignorant evangelists and a flock devoid of any kind of general culture.

*　　*　　*

In *some* recent editions of the Bible – for example, in the popular edition of the Zurich Bible – it is at least admitted that some passages were added by a later hand. But even this is only a very hesitant indication of the massive manipulation to which the biblical texts have been subjected. In the series *Die Religion des modernen Menschen*[6], Dr Robert Kehl gives a sketch of what really happened. I quote:

Most believers in the Bible have the naïve credo that the Bible has always existed in the form in which they read it today. They believe that the Bible has always contained all the sections which are found in their personal copy of the Bible. They do not know – *and most of them do not want to know* – that for about 200 years the first Christians had no 'scripture' apart from the Old Testament, and that even the Old Testament canon had not been definitively established in the days of the early Christians, that written versions of the New Testament only came into being quite slowly, *that for a long time no one dreamt of considering these New Testament writings as Holy Scripture*, that with the passage of time the custom arose of reading these writings to the congregations, but that *even then no one dreamt of treating them as Holy Scripture with the same status as the Old Testament*, that this idea first occurred to people when the different factions in Christianity were fighting each other and they felt the need to be able to back themselves up with something binding, that in this way people only began to regard these writings as Holy Scripture about AD 200.

In other words, there is nothing there about inspiration by a spirit, not even by the Holy Ghost. 'God's word' sneaks in as if by a secret ballot in which black and white balls are used. Those are facts. It would be more convincing if the world organizations which claim to be guardians of the ultimate and only truth did not limit themselves to dealing with historical facts in discussions that are dialectically perfect, but unintelligible to a layman. What they should do is use a first-class public relations system to bring the facts to the 'common people' in generally intelligible language! Do they lack the courage of their convictions? Are they worried lest the business basis, the paid-up capital as it were, be taken away from their 'limited company' if it were admitted that the Bible is *not* 'God's word', because it *cannot* be so according to the proven way in which it originated? How long are the leaders of the Church going to persist in the error that the faithful can be kept in a state of Christian humility and ingenuousness? How long do they think they can describe contradictions and falsifications as 'willed by God', 'for the salvation of the faithful' or inspired by the 'Holy Ghost'? If that is the way facts are treated, what has theological scholarship to do with knowledge? Nevertheless theology is allotted a special faculty in the universities: it is financed by the taxpayer, who usually calls himself a Christian. I assume that straight-forward scientific knowledge is imparted to the theological students in these faculties. What kind of distortion takes place between academic teaching and what is preached from the pulpit? Where does the 'brainwashing' take place that causes the facts to be forgotten, and the old song of the Bible as the true word of God rung out once more from the pulpit?

* * *

It all began with the councils, the assemblies of senior pastors for dealing with important ecclesiastical affairs. A prerequisite for the appointment of an official of the church is that he have 'charisma', i.e. that he shares the 'divine gift of grace'. Hence when councils with such illustrious members meet, the Holy Ghost is among them, omnipresent and active.

The Assemblies of the first five Ecumenical (which means the whole Catholic Church) Councils of the early Christian world set the standards for the doctrine and organization of the new religion.

The oldest dogmas, which are still valid today, were proclaimed at Nicea (AD 325), Constantinople (381), Ephesus (431), Chalcedon (451) and again at Constantinople (553). It is worthwhile taking a quick look at how the Councils came into being and what decisions were taken at them – presumably for all eternity.

The first Ecumenical Council took place at Nicea. The Council was convened by the Emperor Constantine (who was not crowned until he was on his deathbed), because he wanted to use the rapidly expanding Christian religion, with its great potentialities, to strengthen the Roman Empire. When Constantine picked out and convened the 318 bishops for the Council, the background was pure power politics, religious concerns taking very much of a backseat. Even the charismatic bishops can have been in no doubt about that, for not only did the Emperor preside over the Council, he also expressly proclaimed that his will was ecclesiastical law. The senior pastors accepted him as 'Universal Bishop', even though he was uncrowned, and let him take part in votes on church dogma as a secular prince. Ecclesiastical and earthly interests entered into an astonishing symbiosis even at that early stage!

Constantine was completely ignorant of Jesus' teaching. He was an adherent of the solar cult of Mithras (ancient Iranian god of light), who was portrayed on coins as the 'invincible sun' and worshipped until far into the Christian era. When he gave his name to the old Greek commercial city of Byzantium and made Constantinople (330) the capital of the Roman Empire, he had a mighty column erected for the ceremonial opening of the metropolis, with the Emperor and the invincible sun on top of it, forgetting all about Christian humility. Clouds of incense floated in the air and candle-lit processions made their tortuous way through the streets in his honour. Far from abolishing slavery in the Christian spirit of loving one's neighbour, the Pontifex ordered that slaves caught pilfering food should have molten lead poured down their throats and allowed parents to sell their children in times of need.

What were the ecclesiastical-cum-political decisions that this pasha had a hand in?

Until Nicea, the doctrine of Arius of Alexandria that God and Christ were not identical, but only similar, held good. Constantine forced the Council to proclaim that God the Father and Jesus were of the same essence. This absolutely vital amendment became *church dogma* by imperial decree. That is how Jesus became identical with God. With this as a foundation, the bishops unanimously passed the 'Nicene Creed'.

The non-Christian Constantine did the Church another enormous service. Until that time, the place where Jesus was buried had remained unknown. Then, in the year of grace 326, the Roman Emperor, led by 'divine inspiration', discovered the grave of Jesus, who had just become consubstantial with God. (In 330 Constantine had the Church of the Holy Sepulchre built.) However, this wonderful discovery did not stop Constantine from murdering some of his close relatives during the same year: his son Crispus, his wife Faustina, whom he had plunged into boiling water, and his father-in-law Maximian, whom he imprisoned and forced to commit suicide.

That is the image of the Emperor and Pontifex who stage-managed the Nicene Creed and who, when the Council was over, told the Christian communities in a circular letter that the agreement of the 318 bishops was the 'Decision of God'.

Incidentally, Constantine the Great was canonized by the Armenian, Greek and Russian Churches.

The second Ecumenical Council was at Constantinople. This council was convened by the Emperor Theodosius I (347-395), who was flatteringly nicknamed 'the Great' by the Church. This Roman Emperor did not lag behind his colleague Constantine in moral qualities. He was a veritable oppressor of the poor, so history tells us, who swamped the common people with intolerable burdens, which his tax collectors exacted with brutal tortures. With the full rigour of his imperial power, he forbade anyone to give refuge to any of these downtrodden creatures who might have offended him. If they did so, he had the inhabitants of whole villages slaughtered. In the year 390 (i.e. almost ten years after the holy council) he had 7,000 rebellious citizens murdered in a frightful bloodbath in the circus of the town of Thessalonika – at the same time as the 'Halleluya' (Praise Jehovah) came into use in Christian churches. Theodosius proclaimed the Christian doctrine the state religion (hence 'the Great') and made Ambrosius, Bishop of Milan, raze all heathen sanctuaries to the ground. With his methods Theodosius could well have been the ancestor of the Inquisition. If Jesus preached a joyous message to the poor and oppressed, Theodosius was Antichrist in person. Yet this 'Unholy Ghost' convened the second Council at Constantinople.

What happened there?

The dogma of the Trinity of Father, Son and Holy Ghost, was

introduced into church doctrine by the assembly of senior pastors known by theological experts as the Rump Council. It was turned into the 'Niceno-Constantinopolitan Creed'. Thus – something for connoisseurs of the finer points of theology – was introduced the doctrine of the consubstantiality of Father, Son and Holy Ghost. Today the Church still feeds on the dogma of the Trinity that was added in this way.

The third Ecumenical Council at Ephesus was convened by the East Roman Emperor Theodosius II (408-450) and the West Roman Emperor Valentianus III (425-455). These two emperors did not bother their heads about secular or ecclesiastical problems: they were playboys. So they seldom graced the council with their presence.

Theodosius II was a weakling who devoted himself wholly to his hobbies and tyranically levied taxes from his subjects to pay for his extravagant way of life. The Emperor was lavish in taking 'what was the Emperor's'. It is small wonder that he was completely under the influence of his power-obsessed intriguing elder sister Pulcheria (399-453). For some time she acted as regent for her brother and boasted of being a virgin (which only made her contemporaries laugh) on every suitable and unsuitable occasion. Her pious protestation sufficed to get her made a saint, though this did not stop her, after her brother's death, from having his able and successful rival Chrysophus murdered. As for his West Roman imperial colleague Valentianus, he was under the thumb of his mother Galla Placidia and ultimately assassinated.

What happened at Ephesus?

The Council declared that Mary should be worshipped as the Mother of God. By inclusion in the 'Theodosian Codex', their decision became an imperial law. Thus one thing followed another, and the Holy Ghost was ever present. . . .

The fourth Ecumenical Council at Chalcedon was formally convened by the Byzantine Emperor Marcianus (396-457), but in reality it was run by the virgin Pulcheria, who had married Marcianus after the death of Theodosius. She knew far better than the bishops what she wanted. The theologian Eduard Schwartz[7] came to the conclusion that Pulcheria convened and pushed through the Council against the will of the various churches, and held the reins of the deliberations firmly in her hands.

What happened at Chalcedon?

With his *Epistola dogmatica* (Dogmatic Letter), Pope Leo I initiated the dogmatic formula that Jesus had two natures. The Council proclaimed the doctrine that divine and human nature are unalloyed and inseparably united in the person of Jesus. This double nature still persists today as the 'Chalcedonian Creed'. Last, but not least, the preservation of the unity of the doctrine was entrusted to the Pope, who could intervene whenever he saw fit. That is how the primacy of Rome originated. The foundations for future developments were made official. Today the men in the Vatican must still be grateful to the unholy Pulcheria for pushing through the Council of Chalcedon with her intrigues.

The fifth Ecumenical Council was again at Constantinople. It was staged by the East Roman Emperor Justinian I (483-565). He was no mean despot, but in spite of or because of it he fell in with the whims of his wife and co-regent Theodora (497-548). This daughter of a circus attendant deserved well of her husband, because she saved the throne during the rebellion of Nika (532), when there was an uprising against the tyrannical sovereign. After this service, she was able to give her fanatical will full rein and wipe out the rest of heathendom, a project which the senior pastors of the Council warmly encouraged.

The bishops of the Fifth Council had virtually no work to do. Anything that Justinian had in mind had been achieved long before by imperial decrees and laws. It is not unironical to find this assembly described in theological literature as the 'Council of Acclamation'.

Justinian summoned Pope Vigilius (537-555) – 'Unworthy representative of his office', who was later quoted by opponents of papal infallibility to prove their case – to Constantinople. Vigilius and the bishops submitted themselves to the power-political interests of the Emperor, who found a place in the history books because of his pitiless laws against heretics. Henceforth a 'heretic' was anyone who denied the Christian dogmas. He was subject to savage punishments, and even death. An army of Roman officials tracked down dissenters, rounding them up in droves and forcing them to accept Christian baptism on Justinian's orders.

The Byzantine historian Procopius (circa 490-555) was author of a *History of Justinian's Wars against the Persians, Vandals and Goths,* and a book about Justinian's buildings (*Hagia Sophia!*), but he also wrote a pamphlet against Justinian and his wife Theodora. Procopius, who presumably knew his noble lord well, described Justinian as proud, hypocritical, unrighteous, malicious, cruel and bloodthirsty. Christian interpreters of history like to deviate from Procopius's description. Naturally! For Justinian was canonized like the Emperors Constantine and Theodosius.

What happened at the Council?

The Greek ecclesiastical writer Origen (circa 185-254), a teacher in the catechists' school at Alexandria, was the most important theologian in Christian antiquity and the first advocate of a critical examination of the Bible. With the help of his Platonic training he had to some extent made the scriptures intelligible and spiritualized them by allegorical interpretations. The Council condemned his deviations and said his exegeses were unorthodox. What was to be orthodox in future was exclusively determined by the leaders of the Church, inspired by the Holy Ghost. When this decision was taken by the Council, persecution was not confined to Origen's numerous followers; the *view halloo!* to hunt all the other dissenters was also sounded.

(About this time the ring which bishops wear became a symbol of 'marriage' to the Church. A strange union, in my opinion between man and Holy Ghost.)

*　　*　　*

The Bible is not 'God's word'. Moreover, the dogmas concocted at the first five councils by an army of princes of the church are not inspired by the Holy Ghost — in spite of the participants' supposed charisma. This comes as a severe shock to the average religious layman, because he is usually unprepared for it. What is left?

What is the truth about Jesus? Did he exist? Did he bleed to death on the Cross for our sins? Did he really preach what is recorded in the New Testament? And if the texts put into the mouth of Jesus are not by him, where did the 1,500 copies of copies of the 'original text' originate from? *Something* must have happened. One single figure out of many who were crucified could not kindle and support such a colossal cult of personality. Clever heads were at work.

There are thousands of books about Jesus of Nazareth. Versions of the story of Jesus based on the *latest* research have recently been published by authors such as Johannes Lehmann[8], Joel Carmichael[9] and Rudolf Augstein[10]. Naturally these critics of misleading interpretations of Jesus are contradicted by the theological party, yet when one analyses the prevarications of the group of authors[11] writing about Augstein's *Jesus Menschensohn*, one recognizes only the time-honoured technique that Joachim Kahl called 'camouflage'.

Christian theologians make the dogma of Jesus – the established religious doctrine with the claim to unconditional validity, the unproved proposition[12] – the salient point of the Christian religion. Even that seems understandable, if rash, to me, because the hundreds of thousands of pastors of all the Christian churches would lose their jobs and their personal *raison d'etre* if they could no longer act in the name of Jesus. To be honest they would have to say to the little man in the seventeenth row of the nave that Jesus of Nazareth was *not* 'God's only begotten son' and that he himself never pretended that he was. In fact, it would be asking a lot to expect such a pronouncement from the pulpit. What then was the real Jesus like?

Rudolf Augstein[13] asks: '. . . with what right do the Christian churches refer to a Jesus who did not exist in the form they claim, to doctrines which he did not teach, to an absolute authority which he did not confer and to a filiation with God which he never laid claim to.'

These are no novelties to the initiated, but I am addressing the ignorant, the laymen, who neither know nor understand theological double-Dutch. Once again, I am taking it on my broad back to translate professorial wisdom into generally intelligible language – knowing perfectly well what a sound thrashing by Christian specialists awaits me. It is not in my nature simply to believe *'par ordre du mufti'*.

The wisdom of theologians has been printed in hundreds of thousands of books which can be found in archives and libraries. So that everyone can understand me, I must begin at the beginning.

*   *   *

For nearly two thousand years now the Christian has been given an unbearable burden to carry on his way through life: he is inflicted with original sin from birth and he needs the 'Redeemer' to free himself from it.

We all learnt in school and church that God was the beginning and end of everything, *alpha* and *omega*, that God was almighty, infinitely good, all-righteous, omniscient, omnipresent and eternal.

So far I accept the concept of God without reservations. But because he is eternal God is also timeless: he knows no yesterday, today or tomorrow. Eternal and omnipresent God does not need to await the results of his measures. He does not need to ask how they are going to turn out, for he already knows the answer.

In my Catholic school I listened attentively to the charming story of how God in his goodness made two harmless creatures a present of a stay in Paradise, the home of joy and happiness. Adam and Eve, the chosen ones, lived a carefree existence. They lacked nothing and they had no desires or longings. There was only one thing that was strictly forbidden them by God the Father. They must not eat of the Tree of Knowledge. It was the first case of 'Off limits'!

We are nonplussed. Why did the Almighty make this strict prohibition? Did he enjoy this kindergarten for the first people on earth? Could God share the human *happiness* which Adam and Eve experienced in the Garden of Eden, since he, the sublime, stood high above mankind? Why did he want to keep 'knowledge' from his first-created children?

Theologians have an answer. God wanted to 'bestow love' on them and wished that they should both 'partake' of his kingdom. For heavens' sake! According to that interpretation, God is supposed to have yearned for love . . . and to have felt lonely. In my opinion, those are not feelings that befit God, for he of all people is boundlessly happy in his omnipotence. An inter-mediate condition – 'A little love might be nice' or 'It's boring, playmates wouldn't be a bad idea' – does not exist for an exclusive God. So what was he trying to achieve with his humans in Paradise?

Again, theologians have the answer pat. God wanted to lead

Adam and Eve into temptation, he wanted to test them. That doesn't wash, reverend gentlemen. What kind of low opinion have they of God? 'Temptation' and 'testing' would be mere cardsharper's tricks, since he, the omniscient, must have known the results of the temptation beforehand. Now suppose we play with the idea that they did *not*, having free will, eat the apple. What would have happened if they had not recognized their shameful nakedness – and with it the possibility of procreation? Would God have had to create more and more human beings – on the assembly-line system? People, who, thanks to their free will, would not have striven for 'knowledge', because they obediently observed God's ban? God obviously had the 'Fall' in his calculations, because he was omniscient. Otherwise many countries in the world would not be bursting at the seams with overpopulation today.

Adam and Eve did not pluck the apple from the bough casually. There was a tempter, the devil or snake. But every created thing comes from God. At least, that's what we've learnt. So that logically the devil (or snake) is also a product of God. Was our benevolent God so infamous as to create a devil or snake in order to deceive two innocents? And why is God so shocked after the vegetarian meal to find that from then on sin is ineradicable in his world? HE knew in advance exactly what would happen.

Theologists tug at my sleeve. It wasn't like that! Lucifer, the devil, they say, was a renegade in God's kingdom. A renegade in the kingdom of heaven? If the 'kingdom of heaven' equals bliss (as we are promised), there cannot be any opposition, rebels or renegades in it. Either – or. If God's kingdom guarantees the state of perfect happiness, Lucifer would certainly not have had the idea of disobeying God. However, if absolute happiness did not exist there, it was because God was not almighty enough to create such a state. Here, too, there is a weak point in the theologians' argument. They are unable either to dismiss the struggle between God and Lucifer or to motivate it logically. Before Lucifer approached the inhabitants of Paradise to tempt them, God *must have known* that his devilishness would succeed. And the business of Adam and Eve's 'free will' remains a kind of *deus ex machina*. Even with the interpolation of Lucifer, the snake, Adam and Eve acted at the will and behest of almighty God.

To a man who takes the word that was taught him at its face value, the situation presents itself as follows. God did not live in a perfect heaven, for there was an opposition in it. Lucifer set to work in Paradise and egged on Adam and Eve to commit a sin which God knew was about to happen. Then the apple was eaten. Then came the crowning episode: (omniscient) God was so offended that, beside himself with wrath, he cursed the innocent descendants of the first married couple for all eternity and branded the stain of 'original sin' on to the family tree as a ghastly heritage. Everyone born since then carries 'original sin' with him from the cradle.

How can miserable mankind be freed of this burden? Only by a redeemer. The Bible says: 'God so loved the world, that he gave his only begotten son. . . .'

Not being overcritical, people accepted this son who had cropped up so suddenly, although it is difficult to conceive of the one and only God with a family. This son is to be envied, since he has a 'heavenly' father, full of love, goodness and solicitude. That is what one would think, but it is not the case. He is handed over to mankind (suffering under the burden of original sin), so that he can free his brothers and sisters from their burden. The son of God has to be nailed to the Cross and bled to death in agony. After the death of his 'only begotten son' God is appeased again! Surely this ghastly story contains ideas from barbaric pagan cults? This dogma of redemption seems to me to be a kind of throwback to primitive religions which forced their servants to propitiate their wrathful gods with blood sacrifices.

The crucifixion, theologians assure us, is only to be understood symbolically. Why is this not made quite clear in religious teaching? My daughter Lela learns – like all previous generations – that Jesus was the only begotten son of God made flesh, that he suffered every pain (= the oppressing original sins) as a man. That he died as a man, struggled as a man, with all the attendant torments and miseries. But how can God, who *knowingly* let *his* own son be tortured – because Adam and Eve committed a sin that he could easily have prevented through his foreknowledge – be reconciled by Christ's death with the very men who killed him? (With this macabre end to the story original sin should really have been banished from the world. But it is still about.)

c

Theologians, full of ideas and skilled in dialectics, recently sought a path which would lead out of this dilemma, but it terminated in a dead end.

They now say that God the Father did not so love the world that he sacrificed his only begotten son, but that Jesus sacrificed himself of his own 'free will' out of love of mankind. Unfortunately this about-turn does not produce any significant conclusion.

God the Father and God the Son are unalloyed and inseparable, according to Christian dogma (the Nicene and Chalcedonian creeds). So it makes no difference what one or the other does. Either way the sacrifice remains senseless. Father and Son were (and are) 'one' from the beginning according to current doctrine. Hence both of them knew what was going to happen at any given moment. As this does not resolve the contradiction, the ecclesiastical teachers thought up an – absolutely final? – interpretation. Jesus wanted to show mankind how they should live in order to please God the Father.

Does that bring us back to the beginning again, to zero? If the whole of mankind is supposed to become 'pleasing to God', then the Almighty would simply have had to plan that our ancestors Adam and Eve should become so, according to his divine will. That would have been quite within his powers, wouldn't it?

Surely the dogmas of original sin and redemption lack any kind of foundation when considered in the cold light of reason?

Even in the interests of the Christian churches, I consider blood sacrifices and redemption by the crucifixion to be dangerous doctrines. Made dogmas by the early councils they became the authority for torture and murder during the trials of heretics, they became the approved rituals of the Inquisition and even today they 'inspire' salvation-seeking youth and members of obscure sects to ghastly exorcistic ritual murders with whose sacrifices these criminals still pretend to 'propitiate' God.

*   *   *

Jesus was a Jew. His date of birth is unknown. His name is not to be found in any register of births, yet the Christian west bases its calendar on the ostensible (and accepted) year of Jesus' birth. The first time that his name appears is in one of St Paul's epistles, about the year 50 of the new era.

In the Gospels according to St Matthew and St Luke it says Jesus was 'born at Bethlehem'. St Mark, on the other hand, names Nazareth as the place of birth. Right from the birth of the Redeemer confusion and contradictions make the Bible adventurous reading.

Mary is universally mentioned as his mother. His father, Joseph the carpenter, is not the physical father, for Mary received the sperm by 'immaculate conception' with the co-operation of the Holy Ghost. That is Christian popular *belief*, for reason cannot grasp this process of impregnation. So especially illuminated theologians take great pains to prove what is meant by 'immaculate conception'.

According to the official biography, the New Testament, the trail of the infant Jesus is lost after his birth until he suddenly crops up again in the Temple as a twelve-year-old runaway – in heated theological conversation with scholars. Unfortunately we never know exactly what is true and what is not, what actually happened and what forgers invented (original texts!).

If it is correct, and that is what I am assuming here, that the twelve-year-old could tie the clever temple scholars up in theological discussion, the precocious lad must have been drilled in the Old Testament texts in some contemporary school.

What kind of school was available to him? We must recall the historical background to find the answer.

The territory we call the 'Near East' today belonged at the time we are concerned with to the gigantic Roman Empire. Damascus was conquered in 64 BC by the famous general Pompeius Magnus (106-48), Jerusalem was taken in 37 and Egypt became a Roman province in 30. What happened in this century to Caius Julius Caesar in the conquered and occupied territories is not hidden in historic mist.

Presumably occupying forces have been made of the same stuff in all ages. At all events the Romans brought their way of life with them and propagated their culture in the occupied countries. The Roman soldiers were no saints: they worshipped Apollo (taken over from the Greeks), the god of poetry, music and youth, emptied their beakers to the health of the god Bacchus (Dionysus), wooed the goddess Fortuna for luck, implored pity from Jupiter, god of lightning, thunder and justice, prayed to

Neptune, god of water, for rain, knelt in devotion before Sol, the sun god. Abomination to any orthodox Jew!

For more than 400 years — Ezra compiled the text of the Torah as early as 440 BC — the Jewish people had lived according to the Mosaic Law, the Pentateuch and the Torah. And the patriarch Moses said in the law:

Thou shall have no other gods before me.

Thou shalt not make unto thee any graven image, or any likeness of anything that is in heaven above, or that is in the earth beneath, or that is in the water under the earth.

Thou shalt not bow down thyself to them, nor serve them: for I the Lord thy God am a jealous God. (Exodus 20. 4-5)

Moses was a monotheist. When the founder of the Jewish religion had led the Israelites back into Palestine from Egypt circa 1230 BC, he had the legendary tablets with the commandments set up on Mount Sinai. Thus the recognition and worship of a single god was an old tradition, when the Romans practised polytheism among the Jews.

The Jews could do nothing about it. With gnashing of teeth they lived together with the hated heavily armed occupiers, who, I should remark in passing, neither encouraged nor forced conquered peoples to worship their gods. Very sensibly, they even gave them a measure of self-government. True, the Temple was guarded by Roman soldiers, but it was administered by Jews. In the forecourts money-changers, merchants with their stalls and artisans in their booths carried on their business.

So at the time of the Roman occupation, the time of Jesus, the Torah — the basic law of the Jewish state since 443 BC — was still the religious doctrine of the Jews.

The *Sadducees*, representatives of the conservative religious party, were strict guardians, preservers and teachers of the Mosaic law. *One* possible school for the infant Jesus could be sought among them. . . . The Sadducees' opponents were the *Pharisees*, the progressives, who admittedly also kept the letter of the Mosaic Law, but who accepted angels and resurrection from the dead in their teaching. As scribes they gained considerable influence over Judaism at the time of Jesus with their law schools. Here was a *second* possible answer to the problem of Jesus' schooling.

If we follow the gospels, Jesus did not agree with the Sadducees

or the Pharisees. He often made fun of the 'scribes' and the New
Testament also states that they did not accept the forward
young man as one of their kind. But if Jesus had been a graduate
of a Sadducees' or Pharisees' school, he would have been recognized or expelled as a renegade. Nothing of the kind has been
handed down: the name of Jesus of Bethlehem or Nazareth does
not figure in any writings by the scribes. The disputatious Jesus
must have acquired his knowledge somewhere else. Where? Was
there a *third* school? There was, but it has not been common
knowledge for very long.

Until AD 68 the extraordinarily conservative fraternity of the
Essenes lived deliberately isolated from temple Jewry in a
monastic-like habitat that had been rebuilt after an earthquake.
It was situated at Chirbet Qumran in a fissured mountainous
region on the Dead Sea. The 'Army of Salvation' traced their
origin to a 'Teacher of Righteousness' from the time of the
Maccabees, centuries before Christ. The Essenes concluded their
'New Covenant' in order to prepare the Messianic kingdom. The
oldest reports about this ascetic sect are found in an essay by
Philo of Alexandria (25 BC – AD 50): *'Quod omnis probus liber
sit'*[14]

Palestinian Syria, inhabited by a considerable section of the
very numerous people of the Jews, is also not unfruitful in the
production of virtues. Certain of them, more than 4,000 in
number, are called Essenes; in my view, although it is not
strictly speaking a Greek word, it is connected with the word
'holiness'; these are in fact men who are quite specially devoted to the service of God; but they do not make animal
sacrifices. They find it more advisable to consecrate their
thoughts. . . . They amass neither silver, nor gold, and they do
not cultivate large tracts of land because they want to get
income from them, but limit themselves to providing for the
necessaries of life. Almost alone among men, they live without
goods or property . . . nevertheless they consider themselves
rich because they rate sufficiency and a good disposition as a
genuine excess. . . . They reject everything that could awake
avarice in them. . . . They do not possess a single slave, on the
contrary they are all free and help each other mutually. . . .
Thousands of examples testify to their love of God . . . con-
tempt for wealth and honours, aversion from pleasure. . . .

They have a single fund for all, and communal expenses . . .
and the custom of communal meals . . . nowhere else could one
find a better practical example of men sharing the same roof,
the same way of life and the same table. . . .

The intriguing nature of the Essene community also struck
the Jewish historian and general Flavius Josephus (37-97), who
mentioned them in his books *The Jewish War* and *Antiquities of
the Jews*. In Chapter 7 of Book II of *The Jewish War*[15], he gives
details of this religious community which I quote literally:

Among the Jews there are three schools of thought, whose
adherents are called Pharisees, Sadducees and Essenes respect-
ively. The Essenes profess a severer discipline: they are Jews by
birth and are particularly attached to each other. . . . Scorning
wedlock, *they select other men's children while still pliable and
teachable, and fashion them after their own pattern.* Con-
temptuous of wealth . . . their rule is that novices admitted to
the sect must surrender their property to the order. . . . When
adherents arrive from elsewhere, all local resources are put at
their disposal as if they were their own. . . . In dress and personal appearance they are like children in the care of a stern
tutor. Neither garments nor shoes are changed till they are
dropping to pieces or worn out with age. . . . The priest says
grace before meat. . . . After breakfast he offers a second prayer
. . . (only) two things are left entirely to them . . . personal aid,
and charity . . . they champion good faith and serve the cause
of peace. . . . They are wonderfully devoted to the works of
ancient writers, choosing mostly books that can help soul and
body . . . they . . . conquer pain by sheer will-power: death, if
it comes with honour, they value more than life without end.
Their spirit was tested to the utmost by the war with the
Romans, who racked and twisted, burnt and broke them, sub-
jecting them to every torture yet invented to make them
blaspheme the Lawgiver or eat some forbidden food, but could
not make them do either, or ever once fawn on their tormentors
or shed a tear. . . . It is indeed *their unshakeable conviction that
bodies are corruptible and the material composing them im-
permanent, whereas souls remain immortal for ever.* . . . Some
of them claim to foretell the future . . . rarely if ever do their
predictions prove wrong. . . .

Flavius Josephus, who wrote these words in AD 77, knew all

this about the Essenes, because, by his own account, he himself had lived among them for three years. It is highly probable that he also knew the written traditions and leather scrolls from about 100 BC which the community had packed in jars and hidden in nearby caves during a rebellion that threatened them (66).

This theological bomb with a time-fuse of 2,000 years exploded. In 1947 the original documents hidden by the Essenes, now known as 'The Dead Sea Scrolls'[16], were found by accident in caves at Wadi Qumran. Since then they have had an unshakeable place in theological historical literature. Heinrich Alexander Stoll has told the whole exciting story of the Qumran texts in the book *The Caves by the Dead Sea*[17]. This incredibly valuable *Manual of Discipline*, already supplied with commentaries by the Essenes (!), found its way half way round the world, was appraised in universities and monasteries until it came into the good hands of objective scholars such as Professor André Dupont-Sommer[18] and Professor Millar Burrows, after all kinds of intrigues and haggling[19].

The translations of the Qumran Scrolls show quite unequivocally that vital parts of the Gospels originated from the Essene school; that Jesus' style and way of life followed the customs of the Essenes and that parables, such as Jesus used, indeed whole sermons attributed to him, had been taught by the Essenes long before him.

Textual comparisons of the Qumran Scrolls and the New Testament would be recognized and confirmed as clearly tallying with one another by any normal court of law – not so by Christian theologians. As if there was something reprehensible about the remarks of Jesus of Nazareth or Bethlehem containing the spiritual teachings of the ascetic Essene community! But here Jesus' consubstantiality with God, ordained in Nicea, stands in the way. The Essenes were simple members of an order who had their own doctrine long *before* Christ. Jesus an epigone? Impossible. The Christian guardians of the pure teaching of Jesus find that intolerable. Albert Schweitzer[20] obviously did not speak clearly enough when he said: 'Modern Christianity must always as a matter of course reckon with the possibility of abandoning the authenticity of Jesus.'

Here are some examples of clear agreements between the

teaching of the Essenes and the teaching of Jesus:

The Essenes did not baptize. Neither did Jesus.

The Essenes denounced the theologians of their time, the Sadducees and Pharisees. So did Jesus.

The Essenes preached meekness and humility to please God. So did Jesus.

The Essenes warned of an imminent 'Last Judgment with fire'. So did Jesus.

The Essenes said a man must love his neighbour like himself. That was the *leitmotiv* of all Jesus' speeches.

The Essenes spoke of the 'Sons of Light' who fight against the 'powers of darkness'. Who does not know these metaphors from Jesus' sayings?

The Essenes preached the 'spirit of truth' and promised 'eternal life'. Jesus did so, too.

The Essenes spoke of 'members of the New Covenant' and the 'Holy Ghost'. What did Jesus do?

The Essenes had communal meals preceded by saying grace — like Jesus at the Last Supper.

The Essenes spoke of the foundation 'that will not be shaken' — Jesus of the rock (Peter) against which the gates of hell shall not prevail.

'Beatitudes' were found in the fourth Qumran cave that begin sentence after sentence with the word 'Blessed' — the opening phrase that Jesus used in his Sermon on the Mount.

The Essenes required every member who had just entered their community to confess his sins — an iron law of Christianity.

With so many proofs (they are no mere indications), the question inevitably arises whether Jesus, too, did not spend a period among the Essenes, just like the historian Flavius Josephus. For nineteen Christian centuries clever men puzzled over the accounts of Flavius Josephus: no one knew anything about the Essenes. They are not mentioned in the Gospels or the Acts of the Apostles. Had Flavius Josephus penned a science-fiction story about a non-existent order? The discovery of the Qumran Scrolls posthumously confirmed him as a scrupulous historian.

I still remember perfectly the day when I, as a boarder at the strict Catholic College of Saint-Michel, Fribourg, first heard Jesus' moving speech of farewell to his Apostles, in which he announced the 'Last Judgment' to them and prophesied that the Lord 'shall

set the sheep on his right hand, but the goats on the left'
(Matthew 25, 33 *et seq.*).

> Then shall the King say unto them on his right hand, come,
> ye blessed of my Father, inherit the kingdom prepared for you
> from the foundation of the world.
>
> For I was anhungered, and ye gave me meat. I was thirsty,
> and ye gave me drink: I was a stranger, and you took me in.
>
> Naked, and ye clothed me: I was sick, and ye visited me: I
> was in prison and ye came unto me.

The Prefect of the College exhorted us to live every day in such
a way that we stood before God with a pure heart at every
moment, because we had never doubted his word, because we had
always believed God's word, without deviating one iota from the
scripture.

During the sermon I realized that I would definitely stand on
the left side, for I was full of doubts. How is that, I mused? Is
the Prefect right when he says that God will reward the faithful
who have no doubts? Will those who can believe without temptation stand on the right hand side of God? Simply because they
have always *believed*? True, the Prefect incessantly based himself
on God's word, but he had never been present at a heavenly
selection board or when the faithful were rewarded! The Prefect
might be wrong.

For all my doubts I was nevertheless convinced at the time that
Jesus, the Son of God, had coined the wonderful moving words.
Today I know that this text, too, originated from the so-called
'Testament of Joseph'[21]. I quote:

> I was sold as a slave, but the Lord made me free; I was taken
> prisoner, but his strong hand helped me; I was tormented with
> hunger, but the Lord fed me; I was alone, but God comforted
> me, I was ill, but the All Highest visited me; I was in prison,
> but the Saviour blessed me.

Is further proof needed that Jesus' words were not born of his
'divine spirit'? They were in religious use long before him. (So
far none of the many explanations has interpreted his words as
archetypal memories from the unconscious [C. G. Jung], but even
then they would not be of divine origin.)

To me it seems quite certain that Jesus entered the school of
the Essenes and had an extremely profound knowledge of their
teaching. In that way the man from Nazareth or Bethlehem would

have kindled the torch of Christianity from *traditional* religious genius. Would that be so terrible? Only if the consubstantiality of Jesus has to remain the basis of Christian doctrine.

We look benevolently on the growing crowds of Jesus people as a sign of youth turning towards the faith. We allow musicals like 'Jesus Christ Superstar' to be performed in church. I do not like to experience *my* God in make-up, dancing, singing and bawling. My belief in divine omnipotence is too big, indeed quite old-fashioned. It is sacrosanct. This unnatural buffoonery would not be necessary if the problem of God's word were answered honourably and with brutal frankness according to the latest state of research. Today conviction is more attractive than belief.

*   *   *

Jesus came into the world as the illegitimate child of the Virgin Mary in an unknown place. Mary was poor, but wanted the boy to have a good education; she knew that the Essenes accepted other people's children while *still pliable and teachable*. Mary took her child to the monastery school on the Dead Sea. To the Essenes the polytheism of the Romans was blasphemy and the fraternization of the Temple Jews with the occupiers a disgrace. The Essenes decided to strengthen the Jewish population in their psychological resistance against the occupiers and inoculate them with hate by means of disguised speeches (parables). In the little settlements on the Sea of Genezareth and as far as Jericho a *maquis* came into being, a partisan movement which was mainly fired by John the Baptist, who was a fluent experienced orator. Jesus was a teachable pupil in the desert: he learnt the methods of mass psychology from the preacher John.

At the age of thirty Jesus left the Essene community and himself went round the country as a preacher. He chose (undoubtedly not in the simple way described in the New Testament) his twelve disciples. The 'Apostles' were by no means innocent babes in the wood, they were ringleaders of the local maquis: at least four have been identified as 'Zealots', members of the anti-Roman national party, as dagger-men.[22] This bodyguard was so perfectly organized, so eloquent and possessed by such missionary zeal that Jesus, as their leader, could risk making an appearance in the city. He camouflaged his speeches, which were in fact political, from the Roman soldiers – in case they understood his language or had an interpreter with them – with religious sayings. But the Sadducee and Pharisee theologians also understood his exhortations. Jesus made them nervous, because they fraternized with the Romans and were dead set against this itinerant preacher spoiling things for them politically. A tacit gentleman's agreement existed between the Jewish elite and the Roman officer caste. The local high society kept its sanctuaries and could continue to use the Temple. Agriculture and trade, as well as trafficking in money, functioned in the traditional way. The Romans merely exacted a tribute, a fairly juicy tax. However it may be, the Jewish leadership did not want this comparatively tolerable *status quo* upset, it suited them very well. Then Jesus and his bodyguard suddenly appeared in the busiest places in Jerusalem and made rabble-rousing speeches, even if they were in a religious guise.

How could they get rid of this troublesome itinerant preacher?

It can be assumed that the citizens knew perfectly well that Jesus was an Essene, at any rate one of those who knew how to wrap their maxims of a life of humility, righteousness and love skilfully round their political maxims. The Romans, on the other hand, did not notice what was going on for a long time. They regarded the Essene preacher as a harmless priest, whose speeches did not affect Roman interests and sovereign rights. Someone some time – perhaps even a top man in the Jewish elite – opened the eyes of the occupying power to what was going on. From that day on Jesus was shadowed.

It is not clear from the Gospels *what* happened. A communication to the Roman Procurator of Judaea, Pontius Pilate (26-36), must have been enough to have steps taken against him at once. Had the Jewish high priest Caiaphas (18-36) given the governor a hint? Had he told Pilate what the pious Essene was trying to achieve with his meek-sounding speeches? Had Jesus and his followers stormed the Temple – as Joel Carmichael asserts[23]? In any case it must have been a case of a political denunciation, for the Romans did not interfere with Jewish religious life. But *it is established* that it was not a matter of a popular uprising, a rebellion or a revolution against the Romans. *That* would have been recorded in Roman history. The event must have been comparatively unimportant. However *it is also established* that Jesus and his disciples had to hide quite suddenly. Why?

The Gospels describe Jesus as a gentle man who is ready to help, whose speeches encourage the pure life, who heals the sick and brings the dead to life. Jesus himself knew that his life was in danger. With his companions he withdrew to the Mount of Olives with its three peaks, east of the valley of Kidron, near Jerusalem. The risky game was up.

Everyone knows the description of the most dramatic happening in world literature. The Romans look for the Nazarenes, assisted by Jews who know the locality well. The disciples, exhausted by the excitement and efforts of the last few days, fall into a deep sleep in their hiding-place. Jesus alone is unable to rest; he sweats 'blood'. The flickering light of pine torches throws an eerie light on the scene. The shouts of soldiers and the clash of weapons. The rebels are surrounded.

Then Judas Iscariot, an apostle, steps out of the crowd of persecutors, goes up to Jesus and kisses him. (The kiss of Judas later became the embodiment of hypocritical treachery.)

A terrible moment. Yet we ought to ask ourselves what could Judas actually betray? A peaceable man who was loved by the people? A man who only did good? On top of that, Jesus acted quite openly. The people, the theologians, the Romans, knew him well. The Romans could have arrested or brought him in for questioning on any day of the week. Why did Judas have to prove the identity of the master by a kiss? The Gospels say that Judas had told the priests and elders: 'Whomsoever I shall kiss, that same is he.' Can we conclude from the identification by a kiss that Jesus was masked and wearing a disguise?

It becomes obvious in the nocturnal scene. It says in the New Testament that Peter grabbed for his sword and cut off the ear of Malchus, a slave of the high priest (John 18, 10). Did Peter, one of the peaceful brotherhood, possess a sword? Probably the whole company was armed.

Jesus was master of the situation. He realized that resistance was useless and said: 'Put up thy sword in thy sheath.' Jesus was arrested and taken away. The apostles escaped into the bushes through the confused mass of bystanders and soldiers. Only the aggressive Peter tried to find out what was going to happen to his master. In disguise, he mingled with the Roman soldiers round their camp fire:

Then took they him, and led him, and brought him into

the high priest's house. And Peter followed afar off.

And when they had kindled a fire in the midst of the hall and were sat down together, Peter sat down among them.

But a certain maid beheld him as he sat by the fire, and earnestly looked upon him, and said, This man was also with him.

And he denied him, saying, Woman, I know him not.

After a little while another saw him, and said, Thou art also of them. And Peter said, Man, I am not.

And about the space of one hour after another confidently affirmed, saying, Of a truth this fellow also was with him: for he is a Galilean.

And Peter said, Man, I know not what thou sayest. . . . (Luke 22, 54 *et seq.*)

The fact that Peter was able to stay by the camp fire among the Roman legionaries for at least two hours shows what a cunning fellow he was.

Jesus was brought before two courts, tried, derided, tortured, found guilty and nailed to the cross. Carmichael[24] has convincingly proved that crucifixion was a Roman method of execution: Roman soldiers carried out the crucifixion according to a Roman judgment. Theologians assume that it happened about the year 32. The inscription on the cross indicates that Jesus was executed for a *political* crime . . . as 'King of the Jews' (John 19, 19-22).

*   *   *

To fill out this outline I should add that Jesus was a sensitive learned man, who was skilled in medicine and a talented orator, besides having parapsychological abilities. No one can doubt his absolute honourableness and humble fear of God, in so far as he is rated as a historical personage. As an Essene or someone who knew the rules of their order inside out, he practised the commandments to love one's neighbour, be continent and help others. But since the appearance of the Qumran Scrolls, we know that the defendants of the Essene doctrine were committed opponents of the Romans, for all their love of peace. They wanted to drive the heathen interlopers and their polytheism out of the promised land. Religious and political interests mingled and that was bound to lead to an explosion at some time. Religion and politics have never been a good mixture.

I do not want to take sides in the discussion about whether Jesus, as Augstein suspects, was 'an apparition synthetically woven into one from several figures and currents'.

For, to follow Professor Günther Bornkamm[25]: 'If we were to reduce tradition critically to what can no longer be doubted on historical grounds, all we would have left would be a torso which had scarcely anything in common with the story testified to in the Gospels.'

Here I am only concerned with establishing that Jesus was a devout man, but not 'God's only begotten son', a political activist, but not a 'Redeemer'. This proved information will give the literally-minded Christian a severe shock, because doubt is a sin 'against the Holy Ghost'. Hundreds of millions of Christians have been kept at a primitive stage of religion for two thousand years by a doctrinal system based on false premises, although well informed theologians could have 'proclaimed' the truth long ago. Yet they have kept silent. Two thousand years of false instruction – that's what I call tradition.

* * *

Brought up as a Roman Catholic, I am dealing with the figure of Jesus as we all accepted it in the Christian tradition, even if 'understandably . . . (we) are so caught in our own tradition, that we can scarcely approach the Gospels and the New Testament in their totality without prejudice.' (Carmichael.)

Faith is defined as inner certainty without regard to proof, an instinctive conviction. People appeal to faith, people demand faith from those who do not know. Faith means 'trust'. This appeal, in the sense of belief in a higher power, in the incomprehensibility of 'Be!' and 'Die!', of the beginning and end of all being, is good, necessary and eternal. *This* faith has given consolation and help, blessing and profit to men in all ages. But *such* faith has *not the remotest connection* with religious insistence on being right. With the fanatical orders 'Thou must!', 'Thou shalt!', 'Thou shalt not!', Christian pastors and exegetes plunged into the great endless war of the faith. With their stubborn insistence on being the only preachers of the one true word of God, they made a claim with most unfortunate effects.

On the other hand it is not true as general opponents of the faith say, that 'religion' *per se* has brought suffering and care on mankind with persecutions, tortures, tears and blood. If believers, egged on by Zealots, had made *no* image of God there would never have been any religious wars. For religion in the spirit of faith in a creative and ordering power does not claim to proclaim the ultimate truth, nor does it have multi-purpose bits of advice for sore places, or drivelling adages for all occasions.

Even before the Dead Sea Qumran texts, discovered in 1947, forced Christian theologians to admit new material to the discussion, critical matter-of-fact men, who wanted accurate knowledge, had discovered irresolvable contradictions in the New Testament. There could be nothing earth-shaking about that, if it were not God's word or Jesus' word that was supposed to be involved. As father and son are consubstantial (second Council of Constantinople) they are omniscient, infinitely wise, omnipresent, without error – in short, infallible. These are the qualifications of the inspired authors which determined the standard by which the Holy Scriptures are to be judged. Is this high standard justified?

The Gospel according to St Matthew begins with the family tree of Jesus, the son of David, the son of Abraham'. (1)* Ancestors are enumerated until 'Jacob begat Joseph the husband of Mary' (16). What purpose does Joseph serve, since he cannot be the father of Jesus? The fact that his wife was supposed to be pregnant by the Holy Ghost did not satisfy the simple carpenter, who knew perfectly well the normal way of bringing children into being. 'Then Joseph her husband, being a just man, and not willing to make her a public example, was minded to put her away privily' (19). An angel in a dream saved their married happiness: 'Joseph, thou son of David, fear not to take unto thee Mary thy wife: for that which is conceived in her is of the Holy Ghost' (20). Joseph accepted the apparition's message.

Joseph's ancestry does not really seem to have been as clear as one would have wished and a certain scepticism as to his being the father of Jesus is hinted at in St Luke: 'And Jesus himself began to be about thirty years of age, being (as was supposed) the son of Joseph, which was the son of Eli' (Luke 3, 23). Luke ascribes seventy-six progenitors to Joseph (Matthew only 42)

---

* The figures in brackets refer to the verses quoted from St Matthew's Gospel.

There are obviously considerable difficulties in tracing the family tree down to Joseph.

Modern theologians[26] say that the 'immaculate conception' should not be taken to mean that Joseph had not touched his Mary. Are they twisting the meaning of the words inspired by God, because the whole process is so implausible? Matthew makes it perfectly clear: 'When as his mother Mary was espoused to Joseph, *before they came together,* she was found to be with child of the Holy Ghost' (1, 18). Nothing could be plainer than that.

Matthew expressly states that John baptized Jesus and how he did it. John knew whom he was dealing with '. . . He it is, who coming after me is preferred before me, whose shoe's latchet I am not worthy to unloose' (1, 27).

'. . . but he that cometh after me is mightier than I, whose shoes I am not worthy to bear' (3, 11). John addressed Jesus directly: 'I have need to be baptized of thee, and comest thou to me?' (3, 14). After the baptism the heavens opened and the spirit of God descended 'like a dove' and a voice from heaven said: 'This is my beloved Son, in whom I am well pleased' (3, 17). John recognized the man he had baptized, who was even identified by heaven as the Son of God: nothing could be clearer.

Herod Antipas (4 BC to AD 40) took John prisoner and even followed his consort's whim when she urged him to have the Baptist beheaded. John suddenly forgot Jesus in prison and sent two disciples to ask him: 'Art thou he that should come, or do we look for another?' (11, 3). The impression that the Nazarene – with all his concentrated charisma – made on John during the baptismal ceremony seemed so lasting that it is difficult to understand his lapse of memory.

Let us consult Matthew, the toll collector (9, 9) of the Sea of Genezareth, later an apostle and presumably an evangelist! Jesus went about 'all Galilee, teaching in their synagogues' (4, 23), which housed the schools in those days. Synagogues came under priests and scribes. No one could just decide *ex cathedra* to teach there: he had to be examined by the scribes and recognized as one of them. Where did Jesus get the audacity to criticize this guild on which his teaching activity depended: 'Except your righteousness shall exceed the righteousness of the scribes and Pharisees, ye shall in no case enter the kingdom of heaven' (5, 20).

In his Gospel Matthew records speeches of Jesus which raise justifiable doubts about his meekness. One recommendation from the mouth of the Son of God says: '. . . but whosoever shall say, Thou fool, shall be in danger of hell fire.' (5, 22). If all Christians who cursed when they were angry were treated like that, hell would be one gigantic crematorium.

In Chapter 5 Matthew quotes counsels that to the best of my knowledge even the most devout Christians of any age have never followed and, although they were divine commandments, could not follow: 'And if thy right eye offend thee, pluck it out and cast it from thee (30) . . . whosoever shall smite thee on the right cheek, turn to him the other also (39). And if any man will sue thee at law, and take away thy coat, let him have thy cloak also (40), and whosever shall compel thee to go a mile, go with him twain . . .' (41).

I am always amazed when distorted quotations by the master are put in the appropriate passage of a 'story taken from everyday life' and then believed as 'God's word'. I have not met a single preacher who has taken these words literally.

Jesus repeatedly urges his hearers to speak clearly, they must never be 'lukewarm': 'But let your communication be, Yea, yea; Nay, nay: for whatsoever is more than these cometh of evil' (8, 37). The Nazarene himself certainly does not follow his own advice for he speaks in veiled parables. For example, when Jesus healed a leper by laying his hands on him, he said (8,4): 'See thou tell no man', but adds in the same breath: '. . . go thy way, show thyself to the priest.' The original command to keep silence was pointless, because 'great multitudes' (8, 1) were present at the miraculous cure. Yea-nay? Nea!

Jesus asserted that he had not come to summon the righteous but the sinners to repentance: 'I will have mercy and not sacrifice.'

But according to Matthew, mercy is in short supply, because Jesus threatens, even for minor sins: '. . . the children of the kingdom shall be cast into outer darkness: there shall be weeping and gnashing of teeth' (8, 12).

Love one another — love thy neighbour as thyself . . . are the slogans under which the Christian churches have presented their doctrine to the people from the beginning down to today. Why and wherefore does not the Bible reader realize that Jesus simply

became a Narcissus who did not follow these categorical impera-
tives in his own example-setting person? Jesus says: 'He that
loveth father or mother more than me is not worthy of me:
and he that loveth son or daughter more than me is not worthy
of me' (10, 37). Can all that be reconciled with 'God's word' or
is the Son of God in need of love?

The citizens of Chorazin, Bethsaida and Capernaum presumably
had not received Jesus and his disciples with due friendliness.
As a result the Son of God unceremoniously condemned them
to hell until the last judgment (11, 20 *et seq*.).

Matthew, presumably chronicling accurately the deeds of the
Son of God, had to write contradictions en masse. Jesus sent
out his messengers with the exhortation: '. . . be ye therefore
wise as serpents, and harmless as doves' (10, 16). That's what I
call two-faced advice! Then he prophesies that they 'shall be
hated by all men for my name's sake' (10, 22), but need not fear
death. Why does Jesus notify his companions of such a frightful
fate, when soon afterwards he claims with raised voice: '. . . my
yoke is easy, and my burden light' (11, 30)? Even in those days,
close to the ostensible events, it was not easy to reduce 'God's
word' to a common denominator.

What is the point of a description by Matthew of a disgraceful
injustice? 'And Jesus answered and spake unto them again by
parables, and said (22, 1): The kingdom of heaven is like unto
a certain king, which made a marriage for his son (2).' This
'parable' introduces a fine wedding with a fine point. The
wedding breakfast was ready, but the guests did not come. Again
the king sent out messengers to invite the guests, but they
spurned the invitation and even killed some of the messengers.
Finally the king gave the order: 'Go ye therefore into the high-
ways and as many as ye shall find, bid to the marriage' (9). People
from the street were driven into the hall. 'And when the king
came in to see the guests, he saw there was a man which had not
a wedding garment . . .' (11). Wild with rage the king said:
'Bind him hand and foot, and take him away, and cast him into
outer darkness: there shall be weeping and gnashing of teeth'
(13). And the point of the parable that Jesus formulated? 'For
many are called, but few are chosen' (14). Commentaries and
recipes for evaluating sermons can twist and turn this example of
God's word to their heart's content. To me as a simple Bible

reader it remains an example of hideously asocial behaviour. I do not want any hints as to what is 'meant', I can read for myself.

Yet another story related by Matthew does not seem to me to be inspired by the divine spirit. I summarize the text, Chapter 25, 14-30. In this 'parable' a rich man goes on a journey and before his departure entrusts his money to his servants. On his return they report to him. One, to whom his master had entrusted five talents (= a silver coin worth 6,000 drachmas), had used the time to make ten out of them. Nothing but praise! Another had made four talents out of the two given him to look after. More praise! All of them had increased their capital except one. This man, obviously an anti-capitalist, had buried the talent in his fear. He gave back the one talent he had received. Then his master said: 'Thou wicked and slothful servant, thou knewest that I reap where I sowed not, and gather where I have not strewed (26). Thou oughtest therefore to have put my money to the exchangers, and then at my coming, I should have received mine own with usury (27). Take therefore the talent from him, and give it unto him which hath ten talents (28). For unto every one that hath shall be given, and he shall have abundance: but from him that hath not shall be taken away even that which he hath (29). And cast ye the unprofitable servant into outer darkness: there shall be weeping and gnashing of teeth (30).' This story cannot suit the Jesus People with their ideology of the anti-capitalist Jesus, but it is the lesson read in church on the 27th Sunday after Trinity. Capitalists of all countries, praise the divine word! Multiply your talents!

One last puzzle from Matthew (28, 16-17). Eleven disciples (twelve minus Judas) climb the mountain near Galilee where Jesus had bidden them go. They saw him and worshipped him. 'But some doubted.' Since my Bible studies I can find no answer to the question *what* they could have doubted when faced with a human being who had been crucified and buried, but now stood before them as large as life. Did they not believe their eyes, did they think he was a ghost?

St Mark tells some remarkable stories. He states plainly that Jesus has *brothers* (3, 31-32), who appeared on the scene with his mother when Jesus was sitting at table with his disciples. The presence of the wonder-worker had spread abroad and crowds were gaping curiously in the street. 'When his friends heard of it' (3, 21), they went out to lay hold of him, saying: 'He is beside himself.' Did they think that Jesus was temporarily sub-normal? (Today psychology could give plausible reasons for this.) The master did not want to have anything to do with his mother and brethren who were asking for him outside. Dismissing them, he put the rhetorical question: 'Who is my mother, or my brethren?' (33) only to answer it in general terms: '. . . whosoever shall do the will of God, the same is my brother, and my sister, and my mother!' (34) We cannot find any feeling here of grati-tude to the mother who had brought him into the world in ticklish circumstances.

John baptized in the Jordan, where people flocked to him. To all of them he preached: '. . . the baptism of repentance for the *remission of sins*' (1, 4). We know – it occurs later in Mark – that Jesus followed this appeal and was baptized. Surely we should ask: Did the Son of God have sins to forgive?

*   *   *

Contradictions due to the distance in time and the antiquity of the texts are excusable. But when they succeed each other in the same breath, it takes theological gymnastics to explain them. According to Mark, Jesus says to his disciples: 'Unto you it is given to know the mystery of the kingdom of God; but unto them that are without, all these things are done in parables' (4, 11), which is as much as to say: You, my friends, understand my every word, but I have to explain things to the people in parables. Already in verse 13, he is angry with his disciples because they do not understand a parable: 'Know ye not this parable? and how then will ye know all parables?'

It is open to question whether the apostles ever undertsood exactly what Jesus meant. According to Matthew (13, 11), Jesus said: '. . . it is given unto you to know the mysteries of the Kingdom of heaven, but to them it is not given.' He raises the disciples above the others who do not understand him, because 'blessed are your eyes, for they see: and your ears, for they hear' (16). Hence we must assume that communication in the inner circle was so immediate that the code in which Jesus spoke every day was understood. Not a bit of it! Even the learned Peter had to ask: 'Declare unto us this parable' (15, 15). Jesus asks in astonishment: 'Are ye also yet without understanding?' (16). Did they understand 'God's word' or not? Presumably not, for even *after* the Resurrection, when they could not ask the master for further explanations, John says that the disciples did not understand.

Mark relates that John had told Jesus that the disciples had seen a man casting out devils in the holy name and that they had forbidden him to do so (9, 38). Jesus readily answered: 'Forbid him not: for there is no man which shall do a miracle in my name, that can lightly speak evil of me' (39). This is put differently in Matthew. In his gospel, others have prophesied, driven out devils and acted *in Jesus' name* (7, 22). Then comes the typically demagogic answer: 'And then I will profess unto them, I never knew you: depart from me, ye that work iniquity' (23). Those may be the methods of the *maquis* – but it is not worthy of God to give people tasks only to deny their existence later.

*　*　*

It is not made easy for the Christian layman to find his way through the thicket of contradictions in the New Testament. It is simpler for informed theologians: they doubtless have a hot line over which they can get information from the highest source. Through their mouths and again through the mouths of those they teach, children in religion classes and believers in church learn how everything is to be understood and how it may on no account be interpreted. If only the theologians were united on the subject! But, depending on their membership of a particular church they get in each other's hair, violently, angrily, hotly in favour of their own angle. And anything that cannot be brought under one head and is completely inexplicable is inflicted on 'those who are without' as a test of faith. How does it go? 'Let your communication be yea, yea; nay, nay.'

In the revelation of the holy word it is said that Jesus is the only begotten son of God, and that he admitted as much at a hearing before the High Council. In fact the correct translation of Jesus' remark is *not*: 'I am', but 'Thou sayest so'. It is twisting reason not to understand what is meant, namely: I have never claimed it, you have attributed it to me! In Mark we also read: 'And Jesus said unto him, why callest thou me good? *there is none good but one, that is, God*' (10, 18). Jesus clearly points out that *he is not* God, but of course he did not know what the decrees of the Councils would soon make out of him.

Opposed to the dogmas that Father and Son are 'one', and the trinity of Father, Son and Holy Ghost, is an honest confession by Jesus: 'But of that day and that hour knowest no man, not the angels which are in heaven, *neither the Son, but the Father*' (Mark 13, 32). If they had been 'one', *each one of them* would have been informed of the day and hour of a distant event.

The High Priests condemned Jesus — for they found no other reason — because he had 'blasphemed' God. The High Priests asked whether he was Christ, the Son of God.

The answer according to Matthew (26, 64): 'Thou hast said.'

The answer according to Mark (14, 62): 'I am.'

The answer according to Luke (22, 70): 'Ye say that I am.'

The contradictions of the evangelists are understandable, none of them was present at the trial; they are merely reporting rumours.

John gives rather more detailed information. Jesus defended himself before the High Council: 'I ever taught in the synagogue, and in the temple, whither Jews always resort: and in secret have I said nothing' (18, 20). Presumably that was only half the truth, the defence of a rebel. Perhaps the Council also knew about some subversive activity of Jesus, as Matthew hints: 'What I tell you in darkness, that speak ye in light, and what ye hear in the ear, that preach ye upon the housetops' (10, 27). Rebels have been convicted in all ages for subversive activity. Perhaps the reason for the accusation is to be sought here?

The evangelists come to the unanimous conclusion that Jesus was arrested without grounds. The High Priests and Council did their best to find charges: 'And the chief priests and all the council sought for witness against Jesus to put him to death: and found none' (Mark 14, 55).

Until now it has not been explained what damaging information Judas could really have betrayed. He does not report at any stage of the trial, is not present at any hearing, nor does he appear as a witness for the prosecution. It does come out that the elders paid him thirty pieces of silver. What for? For the identification of a man who was known all over the town. But had he, and there the affair becomes and remains inexplicable, given concrete grounds for accusation in addition to the kiss of betrayal, the authorities would not have been so helpless. Furthermore, Judas would certainly not have turned traitor for thirty pieces of silver. There must have been something else involved that we shall never know about. Judas could easily come by money, much more than thirty pieces of silver. Just as the Essenes had their communal life organized with a central fund, Judas looked after the money for Jesus' group. No, there must have been something more to it.

Sentence and execution remain shrouded in mystery.

Jesus was handed over to Pontius Pilate, who considered him innocent, but had him crucified in the end. According to St John, the governor defended himself: 'Take ye him, and crucify him: for I find no fault in him' (19, 6). The Roman governor had been in the country long enough to know that Jews would not crucify anybody. Crucifixion was a Roman form of execution, so his offer was meaningless.

The Jews obstinately went on: 'We have a law, and by our law he ought to die, because he made himself the Son of God' (7). Why should the Romans worry about that? Religious disputes did not interest them. Nevertheless, John asserts: 'When Pilate therefore heard that saying, he was the more afraid' (8). What was he afraid of? He possessed the military and political power and was in charge of the police force. He said as much to the silent Jesus: 'Knowest thou that I have power to crucify thee, and have power to release thee?' (10) So why on earth should he be afraid? Pilate ruled so despotically that he was recalled later. If he had really considered Jesus innocent, he could have released him in spite of the Jewish protests. Since a crucifixion subsequently took place, he must have had political grounds, and as we know political grounds are often left unmentioned.

*　　*　　*

'God's word' also shows considerable variations when it comes to Jesus' last words on the cross.

According to Mark (15, 34) and Matthew (27, 46), he cried in a loud voice: 'My God, My God, why hast thou forsaken me?'

According to Luke, he cried: 'Father, into thy hands I commend my spirit.'

According to John (19, 30), his words were: 'It is finished: and he bowed his head, and gave up the ghost.'

The four gospel accounts also differ about the women's visits to the tomb of Jesus.

Mark (16, 1-8) says that Mary Magdalene, Mary the mother of James and Salome bought spices to anoint Jesus. On the way they were wondering how they would move the stone from the tomb, when they saw that it was already open and that a young man in a long white garment sat inside. He told them not to be afraid, for Jesus whom they sought had risen from the dead. They were to tell the disciples this. But the women fled in a panic, 'neither said they anything to any man; for they were afraid.'

John (20, 1-2) describes things differently. According to him, only Mary Magdalene went to the grave early on the first day of the week and found the stone already removed. In a panic she ran to Simon Peter and the other apostles, telling them that they had taken Jesus away to an unknown place.

Luke (24, 1-6) only mentions 'women' (not mentioned by name), who went to the open tomb and found it empty. While they stood there sadly, two men in 'shining garments' said to them: 'Why seek ye the living among the dead? He is not here, but is risen.'

Matthew makes the whole scene very dramatic (28, 1-9). Mary Magdalene and Mary the mother of James went to the tomb, which was closed. Fortunately an earthquake began at that moment and the angel of the Lord, his face like lightning and his robe as white as snow, came down from heaven, moved the stone, sat on it and spoke to the women. He showed them the place where Jesus lay and said that he had risen, and that they were to inform the disciples quickly. The fact that they also met Jesus on the way is no longer connected with the visit to the tomb.

Should not the countless collaborators on the Bible at least have taken care to synchronize the central event of the resurrection in the accounts? If, for some incomprehensible reason, the legendary 'original texts' of 'God's word' did not contain a unified description they should have been edited for the good of the simple Bible reader who must now ask for all eternity: what really happened?

The apostles' reaction to the phenomenal events is also most remarkable. They did not believe a word of the story told by the women, among whom were the two Marys and Joanna. 'And their words seemed to them idle tales, and they believed them not' (Luke 24, 11). John (20, 9) even affirms: 'For as yet they knew not the scripture, that he must rise from the dead.' *This is quite incomprehensible.* Throughout their four books the evangelists noted down Jesus' pronouncements that he would die and rise again, yet at the end they knew nothing about it.

Even without divine inspiration of the ultimate truth the account of Jesus' ascent into heaven is also contradictory.

According to Matthew (28, 16-17), Jesus had summoned the disciples to a mountain near Galilee for the appearance. When they saw him, they worshipped him, 'but some doubted'. Still? Matthew has nothing further to say about an ascent into heaven.

Mark (16, 19) has only one sentence to cover the important event: 'So then after the Lord had spoken unto them, he was received up into heaven, and sat on the right hand of God.' It was as simple as that.

Luke (24, 50-51) makes Jesus himself lead the disciples 'out as far as Bethany'. While he was blessing them, 'he was parted from them, and carried up into heaven.'

John (21) has nothing to say about the ascension into heaven.

The most important events in Jesus' life (as recorded by 'God's word' — a fact I have devoutly acknowledged in this textual comparison) were undoubtedly the resurrection and the ascent into heaven. The evangelists recorded so many unimportant details that one cannot understand why they did not describe the two central events on which the Christian dogma is based in colourful gripping images and genuinely inspired language.

If Jesus had ascended into heaven in full view of everybody, or at least in the circle of his disciples, the news would have spread through the streets of Jerusalem like a forest fire on the very same day, for the people had taken a lively interest in the trial and crucifixion. But not a single Roman or Jewish historian noted down a single word about these earth-shaking events! The evangelists show only the most rudimentary knowledge of them and they were not eyewitnesses. It is a *crux interpretum.*

*   *   *

I am one of many hundreds of millions of 'Christians', who are dictated to from the cradle and pay taxes for the privilege, but cannot believe in a dictatorial religion. I am not an atheist. I admire the magnificent drama which was written around the central figure of Jesus of Nazareth; I admire the products of Christian culture in painting, sculpture and music. I recognize most of the laws and rules governing human conduct in the codex of the Christian faith (as they are in essence peculiar to all religions, myths and legends).

But I deny the claim of the church into which I was born to be the only one offering salvation, because I – to name only two examples – consider the dogmas and tenets of Buddha and Mohammed to be of no less value.

Millions of devout Christians know nothing or too little of the background of the Bible. Consequently, they accept it as *the* 'Word of God' from generation to generation: they take Jesus for the original preacher of his doctrine. But it has been proved that he adapted essential parts of it from the Essenes by the Dead Sea. The fact that the Christian doctrines and customs are mostly borrowed from older religions is shown by documentation put at my disposal by Dr Robert Kehl[27]. From it I take the following details, which are but a fraction of the material available.

* * *

The Bible does not contain a single religious or moral idea which was not already contained in some form in the holy scriptures of earlier or contemporary religions. The immediate soil – not to say armoury and arsenal – for the present-day 'Christian', i.e. Pauline religious, communal and cult life was in particular the *Hellenistic mystery cults* (for their part largely taken over from the Egyptian and oriental cults). Practically everything that forms present-day Pauline Christianity is to be found in the cults of Attis, Dionysus, Mithras and Isis (a). (The letters (a) to (i) are referred to separately in the Bibliography.)

The central figure of the individual mystery cults was always a saviour corresponding to the Pauline Christos, a 'Son of God', who was described as 'the Lord'. The suffering and death of the 'Son of God' plays a decisive role in these cults, and there is also mention of crucified gods. A god's going down into hell ('. . . descended into hell') was a widespread idea, just as the ascent into heaven formed part of the salvation story in all mystery cults. The Trinity was known too, as it was in ancient Egypt. The sick were healed in the names of Mithras and Dionysus, and the dead woken, the sea calmed, water turned into wine etc. There was also the festival of Easter (celebration of the resurrection), in which the resurrection of the god concerned was conceived of in exactly the same way as in later Christianity (resurrection on the third day, empty tomb, stone rolled away). The doctrine of salvation, which is considered as peculiar to the Christian religion, is found in all its details in the mystery religions. Even the basic Christian dogma of original sin was not really new (Mithras). Baptism with fasting and penitential exercises beforehand was known in the Hellenistic mystery religions. The holy supper, also called 'Table of the Lord', 'Meal of the blessed' or 'Meal of the saints', had a great deal in common with the (later) Christian Last Supper. But it is of special significance that according to the mystery religions, too, this meal represented eating the body and drinking the blood of their god (communion). The bread for the supper was partly prepared in the form of hosts with the sign of the cross. It is demonstrated that this 'Table of the Lord' was also conceived as a bloodless sacramental renewal of the divine sacrifice. Even the words spoken during the transubstantiation in the present-day Catholic Mass are essentially prefigured: 'Say seven times; thou art wine; thou art not wine, but the blood of Athena. Thou art wine; thou art not wine, but the blood of Osiris, the bowels of Jaô.'

The faithful were reborn through this 'meal of the blessed' and, in contrast to the lost, who could expect a miserable fate, were described as 'redeemed, saved, immortal'. The initiates of the mystery religions became 'children of god' through the meal. God took them into his dwelling; they were united with him. The meal is also to be conceived of as actually sharing a meal with god.

The life of the son of god or the founder of the religion shows striking similarities to the life of Jesus, not only in the mystery religions, but also in the Eastern and Far Eastern pre-Christian religions. This begins already with the prophecies as 'Redeemer and saviour of mankind' (b). For example, the followers of the Zoroastrian religion were also told: 'The world is full of expectation of him; he is the prophet Mazda.' Generally there is an account of the supernatural begetting (c) of the saviour god, with the virgin birth being widely known long before Jesus, for example in the case of Buddha and Zoroaster. With Buddha the begetting is supposed to have taken place by the penetration of a divine ray into the womb of the virgin mother. Even more striking is the concordance in the descriptions of the birth of the religion's founder (d). Other founders of religion, besides Jesus, were born in a manger, put in a crib and wrapped in swaddling clothes; in other religions, too, the birthplace was lit by a bright light; in the case of other founders of religions, too, heavenly choirs singing praise appeared; even the adoration of the shepherds was not lacking. After the birth of both Jesus and Krishna (eighth terrestrial apparition of Vishnu, one of main epiphanies of the divine in Hinduism), the slaying of all newly-born male children was ordered by a jealous king. The presentation of the child in the temple is also attested to. In particular all founders of religion were tempted by the devil (e), mostly in the desert where they were fasting. Here too details tally with the Bible, in that the devil first offers food and then worldly dominion if his victim will submit.

When Buddha was baptized, there was an earthquake and god proclaimed: 'Immortality is discovered.' (With Jesus '. . . this is my beloved son . . .') A striking similarity can also be observed in the deaths of divine figures who are venerated as universal saviours. When Caesar died, there was talk of a terrible darkness and also of the earth bursting open and the dead returning (f). The resurrection of sons of god who were transformed on this earth, are generally known in antiquity well before Jesus. The risen Apollonius, a contemporary and a kind of *doppleganger* of Jesus, appeared to his disciples. The mystery religions and the Egyptian and Babylonian cultures before them knew both the concept 'I am the vine' and the pastoral slogan 'I am the good shepherd' (g). The persecution of the adherents of the mystery religions by the priests of the established religion was just as customary as the persecution of the Christians. The mocking of the suffering of Dionysus is staggeringly like the mocking of Jesus. Most founders of religions and sons of gods known to the classical and Far Eastern world *before* Jesus were miracle workers just like Jesus (h). The miracle of the turning of the water into wine has its parallel in the Dionysus legend. The sick are healed, old men become sprightly, the hungry are fed, the blind see, cripples walk, the dumb speak. Cures are performed at a distance, as by Jesus. Those who were healed carry their beds, the sea is calmed, 300,000 people are miraculously fed and there are many other instances.

Peter sinking in the water (the man of little faith) appears already in Buddhism. Buddha called himself 'the truth' like Jesus. Zoroaster also proclaimed that he would 'return with the holy angels'. Lastly Krishna also preached that the world 'could not recognize him' (i).

*　　*　　*

In conclusion, a number of texts from the holy scriptures of other older religions are here compared with passages from the Bible, especially the Gospels:

Abbreviations:

B = Buddhism
Hi = Hinduism
M = Mystery religions
T = Taoism
Z = Zoroastrianism

Bible	**Other Holy Scriptures**
There is none like thee, Lord	There is none like thee in the world (H)
For thine is the kingdom, and the power, and the glory, for ever and ever. Amen	Yours is the dominion and yours is the might, O Mazda (Z)
The crooked shall be made straight	That which is crooked shall be made straight (T)
Unto you is born a Saviour	Unto you this day the Saviour is born. The virgin has given birth; the line increases (M)

Bible	Other Holy Scriptures
Blessed art thou among women	Exalted above all earthly women (the reference is to Buddha's mother) (B)
He that seeth me seeth him that sent me	He who sees me sees the teaching (B)
For God sent not his son into the world to condemn the world; but that the world through him might be saved	For the Logos (Herakles) is not there to harm or to punish, but to save (M)
I am the light of the world	I am the eye of the world (B)
This day is (the scripture) fulfilled . . .	The time is fulfilled (Assurbanipal)
Go ye therefore, and teach all nations . . . teaching them to observe all things whatsoever I have commanded you	That which you have seen of me and learnt from me, that shall you preach to all men (Hi)
Who hath ears to hear, let him hear	He who has ears, let him hear the word and believe (B)
He that seeketh findeth	He who seeks shall find it (the Tao) (T)
No man having put his hand to the plough, and looking back, is fit for the Kingdom of God	For he who is occupied (with the things of this world) is unfit to accept the kingdom (T)
They are all under sin	Sin reigns freely over you (Hi)
Though your sins be as scarlet, they shall be as white as snow	Even if thou art a villain and thy sins surge heavily, the raft of knowledge bears you easily away over every sea of sins (Hi)
If God be for us, who can be against us	We fetch strength from god; who shall be against us? (Z)
And whosoever liveth and believeth in me shall never die	For believe me that he who trusts in me shall never die (Hi)
For your Father knowest what things you have need of, before you ask him	. . . For I know thy questions and complaints beforehand (Z)

Bible	Other Holy Scriptures
And as you would that men should be to you, do ye also to them likewise (the 'golden rule')	Do not that for which thou blamest thy neighbour (a tenet of all religions)
Thou shalt love thy neighbour as thyself	
Blessed are the merciful	A man shall love others like himself (M T B)
	He who fights with mercy conquers (T)
Love your enemies, do good to them that hate you – Father, forgive them; for they know not what they do	Even when they tear his body to pieces, the disciple thinks of the liberation of those who rend him and even in thought he does not destroy them (B Hi)
If ye lend to them of whom you hope to receive, what thank have ye?	Do a man a favour without expecting anything in return from him (Z)
Except ye . . . become as little children . . .	Let ideas and thoughts be and become as a little child (Z)
For whosoever exalteth himself shall be abased	He who is too haughty will rise very little (T)
Everyone that hath forsaken . . . wife, or children, or . . . for my name's sake	True knowledge is only this: liberation from dependence on wife and child, on house and home (Hi)
Blessed are the pure in heart: for they shall see God	He who is pure of heart is blessed here and blessed after death (Z)
In my Father's house are many mansions	The angel of love . . . has prepared fair dwellings for us (Z)
The kingdom of heaven is within you	Heaven is inside you (B)
If any man will come after me, let him deny himself, and take up his cross and follow me	A Bodhisattva (a being destined for illumination) said: I take the burden of all suffering upon me. I do not turn round or run away (B)
As thou, Father, art in me, and I in thee	Stay with me in my soul (M)

Bible	Other Holy Scriptures	
Woman, why weepest thou?	Lament not, mother; now I	
I ascend to my Father	ascend into heaven	(M)
Father, into thy hands I	Take my spirit, I pray thee,	
commend my spirit	up to the stars	(M)
It is finished	It is finished	(M)

*   *   *

Roland Puccetti (50), Professor of Philosophy and Theology at Singapore, is concerned with the central problem of the Christian faith, namely whether its claim to universality is justified. According to Puccetti, if this claim were accepted, most of mankind would be excluded from salvation, because they had never had the opportunity to receive 'the joyous message' of Christ's birth and his teaching. Puccetti[28] says that even if the gospel were generally diffused over our planet – which we all know is not true – only an insignificant part of all intelligent beings in the universe would have heard of it, whereas the claim to universality also entails the duty and mission of making the doctrine of salvation known to all living beings, of allowing them to share in it.

Professor E. L. Mascall[29] says that in the tradition of Christian theology the fact has already been emphasized, as the real meaning of salvation, that the Son of God became one with the species he was going to save. The Son of God became man in Mascall's analysis so that men could become God's children through him. But we need not be alarmed by the prospect of innumerable incarnations and crucifixions in the universe. For, says the theologian, 'the very fact that the victorious redemption of mankind was finally achieved on our planet by Christ's resurrection would *justify a repetition in other places*. In other words, if it is possible in one case for the mortal and the eternal to unite in one person, why should not it also be possible in several cases?'

In continuation of this idea Professor Puccetti comes to the conclusion that a single organic person definitely cannot be more than one organic person, however many incorporeal persons he may represent simultaneously. . . . 'Incorporeal persons can be everywhere at any time, *but* corporeal persons can only be in one place in the universe at the same time.' Puccetti, who, very courageously for a theologian, introduces the latest scientific findings into his religio-philosophical interpretations, tries to explain the central question 'how could the Son of God become man in the universe several times – perhaps in 10^{18} places – without simultaneously being more than one organic person? He comes to the conclusion that it is impossible, but adds, if we take as a basis the above-mentioned figure of possible societies of extraterrestrial natural persons in the known galaxies (which make up approximately one-tenth of all galaxies), and if we assume that the lifetime of Jesus of Nazareth represents the average duration of an incarnation of the Son of God, it would take 34×10^{18} years before the Son of God had spent the time from birth to resurrection on each of the planets in succession. The life expectation of stars whose planetary systems possibly offer the prerequisites for the development of intelligent life is only $(1-5) \times 10^{10}$ years in our galaxy. If we also accept this figure for the rest of the known inter-galactic universe, between 680,000,000 and 3,400,000,000 incarnations would have to take place *simultaneously* from today until the extinction of life on all these stars! If we deduct previous incarnations, the figure is reduced a little, but not enough to make any appreciable difference.

If God is supposed not only to have assumed the appearance of a single member of a rational corporeal species, but also to have assumed its essence through his Son, whereby he would have transferred his personality to this species, we would have to infer that there existed *simultaneously* in the universe many organic persons who were 'divine beings' in the Christian sense of the words. The following supposition makes it very clear what that would mean for Christianity. Let us assume that we could establish contact with a society fifty light years away from us and transmit the text of the New Testament to it. In answer we would receive a television picture of *their* Christ. He turns out to have nine fingers on each hand, four legs, a thick blue skin and long bones. We could then scarcely answer 'Yes, that is Christ,' for that would be tantamount to saying, 'That is the Son of God as he *appears to you!*' which would be sheer Docetism.*

---

* Docetism was a second-century heresy which claimed that God only apparently became man in Jesus.

D

On the other hand we could not deny his divine status
(assuming he preached his 'Sermon on the Mount', died on the
cross for their sins, etc.), for he would have the same right to it as
Jesus of Nazareth. What could we do? *We* had Jesus of Nazareth
and *they* had their 'X Christ'; both were beings assumed by God,
and both species would be included in Christ's 'being man' or
'being X' as separate incarnations of God's word. But if the
Son of God happens but once, how can he be simultaneously
wholly man and wholly X, i.e. exist as two different corporeal
persons? Two corporeal persons are not one. A further point is
that we should have quite as much reason for worshipping the
ostensible 'X Christ' as our own Jesus Christ, and Christianity
would no longer embrace a Trinity, but a fourfoldness, a 'Quad-
rinity' as it were.

And the following are not my words (although they form my
opinion, too!), the scholarly theologian Puccetti is saying them,
the professor who worries about the existence of Christianity
in the future:

> What Christianity can do is to disregard the probable
> existence of intelligent extraterrestrial beings completely. In
> fact it could happen that Christianity – possibly alone among
> the great living religions – would be proved false by experi-
> ments in interstellar communication.

*   *   *

The news that Jesus was an astronaut has been haunting the
press and relevant literature for some time, like the Loch Ness
monster, sometimes accepted, sometimes dismissed.

The inventor of the latest Jesus cult is the Soviet philologist
Dr Vyatcheslav Saitsev of the University of Minsk. Saitsev believes
that Jesus came from outer space, that he was a representative
of a higher civilization and that that would partially explain his
supernatural powers and abilities. Saitsev actually says[30]: 'In
other words, God's descent to earth is really a cosmic event.'

Essays by Dr Vyatcheslav Saitsev on 'A Spaceship in the
Himalayas' and 'Angels in Spaceships' in the Soviet periodical
Sputnik spurred me on to travel to Moscow in the summer of
1968. I cannot go along with Saitsev in his latest speculations.

Of course Saitsev appeals to the Gospels. What is there one

cannot prove by them? A little hard work is all that is needed to prove textually that Jesus was a warrior, general or king, politician or seeker of the truth, spirit healer, magician or soothsayer, sectarian preacher or – last but not least – the Son of God. It can also be 'proved' that Jesus was an 'astronaut'.

What grounds did Saitsev find for his thesis? Matthew (1, 20), who makes 'the angel of the Lord' appear for Joseph? In other words the angel is an astronaut.

Or the story of the 'immaculate conception'? In the astronaut version it 'naturally' became artificial insemination. What else?

Or the heavens opening and the voice over Jordan at the baptism of Jesus by John (Matthew 3)?

What else could that be but a spaceship from which a megaphone bellows earthwards?

Or the two 'men in shining garments', who appear in Luke (24)? Astronauts!

Or the angel in Matthew (28) with a face 'like lightning, and his raiment white as snow'? Another extraterrestrial being in a protective suit!

Or Jesus' saying: 'In my Father's house are many mansions'? That can only mean the innumerable inhabited planets in the universe.

Or Mark's assertion (13) about 'the Son of man coming in the clouds with great power and glory'? It's obvious, the Supreme Commander is going to send his son in a spaceship.

Enough of that.

The list could be continued with as many 'proofs' as you want.

This is the position I adopt:

1) We must *believe* the texts of the Gospels if we are going to infer alleged knowledge from them. For example, we must believe that Mary conceived Jesus immaculately, the Spirit of God descended like a dove and alighted on the Lord, and a voice came out of heaven, a gleaming white angel appeared at the tomb, Jesus actually did the deeds and spoke the words which were posthumously put into his mouth. Anyone who does not *believe* the texts literally, anyone who knows how 'God's word' originated, cannot accept the accounts as reality. Anyone who tries to deduce an 'astronaut Jesus' from the Gospels is committing the same error as judges who form and pronounce a verdict of guilty on the basis of forged documents. (As far as the Soviet

citizen Saitsev is concerned, 'belief' is a *contradictio in adjecto*!)

2)   What is the astronaut Jesus supposed to have done on earth? To have brought a religion, Christian or moral precepts? He introduced nothing new. From a comparison of the gospels and the Qumran scrolls we know that the core of Jesus' teaching stems from the Essene community. His other contributions made no advance. It was not necessary to send out the cosmonaut Jesus in order to threaten men with punishment, to spread panic, to make hell the terminus for non-believers!

3)   Interstellar space travellers would have operated according to a precise programme, but the helpers from the spaceship came too late to save their top man from death. If the astronaut Jesus had been able to count on the help of his brothers in the cosmos at the right moment (which he must have known about), he would not have spent his whole life speaking of his unavoidable death. If we imagine that spacetravellers would have left their important special messenger in the lurch, we are really underestimating extraterrestrial beings.

4)   Even if the resurrection were adduced as a proof, it would be absurd. Nevertheless, let us assume that the extraterrestrial visitors had succeeded in revivifying Jesus' corpse with their special advanced medical skills (blood banks, transplants etc.). Would they have missed the chance of a public demonstration of their powers over death itself? Only a few people, and they doubted, knew about the miracle of the resurrection. Would not extraterrestrial visitors who had achieved such a feat have taken Jesus straight back to Jerusalem to show him and let him preach there? Their impressive achievement would have remained unknown *without* a demonstration of their superior abilities. Besides, according to the apostles, the medical reawakening had no consequence. The disciples remained behind in confusion; they did not dare to appear in public.

5)   Extraterrestrial intelligences who had mastered space flight over interstellar distances would not have been so stupid as to visit only one point on the earth in order to introduce one local religious mission. So that they could be more effectively active, they would have made for various geographical locations, which would have meant a little extra effort, but would have been the only possible way to carry out the major operation of founding a religion. Spaceship landings, observations of spaceships, UFOs

or similar oddities have not been registered in the history books during Jesus' lifetime, either in Jewish territory or other countries. All the fantastic sightings by religious fanatics of Jesus after his death – Jesus in India, Jesus in Central America – are to be dismissed as fancies, for these 'founders of religions' *once again* refer to the frequently falsified gospel texts, which first turned Jesus into the 'Son of God' and the 'Redeemer'. He was neither.

6) If the astronaut Jesus, who was on a much higher intellectual plane than the people of Judaea, had wanted to refer to the future, he would have had to conceal words and formulas in the parables that were to be handed down, formulas and codes which distant generations would understand. And should understand! 'Listen, ye sons and daughters,' he might have said, 'when the time is ripe and your scholars know how to split the smallest particle of matter, the Son of God will appear from the clouds.' Even scholars will not dispute that planning extraterrestrial visitors would have endowed an astronaut Jesus with knowledge of the future development of intelligence of our planet. If there were just one formula, only a short one like Einstein's $E = mc^2$, in the gospels, I would be on Saitsev's side.

7) If extraterrestrial beings had really sent their man Jesus to Jerusalem to spread religious doctrines with the help of advanced technical aids they would have kept the development area under control. But obviously there was no control over Jesus' doctrine. Christianity grew out of Paul's embroideries and soon took on a ghastly inhuman form.

The Romans, as we can chillingly read in the history books, were not the only ones to persecute the Christians. Very soon it was the merciful Christians themselves who slaughtered all non-Christians and deviators from the one true faith. There is no saint's list of non-Christian martyrs, there would be far too many.

No, we must forget all about the story of the astronaut Jesus; he did not exist, just as Jesus the Redeemer never existed.

* * *

I should like to make clear four points about the figure of Jesus as presented by the Church:

a) Jesus was not the 'only begotten Son of God', for Almighty

God, the 'creator of heaven and earth', has neither sons nor daughters.

b) Jesus cannot have fulfilled the function of a 'Saviour', because the concept of 'original sin', which can only be 'wiped out' by blood and martyrdom, is irreconcilable with the concept of an almighty and eternal God.

c) The deeds, sermons and teachings of Jesus in so far as they have been handed down correctly, are not divinely inspired; they existed long before the time when Jesus is supposed to have lived.

d) Jesus was – to mention the most recent explanation – no astronaut. The idea is even more absurd than all the other things that have been claimed in the course of the last 2,000 years.

Jesus and the Christianity initiated by his presence on earth are not of divine origin, just as the Bible does not contain 'God's word'. *Without this basis, visions cannot be attributed to God the Father, or God the Son or the Blessed Virgin Mary.*

Their motivation must be sought elsewhere.

Chapter 3

WHEN MIRACLES DO HAPPEN

IF JESUS is not the 'only begotten son of God' if Almighty God had neither sons nor daughters; if Mary cannot belong to the heavenly personnel, and angels or archangels cannot be numbered among the legates of the enlarged Christian family, then all these sacred messengers are excluded as active causers of visions. However, the fact remains that miracles happen and medically inexplicable cures take place at the sites of Christian visions. Does this mean that nevertheless such phenomena are proof of 'heavenly powers' at work and evidence of the 'authenticity' of visions of members of the Christian Hierarchy?

After studying a mass of sophistical theological explanations, one question takes precedence for me. If no genuine apparition has taken place at what is supposedly the scene of a vision – i.e. of the Blessed Virgin, Jesus or the archangels – or if the personified vision is not identical with the figures placed on record by the 'visionaries', how can 'miracles' and 'miraculous' cures happen *in the name* of those who are supposed to have appeared?

I sought clarification on the spot.

Lourdes, in the French Pyrenees, is the world's best known place of pilgrimage. As many as five million pilgrims travel there annually from the four corners of the world. The town is rather like a vast annual fair at which miracles are offered as attractions. The streets of Lourdes seethe with people even at night, although the nightlife offers nothing more than a striptease of tense expectations.

The miracle business is flourishing; it has been booming for 125 years. In the countless shops there are crucifixes of every conceivable kind and the statue of the Madonna is mass-produced in all sizes, for the office and the front garden. Nor are the rosaries the same for all classes: there are expensive models for the rich and cheaper ones for the less well-off. Which are likely to be more effective is beyond me. The objects on offer are fanciful and endless: pictures of the saints and clogs, purses, bells and plates, sunglasses, watches and lockets, candles of all kinds: thick and thin, long and short, violet and pink, straight and artistically twisted and adorned with gold writing. On every single one of them – made in Lourdes – the Madonna! Her face on the candles will flow away as wax tears; it is more permanent on the clogs and plates.

I know a lot of bars all over the world, including the ones in Acapulco which claim to have every conceivable shape and size of bottle on their shelves. But in my opinion no establishment can compete with Lourdes when it comes to shapes. I have never seen such a collection of differently shaped bottles in my life. Pot-bellied and spherical bottles, rectangular and triangular, pocket-sized, litre and gallon bottles, of all colours and all sizes. In contrast to the bottles with delightful contents at the Miracle Bar in Acapulco, none of the bottles contains anything but 'miracle water from Lourdes.'

The shopkeepers know how deeply they are indebted to the place's reputation, know precisely what ensures and raises their turnover.

They call their shops 'Au Paradis', 'Notre Chere Dame de Noel', 'Au St Odile', 'Au St Camille', 'Au St Pape Paul X', 'Au la Paix du Monde', 'Au Rosier de Marie' and, unbeatable in its simplicity, 'Au Sainte Dame de la Grotte'. Since the girl who saw the Madonna was canonized, everything has been given a name with religious associations. Even the hotels are not given the normal names of earthly hostelries: one, for example, is even called *Hotel du Vatican*. Rome's masters wear ample robes beneath which such things are easily hidden and not a cardinal in the Holy Office blushes.

Disgusted by all this commercialism, I parked my car in the holy garage of a holy hotel for an unholy price. Secretly hoping that the inner illumination would come to me in spite of everything, I mingled with the crowds in front of the basilica. Here at least, in the holy precinct, there were no stalls or pavement salesmen. You were drugged, enveloped in the smell of candles and incense. Familiar, internationally known hymns, mingled with prayers, sounded from stereophonic loudspeakers. The impression was confusing. What should one look at first?

Sick people, in identical wheelchairs, pushed or pulled by helpers, went past in mile-long queues. The Lord's Prayer. In the big meadow a procession was forming with flags, cross and a statue of the Madonna at its head; a priest was saying prayers into a hand-megaphone. A vast production, staged several times a day.

In rows of ten, the hopeful miracle-believers and cure-seekers, myself among them, advance at a snail's pace, waiting patiently until they can fill their colourful plastic bottles with holy water from Lourdes at the taps which are set into the wall. Many drink it, catching it in their hands so that they can apply it to head or feet. Although it is all in the open air, there is a solemn atmosphere as if we are in the nave of a cathedral. All around hundreds and thousands of candles are burning in a vast dance of lights. The only sounds are praying, whispering and hymn singing. Signs in several languages warn you that you are on holy ground and that anyone who forgets it will be immediately reprimanded by strict guards: they also see to it that those in a hurry do not jump the queue.

Now I have reached the stream of water: I haven't got a bottle, I let it run into my hands. I watch my nextdoor neighbours. Their faces are marked with pain and rapture, with devotion and worship, with happiness and pride, simply from being here at last, so close to the miracle. Water is collected here in gallon and ten-litre bottles. For personal needs? Or do people finance the cost of a second trip by selling small quantities once they get home?

The phalanx of the hopeful advances step by step to the great goal, the grotto. It is eight metres long, six metres high and twelve metres wide. At a height of about three metres, to the right of the entrance, stands the white marble statue of the Blessed Virgin, on the very spot and supposedly in exactly the same attitude in which she showed herself to the little Bernadette Soubirous[1] in eighteen visions between 11 February and 16 July 1858. The walls are damp and glistening; the faithful kiss them, kneel on the ground and stare entranced at the marble statue. They pray and many of them weep aloud. From time to time envelopes are thrown into a metal basket in the rear part of the grotto — petitions to the Blessed Virgin. No stamps! In the middle of the grotto stands an altar with candles burning in front of it, hundreds of candles which make the damp air stickily hot. The sea of flames which I see shining at this moment has been shining incessantly since 18 February 1858. If there is such a thing as an everlasting flame, it is here in the grotto at Lourdes.

I was as deeply moved by the devout atmosphere at the pilgrims' goal as I was disgusted by the eastern bazaar atmosphere in the town. No one can be so hard-boiled as to be unmoved by what takes place at the water taps, in the grotto, in the big square and the basilica itself. The countless cares and pains that are dragged here, the communal hope that joins the faithful together! The heavy burden of disappointment that many of them will carry on the journey home! I sat on a wall, 100 yards from the grotto. I crouched there for ten hours, until late at night. With the onset of darkness the stream of pilgrims decreased and the shimmer of the candles burning everywhere increased, became one great flame, dazzling one's eyes, heightening the already expectant atmosphere of Lourdes. The weeping of some unknown fellow-man came steadily from the grotto, even long after midnight when I returned to my holy hotel.

What magnet has the immense power to draw millions of pilgrims to this place year after year?

The Madonna appeared to the fourteen-year-old shepherdess Bernadette Soubirous (1844-1879) eighteen times in the grotto and gave her orders and messages. Bernadette was canonized by Pope Pius XI on 8 December 1933. By this act the Church recognized the authenticity of the visions and of certain miraculous cures which had been recorded at Lourdes. More effective publicity could not have been set in motion by headquarters at Rome. As far as the arm of the Church reached, pilgrimages and processions (with tickets at reduced rates) were organized in all dioceses.

In 1858 more than 100 cures were recorded, seven of them being recognized as 'miracles' by the Holy Office. (By Catholic definition 'miracle' has always meant the 'breaking of the laws of nature'; as this concept is scientifically dubious today, the Church now interprets a 'miracle' as something 'completely inexplicable'.)

Since 1866 cures have been constantly publicized in the *Journal de la Grotte*. Out of thousands of ostensible cures the Church gave the official title of 'miracle' to sixty-three cases. Dr Aphoriso Olivieri, for many years President of the *Bureau des Constatations Médicales*, said in 1969 that even then an average of thirty cures a year were recorded[2]. However, the Medical Bureau at Lourdes does not possess all the data of genuine or ostensible cures, because it only has details of patients who were admitted to the Asylum of Notre Dame or the Hospital of Our Dear Lady of the Seven Sorrows. Between them 49,036 sick and ailing people were housed there in 1970, and 44,731 in 1971.

How does an 'ecclesiastically recognized miracle' evolve?

In May 1952 Mrs Alice Couteault travelled from Poitiers to Lourdes with an organized pilgrimage. She was thirty-four years old and had been suffering from multiple sclerosis* for three years. The journey in the pilgrims' train with many other very sick people was sheer torture for Mrs Couteault. They prayed, lamented and sang hymns to Mary all the way. Relations and attendants looked after the sufferers. The atmosphere of pain and suffering was oppressive, nevertheless the hope they placed in Lourdes was alive and present and consoled them all. Mrs Couteault felt better as soon as she arrived.

In the early morning of 15 May Mrs Couteault, who could neither walk nor speak, was taken to the bathing-pool in a wheelchair. When she was immersed she was on the point of fainting: all her limbs twitched. After the bath she felt like a new woman. She was taken back to the Asylum of Notre Dame in the wheelchair. In the afternoon she went for a short walk alone in the hall: no doctor would have thought it possible.

In the late afternoon she took part in the sacramental procession at which all pilgrims were blessed. Suddenly Mrs Couteault felt as if she could speak again, but did not risk it, because she was afraid 'she might utter a hotch-potch of separate words and make herself ridiculous'. The attendants took her back. Outside the front door she got out of her wheelchair and walked into the Asylum unassisted.

On 16 May Mrs Couteault presented herself at the medical bureau. Under the direction of the President – it was Dr Alphoriso Olivieri – various doctors from various countries diagnosed the patient's condition. (Any doctor who goes to Lourdes can take part in the examinations.) The certificates and diagnoses of doctors who had treated Mrs Couteault *before* the pilgrimage were read. There were opinions by Dr Chauvenet, a surgeon, Dr Delams-Marsalat, a neurologist, and Professor Beauchant from her home

* A chronic progressive disease in which patches of thickening appear throughout the central nervous system, resulting in various forms of paralysis. Cause unknown.

town, Poitiers. Laboratory analyses were in the file. The unanimous diagnosis: multiple sclerosis, incurable. On this 16 May the doctors put on record: 'Her gait and posture while walking are normal. There are no muscular contractions. The patella reflexes are normal. . . .'

During the following years the patient was examined and re-examined at Lourdes: her cure was medically confirmed. On 10 May 1955, fifteen examining doctors certified that 'all subjective signs of the illness have disappeared'.

Such cases of cures are communicated to an international committee to which some 10,000 doctors, dentists, medical students and chemists etc. belong. Another larger group received detailed reports on the history of the disease and the cure at Lourdes. On 15 August 1955 Professor Thiébaud of the University of Strasbourg, declared: 'Examination of the patient showed no disturbances of functions. In particular she hears and sees well, and articulates correctly when speaking. . . .'

On 23 June 1956 the Commission appointed by Monsignore Vion, Bishop of Poitiers, met at Poitiers. Following the doctors' opinion, the Commission pronounced Mrs Alice Couteault's cure to be 'outside and above the laws of nature'.

On 16 July 1956 Monsignore Vion ceremonially announced:

'By virtue of the authority conferred on us in this respect by the Pridentine Council (= inspiration by the Holy Scriptures), with our decision being subject to the authority of the Pope, we hereby solemnly declare that the cure of Mrs Alice Couteault, which took place at Lourdes on 16 May 1952, is miraculous and must be acknowledged as a special manifestation of the most blessed Virgin and Mother of God, Mary.'

* * *

What are we to say about that?

It is well known that the Medical Bureau carries out very strict and accurate examinations and that there are unbelievers and sceptics among the doctors. No case of a cure is recorded unless the clinical picture *before* the event is given in medical certificates. The trouble with certificates is that they are rarely of recent date; they often go back years – to the origin and development of the disease. At best they are issued a few weeks before the decision to make a pilgrimage to Lourdes. But the question also arises whether doctors can give an 'infallible' diagnosis, embracing all symptoms. For example, what diagnostic value has the pronouncement that Mrs Couteault appeared to be cured on 16 May 1952? The findings of the Lourdes Medical Bureau could be ascribed a higher degree of scientific certainty only if the *same* doctors who certified the spontaneous healing process had *themselves* been observing the patient for a long time *before* the miracle. But this strictly scientific method is not feasible with the thousands of sick people who converge on Lourdes from all over the world.

Since the theory of psychosomatic effects developed first by F. G. Alexander in America and later by V. von Weizsäcker in Germany, was introduced into medicine, it has been proved in many clinical experiments that bodily procesess and organic suffering can be directly influenced by psychic stimuli. Muscular performance, cardial activity and the separation of digestive secretions, etc., can be altered by suggestion (hypnosis).

Accurate observations have shown that organic diseases often develop in critical life situations – indeed, it is beyond doubt that specific diseases of organs are subject to specific psychic situations. 'Psychosomatics concern a subject who forms "his" disease himself and is not passively "attacked" by it; every disease has its characteristic expression in the living organism's outward manifestation of the psyche.'

Diagnoses (Greek: deciding between) establish typical symptoms of a condition; from them doctors infer therapies which are possible and likely to be successful. Diagnoses do not and cannot always show *the cause* of a disease or ailment, but only such ultimate absolute knowledge can effect a cure with certainty. If doctors could always recognize all the causes of illness, there would soon be no patients left.

When the Medical Committee at Lourdes examines the findings before and after a cure, it is comparing two different conditions: with the best will in the world it cannot communicate the *reasons* for the change on the basis of this comparison.

Does the hope of a cure at Lourdes already pave the way for a miracle?

Before a sufferer makes up his mind to make the laborious journey, questions, doubts and hopes have been spinning through

his brain for a long time. Has he not long since acquiesced in his
fate? Has he not already visited every doctor who was recommended to him? Without success? Should he risk one last
attempt to change his destiny on a pilgrimage? Could a miracle
actually bring him relief from his pains? If the decision to go on
the pilgrimage ripens in this struggle between doubt and hope,
does not the miraculous cure begin at this moment? Is not a
change in his psychological attitude to the disease initiated?

Dr Alphoriso Olivieri[3] says of this possibility, 'that the
hypothesis of autosuggestion or heterosuggestion (is) quite im-
probable'. He points to Mrs Couteault, who clearly recognized
that she was suffering from an incurable disease, but adds that
she had 'boundless confidence in the efficiency of the baths (at
Lourdes) from the time of her departure and during her pilgrimage.'

There is a big contradiction in these lines! Why and wherefore
can autosuggestion or heterosuggestion be categorically excluded
as causes of the cure, if it is simultaneously admitted that the
patient had 'boundless confidence in the efficiency of the baths'?
'Boundless confidence' is an academically toned-down circum-
locution for 'faith' and 'faith', according to the Church, is
personal conviction, an assumption as opposed to knowledge.
Hence 'faith' is a matter of influencing oneself, in other words
autosuggestion. Then why explain away a crucial explanation of
the cause of cures with a cleft tongue?

*   *   *

The miraculous cure of Gabriel Gargam takes a special place
in the annals of Lourdes, for Gargam was not a believer and went
to Lourdes against his better judgment. So was it a miracle?

Dr Franz L. Schleyer[5], who investigated 232 cures with the
collaboration of medical experts, came to the conclusion that in
the case of Gabriel Gargam 'psychogenous mechanisms were
obviously set in motion on the basis of a severe trauma, and that
these disorders were finally completely eliminated at Lourdes,
after the organic consequences of the trauma had been largely
cured beforehand'.

Psychogenous troubles are physically controlled. During his
long stay in hospital and afterwards Gargam had inwardly resisted

a cure: he was depressed and convinced that he would have to spend the rest of his life in a wheelchair. He himself had given up the struggle. (This kind of 'flight into sickness' is a significant symptom of our time!) But Gargam's resistance to being cured was already broken when he agreed to be taken to Lourdes. Gradually the motor nervous system resumed its functions. The 'shock' of bathing in Lourdes water did the (positive) rest: the will to a healthy life was there again. A miracle? The end of an ailment, effected by a means that no doctor can give a prescription for.

*   *   *

In the course of his investigations Dr Schleyer stated that 'women between the ages of sixteen and forty-five form the majority of sick people at Lourdes'. Out of 232 cases examined, 185 were female. Dr Schleyer explains this as follows:

Obviously the sick people at Lourdes consist predominantly of a quite definite type of young woman, characterized by an abnormal facility for the release of involuntary reactions of the nervous system, with a long history of suffering, in the course of which these asthenic women (people of slight build) have had many serious diseases diagnosed – often with little justification. (It is sometimes astonishing how many different diseases a single female patient is supposed to have had before her pilgrimage to Lourdes.)

At first the Church laid down that the cure of nervous diseases could not be recognized in the category of miraculous cures. Medical research has thwarted it. Since doctors know that neuroses can unleash organic diseases, whose causes can be clearly explained by the patient's life and conflict situations, that neuroses are motivated by the personality of the patient and are mostly inaccessible medically or surgically, miraculous cures are no longer miraculous. With the progress of medicine genuine miraculous cures will become rarer and rarer. I am reminded of the wise saying of old Seneca that we learnt at school: *'Felix, qui potuit rerum cognoscere causas'* – Happy the man who has been able to know the causes of things!

*   *   *

Water (especially springs that have appeared suddenly) plays a legendary role at pilgrim shrines. The Hydrological Institute which made a physical and chemical examination of Lourdes' wonder-working water, issued the following analysis on 8 October 1964:

Water with an almost neutral pH-value (measurement of the concentration of free hydrogenions)

Free carbon dioxide content weak

Gaseous carbon dioxide nil

Water of average hardness (about 14')

Slight mineralization, essentially from calcium carbonate

Sulphate and chloride contents very low

Soluble iron and organic materials content normal

No effects from building materials or sewers

In other words: absolutely normal drinking water that *cannot* have any balneological effect!

*   *   *

Lourdes is world famous for its miraculous cures, but it is not unique. Wherever a 'wonderworking Madonna' is set up at pilgrimage shrines, miracles of all kinds immediately happen and cures are soon reported.

Yet, I do not know of any case of an *authentic* miracle, for example of a patient getting an amputated leg or arm back again. But at the first-class addresses of the wonder workers who all trace themselves back to almighty God such *authentic* miracles should be neither impossible nor black magic.

The orthodox Lourdes historians [6, 7, 8, 9] object that even that sort of miracle would not convince the sceptics. Jesus raised Lazarus from the dead, yet those who were not present did not believe in that unique miracle (John 11, 1 *et seq*.). The fact that scepticism even applied to Jesus himself is quite understandable given the way in which 'God's word' originated. The apostle Thomas was among the sceptics who refused to admit that Jesus had risen from the dead: 'Except I shall see in his hands the print of the nails and put my fingers into the print of the nails, and thrust my hand into his side, I will not believe' (John 20, 25, *et seq*.).

Jesus appeared and challenged the unbelievers to plunge their hands into his wounds. If we follow the gospels, the Son of God was determined to convince a sceptic. Why should not, in the case of a presumptuous claim to be able to work unverifiable miracles, just one sceptical, scientifically trained doctor, a man without *faith*, but plenty of knowledge, be convinced by an unequivocal obvious miracle?

*   *   *

Miraculous cures have taken place at Fatima, about 100 miles north of Lisbon, since October 1917. Here are only two absurd examples from the records:

As Miss Cecilia Augusta Goveia Trestes of Torres Novas had been suffering from pulmonary tuberculosis, peritonitis and dropsy for years, her family, correctly assessing the situation, had already ordered a coffin for her. Although the doctors could do nothing, Miss Trestes was taken to Fatima on 13 July 1923.

Nothing happened at the miracle shrine. However, on the way home Miss Trestes, who normally had hardly any appetite, became as hungry as a hunter. She greedily gulped down her attendants' provisions. After half an hour's pause for digestion, the taciturn Cecilia Augusta grew loquacious and even began to laugh and sing. A week later she was better[10].

Whether this surprising change was provoked by a type of euphoria well-known in medicine, the sudden subjective sense of well-being of severely ill patients – and all the signs point to it – is not stated in the records, nor when or where she finally got rid of her ailments.

*   *   *

A thirty-year-old man from Camara de Lobos on the island of Madeira was a chronic alcoholic. Doctors prophesied that he would certainly get cirrhosis of the liver with a fatal outcome. The young man went on carefully boozing his bottle of spirits a day. Then his religious wife took a hand. She mixed a few drops of Fatima water with his daily ration of spirits. Wonder of wonders, from that moment alcohol repelled the former drunkard. He lived to the age of seventy[11].

'Cures' of this sort are always unverifiable, yet they obstinately assert themselves in the fairytale literature of miracles. The relevant people whom one could question have long since died – relatives, flattered by having a miraculous cure in the family nod sagely: yes, yes, that's the story told about the dead man. . . .

The round figure of 1,500 supposed cures has been recorded at Fatima since 1940. As at Lourdes, the Medical Commission has only recognized a comparatively small number of 'cures' and here, too, the ratio of cures is women 70 : 30 men. What is the reason for that? Do women pray more frequently? Or do Eve's daughters contribute more (imaginary) illnesses, confirmed by desperate doctors unable to find anything concrete, to the Madonna?

Let me make it clear that exceptional cures at the scene of visions are not denied. But let me also make it clear that as members of the Holy Family are not *the cause* of the visions, neither can they be *the cause* of the miraculous cures which indeed happen by virtue of visions.

Nevertheless miracles are performed in the name of holy figures. The periodical *Children of Fatima*[12] prints regular reports of cures, confirms the addition of votive tablets or quotes from letters by people who certify that they have received help from or been cured by praying to and invoking the Christian hierarchy. And the bulletins in this periodical do not only contain the names of Mary, Jesus, archangels and saints! Frequently letters of thanks are addressed to the dead visionary children, who promptly grant requests of all kinds, although they have not been beatified or canonized by the Church, in other words, are active without religious approval.

The Church not only decides which visions are 'genuine', it also defines what a 'miracle' is. In 1870 the definition of what should count as a miracle was laid down by the Vatican. A miracle is 'in contradiction to the laws of nature'. Full stop. But this definition is over 100 years old, it has acquired a patina, like many church towers. Man is getting to know more and more about nature's tricks, he is even learning to manipulate the laws of nature at will. So I have a well-founded hope that in 100 years' time there will be nothing left that we can call a miracle.

At the time of writing about 1,200 (!) cases for beatification or canonization are under consideration in the Vatican.

There are already some 12,000 saints (!).

Since Pope Benedict XIV published his work 'On the Beatification and Canonization of God's Servants' in 1738, the rule applies that each saint must be shown to have performed at least two miracles *after* his or her death. All those who are now on the waiting list of 1,200 'near-saints' have a very much harder time of it than their predecessors. Things that were readily accepted as miracles before are performed today by every competent medical practitioner. It is no longer so easy to become a saint as it was before. I remember the Latin tag from my schooldays: *Tempora Mutantur, nos et mutamur in illis* (Times change and we change with them.)

What does the Church do when one of its servants performs miracle after miracle during his lifetime? If he is venerated . . . and prayed to as a saint by the faithful without its supreme blessing? It tolerates the situation.

In initiated circles it is considered quite certain that Francesco Forgione, who became world-famous under the name of Pater Pio, will be summoned into the community of the saints. Pater Pio performed so many miracles during his lifetime that he was turned into a (living) saint long before there was any question of canonization.

Francesco Forgione was born in Pietrelcina on 25 May 1887. He died as Peter Pio in the monastery of San Giovanni Rotondo on 23 September 1968, 'almost fifty years to the day when he received the stigmata of Our Lord'.[13]

Deliberately or by chance, little is known about Francesco's youth. He said of himself that he had been a *'maccherone senza sale'* (lazy lad). The Capuchins do not speak about the development of their saintly brother, but even during his novitiate rumours reached the outside world that 'strange phenomena' distinguished the young brother, for 'this pale emaciated novice dispenses with food for days on end. . . . In Venefro he lived for twenty-one days solely on the Holy Eucharist.' His weak health made him suffer from sudden attacks of fever which 'constantly burst the monastery thermometers': the brother in charge of nursing tried him with a strong bath thermometer and the mercury rose to 48° (!). Nights in the monastery cell were exciting. 'Horrible monsters appeared from all sides, when he, obeying the holy rule, tried to get some rest.'

Pater Pio was staying on his parents' farm to convalesce. On 20 September 1915, when his mother called him to lunch, he came out of a hut in the vineyard, 'waving his hands about as if they were burnt'. His mother asked what had happened and Pio answered that all he could feel were slight pricking pains. But according to the book which bears the highest ecclesiastical imprimatur, 'Pater Pio had really received invisible stigmata'. The invisible marks later began to bleed while he was sitting in the last row of the choir with his fellow brothers. When Pio stepped forward, his hands bled, there were stigmata on his feet and a deep cut in his right side.

'*Pater Pio è un santo*' cried the multitude. Pater Pio is a saint.

Photographs of the stigmata reached the Holy Office. (Today the Office of the Congregation of the Faith, formerly the Holy Inquisition.) Pater Pio was ordered to undergo medical examination and so still the curiosity of the faithful. Doctors examined him and sealed bandages over the wounds. They finally stated that 'this kind of lesion was beyond the comprehension of science'. Pater Pio lost a cup full of blood every day. Every day he wore brown gloves over the visible lesions.

Apparently Pater Pio possessed all the faculties that science now sums up under the heading of 'parapsychological phenomena'. He was visionary and prophet, telekinetist and telepathist, wonder-worker and long-distance healer all in one. Pater Pio could not speak a word of English, but he understood what American children said to him. He knew in advance what the penitent children who were ripe for penance would confess or keep silent from him. He told one man to his face that he harboured thoughts of killing his wife. In the case of a woman who was faced with a major gynaecological operation, the haemorrhages stopped spontaneously, and Pater Pio prophesied that she would give birth to a son. A year later she brought the boy to him in the monastery.

Alberto de Fante, the official chronicler of San Giovanni Rotondo, relates that a man prayed for help at Pio's confessional box for his nephew who was at death's door and had been given up by the doctors. Twenty-four hours later the nephew was well again; an 'undeniable' cure had taken place.

A woman wanted to speed up the appointment given her by the booking-office for three days hence – Pio was always booked up for weeks ahead – but when she was pushing her way through the crowd and weeping bitterly, Pater Pio stopped her and told her to go home quickly, for everything would be all right. When the woman got home, her husband, for whom she had been going to intercede, was cured.

The number of 'miraculous' reports is large. Once a man left the monastery in the evening after confession and was faced with a cloudburst. He waited, because he did not want to get soaked. Then Pater Pio approached him and told him not to worry, for he would accompany him. When the stranger reached his inn, people wondered why he had not got drenched through. The innkeeper understood at once: 'Of course, if Pater Pio was with you. . . .' But Pater Pio was also able to do magic the opposite way round. One winter morning a female penitent arrived at the monastery in a downpour of rain. Pio touched her on the shoulder and to her astonishment the signora's clothes 'were bone dry in a moment'.

Bilocation* was obviously also within Pater Pio's powers. The authoress of the approved account says that the father could 'pass through closed doors' to the great astonishment of the crowd who were waiting for him. In the process he was able 'to mislead insistent enquirers and put off the curious. "Where were you, father? We were looking for you everywhere!" Pater Pio chuckled: "I was walking to and fro in front of you, but you didn't take any notice." '

The suffering father ('I suffer when I do not suffer' – Pio on Pio), even conjured up sweet smells in frowsty rooms. Dr Romanelli thought it unseemly of Pater Pio to use scent, as he imagined he did. A Capuchin explained to him that Pio's blood was impregnated with the 'sweet scent'. When a Dr Festa took a piece of linen soaked in Pater Pio's blood to Rome to have it examined in a laboratory, his fellow travellers asked him what it was that smelt so nice. In July 1930 a living-room in Bologna suddenly smelt of roses and narcissi. A sick girl had just returned from San Giovanni Rotondo. The heavenly aroma lasted for a quarter of an hour and then the sick girl was able to move her paralysed arm again. There can be no doubt about the phenomena of smell, because the number of witnesses has been very large over four decades. In the words of Michael Faraday (1791-1867), there is obviously 'nothing too miraculous to be true'.

---

* Being bodily present at two different places simultaneously.

Pope Benedict XV anticipated all requests for canonization by saying: 'Pater Pio is truly a man of God.'

Pater Pio bore the stigmata of Christ before the eyes of contemporaries. His famous predecessor, Francis of Assisi (1182-1226), was the first person to be afflicted with officially attested stigmata. And he was canonized two years after his death. His stigmata are legendary; the saint who talked to the birds has long been singing in the choir of angels. Since St Francis was marked by the stigmata, about 350 people are supposed to have been similarly afflicted. Not all stigmatics bear genuine signs. For example, Therese Neumann (1898-1962) from Konnersreuth in Oberpfalz, Germany, who hit the headlines, is reputed to have been a fake. The theologian Dr Joseph Hanauer[14] suspects that Therese scratched the wounds on her own body, because she often sent visitors out of her room and then showed them the bleeding wounds when they returned. Unofficially it is said that Therese received the stigmata during Lent 1926, and had visions of the Passion of Our Lord on every Friday except for Christian holidays.

Reports however of devout people who have borne the marks of the crucifixion on hands, feet and below the heart are announced too often and by too many witnesses to be dismissed as nonsense.

The 'marks of the Lord Jesus' (Galatians 6, 17) are reputed to hurt like the wounds of the crowning with thorns and nailing to the cross; they bleed on Fridays for preference and are incurable by normal treatment.

Are we faced with confirmation of an unassailable miracle? I must admit in advance that no proven explanation of the stigmatic phenomena exists *as yet*, that is why they are still surrounded by a thick, well-protected occult veil.

*　　*　　*

The reader should know that in the past cult and religious happenings provably arose around people ostensibly possessed by demons. Epilepsy (sudden insensibility accompanied by convulsive seizures) was called *morbus sanctor*, the 'holy disease', because those affected by it often had visions of Lucifer, spirits, gods and angels. 'It is well known that Mohammed, too, suffered from epileptic attacks and was considered divine by his people for this reason. He himself recounts his stay in Paradise in the Koran.'[15]

Professor O. Prokop says that experiences in epileptic states are mostly of a religious nature and that people subject to them tend to asceticism. (A characteristic of stigmatics!) They are able to induce the demonic attacks by breathing techniques – 'by shifting the balance of the acid bases'.

Catatonia, a form of schizophrenia characterized by restlessness and excitement with periodic states of stupor, develops special powers in religiously fixated persons. 'The fascination is all the more effective . . . as the schizophrenic works on his environment without loss of intelligence.'

Professor Prokop and others also mention *hysteria* as a genuine ailment of a psychic nature. They attribute to hysterics a 'marked desire to be honoured, loved, praised and recognized, and also their joy in the ability to attract people to them by their own charms . . . and in this way explain why the religious martyrs not only bore their martyrdom but also went to meet it gladly'. In addition there is the frequently proved fact that hysterics are virtually insensible to pain.

In my opinion the brief description of the clinical pictures gives essential hints about the predisposed state of people who are sought out by stigmata. All three symptoms of illness point to damage or disturbance of the nervous system. Simple reference books describe a 'stigmatic' as a man with a hypersensitive nervous system who tends to react to psychic and other stimuli with disorders (stigmata). The *parasympatheticus*, a part of the vegetative nervous system, acting on stimuli or orders from the brain, makes the eyelids close, tears flow and spittle run, but it also controls the sexual organs, etc.

In a state of heightened tension (*vagotonia*) the organs looked after by the parasympathetic nervous system require very small stimuli; organic disorders can arise. Abnormal states of tension (*dystonia*) of muscles and vessels are typical of weakened vegetative nervous systems; they are expressed by organic troubles . . . and in the skin by excess or congestion of the blood (*hyperaemia*). To round off the brief medical discursion, I should mention *hyperaesthesia* with its morbidly increased sensitivity to touch as a result of the most varied diseases of the nervous system.

To sum up. In all the cases of stigmatics known to me spontaneous excitability was as marked as the development of special powers. There can be no doubt that without exception they exercised a – deliberate or involuntary – fascination on their fellow humans. Did they not also feel a humble joy in 'being honoured, loved, praised and recognized'? Could they deny their ability to draw men to them by their own 'attractions' (= stigmata)? How could they bear pain except as a result of a specific medical condition? Were not their bodily functions also subject to the orders and stimuli of the nervous system?

The sum total of these clinical pictures, in my opinion, puts stigmatics in a stress situation which influences their whole bodies. Professor Dr Hans Selye, Director of the Institute for Experimental Medicine and Surgery in the University of Montreal, the 'father of stress research', describes such states: 'Stress is always expressed by a syndrome, i.e. a sum total of alterations, not by a single alteration. An isolated effect on a single part of the body either causes damage or stimulates higher achievement.'[16] In the present-day state of knowledge it need only be mentioned in passing that every conceivable ramification is bound to the end effect by autosuggestion.

*   *   *

On 14 October 1973, I talked to Professor Josef Brudny, rehabilitation expert at New York University, in the Plaza Hotel in New York.

'You cured a young man who had been tied to a wheelchair for years with a broken spine, without an operation. Are you a miracle doctor?'

'There was no question of a miracle. If one can speak of miracles in this connection, it is the power of mind over the body. I literally mean that the power of the brain is the last untamed beast on this planet.'

'How were you able to cure the patient of his paralysis?'

'I coupled him to an electromyographic Feedback and trained him to respond with great patience'.

'What is this machine exactly?'

'It's an electronic apparatus which can be compared to an encephalograph. It registers certain biological processes, e.g. heart beats or blood-pressure, but also gives the patient signals as soon as a change in the current is registered. For example, if the heart beats more slowly than it should, the patient hears a rhythmic peep-peep through his headphones showing what his heartbeat should actually be. The brain reacts at once and orders the heart to beat in the rhythm recommended.'

'In other words the brain tells the heart how quickly it must beat?'

The human organism is like a cybernetic system with its control and regulatory mechanisms, a permanently self-contained cycle of functions. The brain orders the muscles to react in such and such a way. It itself obtains its information from sensors of all kinds, through taste, touch, sight, smell, hearing, feelings of pain etc. For example, if the heart starts to beat irregularly, the brain immediately records a panic situation. There are intensive orders to the heart muscle and it obeys, providing there are no special circumstances to prevent it, such as a blockage of an artery.

'My colleague, Dr B. Engle of the San Francisco Medical Centre in the University of California, has succeeded in deliberately, i.e. suggestively, slowing down or speeding up the heart beats of several patients. The "guinea-pig" sits in front of red, green and yellow signals. "Yellow" corresponds to the patient's normal heart rhythm. If the doctor orders a quicker heart beat, the red lamp lights up and a simulated quicker heart beat plays through the patient's headphones. The patients experimented on are affected audovisually. They try to follow the order of the red lights and the beats in their headphones. In a few seconds the recorded heart curve shows a diagram with a quicker heart rhythm than the person should normally have. In this way it is possible to slow down the pulse, alter blood-pressure, order heat or cold on the surface of the skin . . . or even, as in the case of the young paralytic, successively overcome the paralysis. These are proven medical experiments, not miracles. This method is known as "Bio Feedback".'

*   *   *

Of course we cannot attach the slightest blame to stigmatics for having no idea of the reasons and origins of their signs, or for their knowing nothing about Bio Feedback, a method which permits direct conclusions.

In the case of persons living in a state of religious ecstasy we do not know how gradual pathological changes in their body cells and tissues are caused by their psychic fixation on the revered figures they are so keen to resemble. It is quite possible medically that heterosuggestion which is active for years and becomes so natural that it is an unconscious part of existence can finally produce stigmata.

Women predominate when it comes to stigmata, as they did in the case of miraculous cures. Possible motivations have already been mentioned. If religious fanatics, whether men or women, desire the mark of the Lord with a devouring ardour – stimulated by *visual signs* which constantly provide them with images of our wounded Lord on the cross stimulated by *acoustic signals*, which represent the crucified one in prayer and song – at some time the 'beast brain' will obey and give orders to supply the arteries and veins so richly with blood that they swell up and finally allow small drops to appear on the epidermis. Above all the will *to suffer* and the inner wish to feel the pains of the Redeemer dominates.

The prominent English surgeon Richard Sergeant[17] asks 'Is it really necessary to suffer to achieve salvation? . . . Does salvation justify pain? In the lay hierarchy of the Christian heaven the host of the martyrs takes third place after the apostles and the prophets. In other words martyrdom is the only way for the ordinary man to enter the kingdom.'

The will to join the community of the blessed through suffering, pain and asceticism, in brief through martyrdom, is clearly the essence of stigmatics. Those who bear the stigmata have iron wills.

Let us leave the religious enclave to demonstrate by a profane example what an iron will can achieve. . . . During the twenties August Dieber, a miner, was buried alive when a gallery collapsed owing to bad weather. He waited two days and two nights to be rescued. His right thigh and part of his foot were jammed by blocks of stone. The miner first willed himself not to feel the pain, but he sensed that his limbs had grown cold and lost sensation. Then he concentrated the whole of his will on sending blood to the 'numb' thigh. At first he felt severe pains which he rejected, then he noticed the return of heat and sensation. When he was medically examined, both thigh and foot were found to be well supplied with blood, to the general astonishment of the doctors. Amputation was unnecessary.

The miner had discovered a new faculty during the accident. By will power and suggestion he could make parts of his body insensitive to pain (fakirs!), and even send blood to parts of the body chosen by him. He trained these faculties and became an international variety attraction.

It was no novelty for artists to have their bodies pierced with needles and swords on the stage. But by dint of intense concentration this man produced the classical stigmata on his skin while the public watched in breathless excitement. He did this at every performance, and twice on Wednesdays and Sundays.

The variety 'miracle' ended in a nervous breakdown. Smart managers wanted to make the performance hyper-perfect. The artist was to weep tears of blood, too. As he could not force any blood through the cornea, even with the greatest effort of will, the mercenary manager had an obscure ophthalmalogist come to his dressing-room before every performance and make tiny perforations in the eyeballs. August Dieber did weep tears of blood on a few occasions, but then his nerve gave way. The tears have nothing to do with my subject but the story shows that a man possessed of an iron will can force stigmata to appear on his body.

Professor H. J. Campbell, a physiologist at London University, has convincingly demonstrated that the brain in men and animals is devoted to procuring pleasure. The embryo begins its intrauterine growth with a head that is comparatively out of proportion. In it the grey matter of the brain makes the body grow according to programmed patterns. The nerve paths which strive to procure pleasure are already formed at birth. From the baby's first cries the process of experience with its reactions to feeling pleasure or pain begins.

The environment – parents, uncles, aunts, teachers and parsons – continually and rather thoughtlessly nourishes the 'beast brain' computer with rules for human behaviour and moral laws. In addition discoveries which the sensory organs report to it must be stored in the tiniest cells of the brain. Fixed reactions for future behaviour are programmed from all 'reports' to the brain. You may not do that, you must do that, you may say this but not that, you must and shall believe this, it is forbidden to believe that etc. Or experiences such as these: that is hot, you are getting burnt, this is cold, you are freezing, sing for it cheers you up, smell a rose for its scent is pleasant, etc.

As the striving to procure pleasure still dominates, even after education, learning and religious teaching, Campbell says that a single order was given to the brain computer of our first ancestors: 'Activate pleasure procurement!' Campbell uses the concept 'pleasure' in a strictly scientific sense. By it he means the feeling arising from increased stimulation of the pleasure areas which occur in the higher brain layers. In such a sense, thought 'can lead to the setting up and transformation of preferred paths in the brain and thus give the individual the power to shape his mind with forethought'. What the individual registers and selects as procurement of pleasure for himself, he himself determines according to inclination and taste. The work of Campbell, who worked as guest professor at the Max Planck Institute of Brain Research at Frankfurt, and the Collège de France, Paris, provides important hints for our theme.

From his first vague thoughts the Christian's presumptuous 'faith' forces him to believe that he is the Lord of Creation, 'chosen' before men of other faiths because the Redeemer died for him; that special mercies are reserved for him, because the heaven of the blessed is assured him in return for behaviour pleasing to God (and the Church); and on top of all this, that there is an infallible judicial tribunal over good and bad, namely the Pope, governing his earthly (Catholic) existence.

This doctrinaire 'upbringing' goes hand in glove with the suggestive visual infiltration of religious doctrine, e.g. by illustrations of the text of the rosary learnt by children, by Christ's stations of the cross, by gifts of sentimental coloured prints of Mary on the occasion of one's first Communion (children of eight or nine take part in the Eucharist for the first time). Church interiors present the whole pomp of a kingdom of heaven 'on earth' with images of Christ on the cross artistically carved in wood or sculptured in marble, the stigmata generally dripping with blood in a most realistic way. They display statues and pictures of Mary, with and without the infant Jesus, Mary kneeling at the cross in Gethsemane or sheltering the head of the sufferer in her lap. They offer statues and paintings of the saints. Martyrs and patron saints lie in state under countless glass cases. And everywhere we see the brilliant graphic emblems of the cross.

Visual signals of the 'only true faith' follow the faithful every-where, for it is a *pleasure* to partake of the holy life.

The vast size of the churches, in which man appears so minute, and the reverent atmosphere in small intimate chapels induce complete repose, relaxation, meditation. Prayers lull those kneel-ing in the pews. During the mass or high mass fascinating stage management forcibly attracts the attention of the congregation to the mystery of the transubstantiation, the changing of the wine into the blood of our Lord. The liturgy is the form of divine service, the 'religious realization of Christ's work of redemption through the Church'. *Acoustic signals*, with the antiphonal sing-ing of priests and congregation, magnified and intensified by the peal of the organ (whose almost exclusive adoption is one of the church's cleverest 'effects'), sensitize the congregation, which is already receptive to the great spectacle. The texts of the hymns literally teem with painful suffering: indeed, they immerse the faithful in a feeling of perceiving pain as a pleasure to be sought for, so that thereby they can come closer to the Redeemer. Naturally they end, mostly in a chorus, with a promise of heavenly happiness! It is a *pleasure* to suffer and participate in pain.

The visual and acoustic signals, as introduced by modern medicine in Bio Feedback, and the wish to procure pleasure pro-grammed in the human brain demonstrated by Campbell provide illuminating explanations, in my view, of the detailed accounts which visionary children (and the few adult visionaries, too) put on official record. They are 'visions' of pictures and images that have followed them around since they were tiny. Their 'messages' contain texts and vocables which are really childish simplifications of the theological double-dutch pumped into them from pulpit and schoolmaster's desk . . . because they have frequently mis-understood what they heard and learnt, they bowdlerize sermons and catechist texts. The result is mysterious incomprehensible communication in which supernatural ideas, soothsayings and prophecies are hopelessly confused.

It is not surprising to anyone familiar with the infantile psyche that it is mostly the youngest of all who are able to enjoy visions. They live in fear of purgatory, 'the place of purification', 'the fire . . . for punishing those who have not done penance for their sins (1 Corinthians, 3, 15, German version.) Children fear the threatened punishment, so they do everything in their power to avoid the torments of hell. With naïve passion and unbridled childish imagination they become inflated and involved in fantastic ideas and undertakings. There is nothing they long for more than to meet the wondrous figures of the religious world face to face. Every day they learn from beautiful legends about favoured people who have met members of the Holy Family. Parsons and Sunday school teachers have told them these legends, and the Church does not lie. (Stories with ghastly contents, as every psychologist knows, can cause anxiety neuroses in children.) Out of the fantasy grows the enjoyment of forcing miraculous experiences to occur. Then the children 'suddenly' experience, but with full sensory perception, true dreams, which have a surprising content of truth (namely the figures, symbols and words of their religion) 'which appear to lie outside the normal apparition. The objects of the true dreams have long before been recorded by the dreaming psyche. Now, in a flash, they become the "revelation of the reality of the conscious".' (Herder.) The striving for pleasure, in the case of the children their joy in the vision, is fulfilled.

It is unfair to dispute the subjective 'truth' of their visions. If the Church does not want visions to exist on a large scale, it must change or exclude the training in readiness to receive experiences, the wish to be confronted with the Holy Family. That is something it will certainly not do, as it can make very good use of the so-called 'genuine' visions in its proselytizing work. Walter Nigg, the hagiographer already mentioned, who wanted to see the return of the saints, expresses a pious hope that is equally applicable to the 'necessity' of visions: 'Admittedly they are virtually forgotten nowadays; they are spoken of infrequently or not at all. Yet the silence will not endure, for suddenly they will speak to men again.' The Church, too, has its specific wish for pleasure, for *pleasure in miracles*.

*　　*　　*

In order to increase the procurement of pleasure in the faith, some tricks have been integrated into the Mass. The American Leslie M. LeCron[19] says that a burning candle is best suited for the stimulation of heterosuggestion (and what else is devotion?). It should be set up in such a way that it is pleasant to watch. 'The flickering flame of a candle has a hypnotic effect.'

Campbell proved by experiments that white, with its many frequencies, provoked intense feelings of pleasure. 'Brightness contrasts with the boring monotony of the surroundings and hence produces pleasure.'

Naturally the smart ecclesiastical bigwigs had no academic justification when they installed the *Lucerna*, or eternal lamp, before the altar as a 'sign of the presence of Christ as light of the world' (John 8, 12). But during its 2,000 years of history the Church has shown an infallible instinct, a sixth and seventh sense, for 'effect'. For a long time now, the eternal lamp has not been confined to the interior of the Church. Candle stands offer the effective illumination for sale right at the entrance. There is not a single church without countless candles burning away before altar and high altar, before pictures of the Madonna and saints. They excite the desired raptures.

At places of pilgrimage candle orgies create Orphic mysteries which stimulate a state of preparedness for miracles with their sea of light. Torch- and candle-bearing processions are common on high holidays. In the light of present-day psychological knowledge, they effectively stimulate that state of 'being outside one's self' in which even miracles still have a chance of being believed.

*   *   *

I have no intention of entering the boundless territory of psychology, but I should like to illuminate one sector which can answer some questions — I refer to the psychotherapeutic method of psychodrama. A group of patients act out their conflicts to liberate themselves from their frustrations and neuroses. The therapy effects a healing process.

Actually this highly modern concept can be found as early as the Greek philosopher Aristotle (384 BC-322 BC). Aristotle realized that ideas do not work outside, but in, the body as an effective force. His idea of entelechy (= forming power) which he took over from physics, was introduced into his moral philosophy, which survived for centuries. According to it, the mind is matterless energy (= the first forming power). Tragedy, says Aristotle, achieves through catharsis (= purification), the decision between good and bad, a miraculous healing effect (Psychodrama!).

Dr Ploèger, a university lecturer[20] explains the process as follows: 'An implicit condition for it among the spectators is their identification with the hero, whose actions they accept and find in agreement with their own ideals and motives.' (Such identifications exist at all places of pilgrimage – with members of the Holy Family!) Dramatic representation of the conflicts effecting a cure in the Aristotelean sense produces effects much like those obtained by psychodrama as practised in western and eastern countries today.

In Chinese philosophy of the fourth and third centuries BC there existed the concept of the Tao, which means something like path or way. Tao was the world's primal cause, which was at the root of all phenomena, but was beyond rational perception. In this philosophy the Yin and Yang (dark and light) stand for positive and negative values. As Professor Ilza Veith[21] says in his essay 'Psychiatric Thought in Chinese Medicine', the Chinese have never, like other cultures, imagined their creator as a figure who demanded obedience and devotion. Undisturbed by a punitive vengeful god at the beginning of things, the Chinese sought edification *and* healing in the additive power of likeminded 'souls', in the grouping of family and friends. Here, too, the mind of a community which was fixated on an idea did its work and the cure was accepted as a miracle.

Those are examples of the stages of the development on the way to psychodrama with its 'mechanisms of inter-human reference'[22].

Autogene training, which is relevant in this connection, also has a solid tradition. The Gottingen neurologist Johannes Heinrich Schultz (1884-1970) introduced this kind of self-hypnosis, which leads to relaxation through a certain inner attitude, into general use. It has an approximate counterpart in the incubation or temple sleep of antiquity. Incubation effected divine revelations and the cure of diseases in dreams. (*incubare*: to lie down in a consecrated place.)

In classical times incubation leading to relaxation was preceded by bathing. (Lourdes and elsewhere!) 'The actual incubation was carried out peacefully in the *abaton*, the holy of holies of the temple.' (What other effect do churches and altars have?) Dr Von Schumann[23] says that muscle relaxation and falling asleep during incubation (as in autogene training) must be in close correlation, for then the suggestible and credulous patients, uncritically

One of the branches of the 'Bank of the Holy Ghost' in Rome. It is owned by the Vatican. Anyone who believes should feel safe in opening an account there!

The dark clouds opened and the whirling sun began its firework display against a background of clear blue sky. Fatima is one great garden of expectation on 13 May and 13 October every year.

Fatima. The children Jacinta Martos, Francesco and Lucia Santos had their first vision of Mary around noon on 13 July, 1917. 70,000–80,000 pilgrims saw the solar miracle on 13 October, 1917.

From 11 February to 16 July, 1858, Bernadette Soubirous had a total of 18 visions of Mary in this grotto on the spot where the marble statue is worshipped by the hopeful today.

At night searchlights illuminate the row of taps from which bottles of all shapes and sizes are filled with 'miraculous water'. According to analysis it is ordinary tap-water.

A candle stall with a notice in German. (There are others in all known languages.) The sea of candles has been shining since 1858. The massive turnover also helps the Church.

Day after day the concourse below the basilica teems with thousands of pilgrims – Five million a year.

In the square in front of the basilica male and female helpers push incapacitated patients towards the miracle in wheel-chairs.

One of the many daily rosary processions, with megaphones and singing. They follow a strict timetable.

St Odile, Au Saint Basque. . . . At Lourdes the saints are invoked to sell you everything — bottles, rosaries, clogs . . .

Profane commerce flourishes side by side with prayer and hope.

Cars from all over the world. Shops with religious items by the dozen and in every one of them the Madonna, 'made in Lourdes'.

Nowhere else in the world have I seen such a collection of differently shaped bottles: potbellied and spherical, rectangular and triangular, pocket-sized and gallon-sized, in every conceivable colour — all for the wonder-working water.

There is nothing they haven't got in the religious shops: pictures of the saints and clogs, purses, bells, plates and sunglasses, with the Madonna on every one.

A reconstruction of the temples at Epidaurus.

The ruins give some idea of the enormous size of the sacred precinct, in which the god Asclepios cured the sick in a healing sleep. Miraculous cures 2,350 years before Lourdes!

The layout of the temples at Epidaurus, even though in ruins, still give an idea of the gigantic 'polyclinic' which the friendly gods of healing successfully ran with the wonderful therapy of healing sleep. The gods of healing were first-class doctors.

Statue of Asclepios, god of healing and head of the divine polyclinic.

Votive tablets from pre-Christian times. The desire to offer thanks for miracles is as old as the hills.

Votive tablets. La Madonna della Guardia, Genoa. Santuario della Rivelazione, Rome, Madonna del Divino Amore, near Rome. That is how people offer thanks in the Christian era.

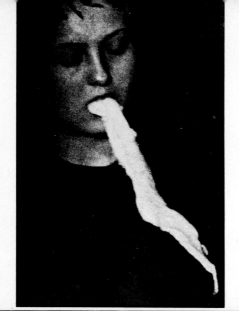

During his experiments Dr von Schrenck-Notzing took flashlight photographs which show materialisations by the medium Eva Ç. The Society for Psychic Research, London, under the leadership of Sir William Crooks, took such exposures with four cameras simultaneously.

In 1938 Mr Colin Evans, a medium, floated several feet above the ground before 300 spectators in Rochester Square Temple, London.

Hellenistic mystery cults already had the 'Last Supper', when bread with the sign of the cross (later the host) was served. The meal was eating and drinking the body and blood of their god. And that was at a time when no one had ever heard of Jesus. – The Madonna and child were worshipped in several religions long before the invention of this Christian cult. Two Asian statues of Madonna and child – models for the Catholic cult of Mary?

At Mama Rosa's, San Damiano.

'Mama Rosa' is obviously successful in her work. The south wall of the farm is covered with votive tablets saying 'Mary has helped!' The messages of thanks are written in all languages known to me. Even without the Church's official blessing, 'Mama Rosa' seems to be on good terms with miracles.

Bruno Cornacchiola, a tram-conductor, had visions of Mary in this grotto near Tre Fontane, Rome, in 1947. It is a popular and successful place of pilgrimage – the votive tablets prove it!

5 May, 1974. A visit to the clairvoyant Jeane Dixon in Washington, D.C.

With the exception of 2, 3, 4, 31, 32, 33 (historical photographs), *all* photographs were taken by Erich von Däniken.

This is how little Conchita experienced the 'miracle of the Host' at Carabandal.

Processions of the cross-bearing pilgrims wind through the fields of Heroldsbach in spite of the ecclesiastical ban.

Heroldsbach, a quiet Bavarian village.

'The biggest visionary shrine in the world', a grotesque record.

This is surely the first photograph ever of a vision of Mary. An Egyptian reporter snapped the nebulous figure which floated above the Coptic Church near Cairo on 12 April. 1968. The authenticity and value of this picture have not been investigated.

wide open for a religio-magical cure, can be healed and liberated
of their disorders. The person seeking a cure behaves passively
during incubation and 'awaits . . . a magical cure from the God
Asclepios'. If for example we substitute the name 'Bernadette
Soubirous' for the god Asclepios, we think we are reading an
account of what goes on at Lourdes.

The god Asclepios (Aesculapius) was active in the sanctuary
dedicated to him at Epidaurus, a city on the Saronic gulf famous
in antiquity. But he also 'worked' in the temples of Cnidos, Cos,
Pergamon, Sikyon, Naupaktos and Athens. He ran many branch
sanctuaries in which cures were effected for every kind of thing
that cropped up. They were visited by blind, crippled and dumb
people, by dropsical patients, by those with organic diseases,
patients who had tape-worms and those plagued with falling hair.
The busy god had to keep on performing miracles – just like the
statues of saints at modern pilgrimage shrines. Rabbi Ben Akiba
used to say: It has all been done before. . . .

The temple of Epidaurus with its inscription 'Enter as a good
man, depart as a better one', was a place of pilgrimage by cure-
seekers from 500 BC onwards, the Lourdes of the 'Golden Age' of
Greek civilization. In addition to the head 'doctor' – Asclepios –
'friendly gods of healing' also worked miracles during the healing
sleep.

Kurt Pollack[24] writes: 'The miraculous cures mainly took
place in the case of the blind, deaf, crippled, sleepless and other
sufferers, *who would be classified today in the great army of
neurotics and vegetatively stigmatized.* The divine doctor cured
many people whom earthly practitioners had not been able to
help. . . . The able members of the Asclepian priesthood became
experienced observers of human nature who knew exactly how to
exercise psychic influence on the sick. In a certain sense, whether
they knew it or not, they were predecessors of present-day psycho-
therapists.' Need one comment on this kind of miracle? The
Church knows its history.

The psychotherapeutic effect of music too was well known to
the Pythagoreans of the sixth century BC. (I can hear the laments
at Lourdes!) The Syrian philosopher Iamblichus tells us:

The Pythagoreans used music as a cure; and there were
special melodies against psychic suffering, namely those against
depression and anxiety, which were considered the most helpful

E

– others against violent emotions and passions and against every kind of psychic confusion. In certain kinds of tones and rhythms, by which the disposition and mood of men is improved and their psychic state restored to its original state, Pythagoras found the means for pacifying and healing illnesses of body and soul.

How similar the two pictures are!

The miracles that saints and their adjurants perform today were performed by Asclepios and his disciples at Epidaurus with identical or similar methods, and without any Christian help!

Fortunately, because it is demonstrable, those cured in classical temples also felt themselves obliged to express their thanks in a similar way to those cured at the shrines of visions and miracles. They, too, put up votive tablets. In AD 165 the Greek writer Pausanias from Magnesia in Asia Minor stood before the ruins of Epidaurus. In the second volume of his descriptions of Greece (*Periegeses tes Hellados*), he observed:

In olden times there were even more inscribed plaques within the enclosure of the sanctuary than there are today. Now there are only six left. On them are recorded the names of men and women who were cured by Asclepios, and also the diseases which each of them suffered from, and how they were cured. The tablets are written in the Doric language.

During excavations at Epidaurus in 1928 these six stone tablets were found, with the following messages of thanks:

Ambrosia of Athens, one-eyed. Came to intercede with the god. When she walked about the sanctuary, she laughed at some of the cures and thought it impossible that lame and blind people could become healthy when they had only a dream. After she had slept in the cure room, she came out cured.

Euhippos has had a lance point in his jaw for six years and slept in the cure room. . . . When day broke, he came out cured, with the lance point in his hands.

Hermodikos of Lampsakos, crippled in body. Asclepios healed him when he slept in the cure room and ordered him when he came out to bring the biggest stone he could find to the sanctuary. Then he brought the stone that now lies in front of the sanctuary.

Alketas of Halieis. He was blind and slept in the sanctuary. When day broke, he came out cured.

Arate of Laconia, dropsical. Her mother slept for her, while she herself was in Lacedaemon, and had a dream. . . . When she returned to Lacedaemon, she found her daughter cured; she had had the same dream.

Aristokritos to Halieis. He had swum out to sea and while diving reached a place from which there was no way out. So his father, as he could not find his son anywhere, slept in the cure room of Asclepios. . . . When he came out of the room . . . he found the boy on the seventh day.

The people who were miraculously cured 500 years BC behaved just the same as their counterparts today, and even the miracles were of the same quality as today, although the Christian guardians of 'genuine' miracles are not at all keen to hear that. The god Asclepios does not stand alone as the chief witness for pre-Christian miraculous cures; he is in illustrious company.

It is occasionally forgotten that Apollo was not only the god of radiant youth, poetry and music, but also the god of medicine and soothsaying . . . and the son of Asclepios. So he had been well trained. Apollo was a venerated god of healing, to whom a temple was erected in the sanctuary of Delphi in the eighth century BC. Naturally miracles happened in it. The dumb learnt to speak. Kidney-stones disappeared through the ureter in a mysteriously natural way. Shiny-headed Greeks prayed and hair grew luxuriantly on their pates[25]. (A clever speculator told me that after the invention of knitting needles and the zip fastener, there was only one invention left that could make anyone a millionaire − a genuine hair-restorer. Prayers to Asclepios and Apollo cannot be sold as cosmetic miracle workers by the most talkative Figaros in the world.)

In the great sanctuaries of Thebes, the Egyptian city of the Dead, the god of healing, Amphiraos, was worshipped − in the temple of Ptah at Memphis votive stones were found on which cured patients extolled their gods. Frequently feet, legs and hands were perpetuated in stone to make their gratitude permanent. 376 stone ears were carved next to the image of the Ptah at Memphis[26]. A polyclinic for otology (ear therapy) must have been working overtime on miracles there.

*　*　*

Group experience is common to all these classical places of healing. I see in them predecessors of the psychodrama practised today in the sense in which Dr Samuel Warner[27] describes group therapy:

> Group therapy is often especially helpful, for it is easier to recognize something mutually, and during the reciprocal relationship one hand washes the other so to speak. . . . This therapy is not only an intellectual experience; it also embraces the emotional life, for personality is formed by emotional experiences which are caused by the reaction of the glands and other subsidiary corporeal symptoms. In order to achieve a basic change of personality the therapy must make contact with these intensive, repeated and continuing emotional experiences, so that the emotional spheres of the personality are affected again and undergo a transformation.

This kind of group experience with a deliberate goal could be sensed at all the places of pilgrimage I visited. The longing for a miracle − as a common emotional experience − released among complete strangers reciprocal relationships which extinguished any inhibitions, even against crying and lamenting aloud. People who were normally rather introverted underwent a change of personality. They surrendered themselves completely to the general feeling. Here, at the goal of their hopes, among the mass of anonymous sufferers a change in their attitude to their illness took place. It was now or never! At places of pilgrimage ecstatic emotions are the humus on which the apparently incredible can materialize.

*   *   *

In this connection I should mention briefly 'animal magnetism' which was practised by the doctor Franz Anton Mesmer (1734-1815). Mesmer looked his patients fixedly in the eyes and then by laying on of hands used the powers radiating from people for suggestive cures. The Catholic Church has canonized thirty-five chirotetes (layers on of hands). The English surgeon James Braid (1795-1860) realized that there was no occult hocus-pocus about successful healing by this method. He christened it hypnosis (Greek, sleep). Mesmerism became a European scourge, because people who did not possess healing magnetic powers also did a roaring trade in it.

We can read in a report[28] published in 1784 the extent to which mass suggestion and mass hypnosis could effect 'miraculous cures':

The Marquis of Puiségur had turned his chateau near Soissons into a 'magnetic sanatorium'. A fanatic follower of Mesmer's methods, he used it to house people in search of a cure. The afflux of patients was enormous; people were bursting out of the castle rooms. What could be done? The Marquis had a bright idea. He magnetised a stately elm tree in the village! 'suffering humanity from both sides of the Rhine flocked to this magnetic tree as if to a wonder-working sacred image.'

No comment. But reliquaries, mummified saints and miracle-working statues of saints are not always necessary to effect miraculous cures. Old elm trees can do it too so long as the cure seekers 'believe' in them.

Suggestion and hypnosis (as a form of suggestion) are always present when miraculous cures take place at pilgrimage shrines, whether the Church admits it or not (and this applies equally to the 'genuine' miracles attested). Suggestion, to define it more accurately, is an influencing of the processes of thought, feeling and will, which 'leads to the uncritical acceptance of convictions, the suggestion of values and patterns of behaviour'. In the case of affective sympathy 'man involuntarily opens himself to . . . phenomenal forms and ideas. . . . Mass situations, as well as states of heightened excitement of the affects, have a strengthening effect. . . . Autosuggestion is self-influencing by emotional hope and wishful thinking.' What can hypnosis do? It can 'easily summon up illusions and hallucinations. Memory is released. Most people can be hypnotized if they are inwardly prepared.'

These definitions are diagnoses of pilgrims at pilgrimage shrines.

What does the Church say about this?

It claims that 'the fact of the major miracle in the Catholic Church (must) be established beyond doubt to the unprejudiced investigator'[29]. I find this assessment by the Church to be inept, to say the least. If in our age that is so overloaded with neurotic organic diseases and physically harmful states of depression, only 100 cures (even if they are not 'miracles') effected by suggestion, autosuggestion and mass hypnosis are reported annually from all the places of pilrimage, the church's media – Madonnas, relics, springs, etc. – fulfil a useful miraculous purpose.

*   *   *

Miraculous cures have been known since time immemorial. Professor D. Langen[30] writes:

Hypnosis as a psychic treatment of disease is extremely ancient and can be found both in the medicine of the ethnic cultures (shamans) and in the lofty civilizations of Egypt, Greece and Rome. . . . The trail was lost in the Middle Ages. . . . Franz Anton Mesmer marked the beginning of a new period that led to the still valid suggestion theory of hypnosis by way of the theory of fluidum and *magnetismus animalis*. . . . Thought is concentrated on a narrowly defined point so that a relation between a hyper-awake core of consciousness and the remaining lowered states of consciousness arises. While this state is maintained, thought is ordered to direct itself to a point or a complex of ideas and remain there. . . . Consequently meditation is thought concentrated on a point in a sub-waking state of consciousness.

By all the 12,000 saints! Cannot you see that all the masses at places of pilgrimage concentrate their gaze on a 'point', say a statue of the Madonna? How they fall into a hypnotic trance by autosuggestion? Do you not feel in your bones how the general layer of consciousness sinks and simultaneously dwells on the miracle in a hyperactive state? Nearly every pilgrim has fallen into the power of mass suggestion from the start; should one of them remain outside it, he would be caught in the undertow of the state of consciousness of the others. 'Human individuals have an immediate effect on the *sensorium commune* (common emotions)'[31].

These are not Mr von Däniken's suppositions, but a logical chain of evidence forged by doctors as the result of research. . . . It is true that the Church *also* admits 'natural' explanations, but it reserves to itself the recognition of 'genuine' miraculous cures performed by visions, with the co-operation of the Holy Family and the halleluya singing choir.

*   *   *

Yogananda Paramahamsa[32] was one of the most famous Yogis of our day. The world-wide Self Realization Fellowship he founded in 1917 championed thoroughly sensible views which centre round one of the great Yogi's basic utterances:

God helps those who help themselves. He has endowed you with will power and concentration, faith, reason and healthy commonsense so that you can help yourselves in all corporeal and mental suffering. You must apply all your faculties at the same time as you call on him for help. When you pray or practise healing meditation, always say to yourselves that he needs *your* own, but God-given, powers in order to heal you or others.

Yogananda knows psychology's laws of effect inside out.

We can never know in advance when we shall be cured and so should not set any time limits to the process. *Faith* and not time will determine when the cure is to take place. The end result depends on the correct awakening of the vital force and the conscious and unconscious disposition of the person concerned.

These insights of the Yogi's, to whom consecrated water (considered sacramental; it has a little salt mixed with it) is as alien as the joy of marriage still is to a Catholic priest, get to the very essence of miraculous cures, even though they stem from a totally unchristian faith, which is if anything a *knowledge* of the vital processes of autosuggestive cures. Yogananda gives his fellowmen a hint about how it is exercised at all the sites of visions and miracles:

Do not forget that you must say the healing words with the right emphasis, loudly at first and then more and more softly until you are only whispering, that close attention and concentration are especially necessary. In this way you lead your thoughts, the truth of which you are deeply convinced of, from the aural sense into consciousness . . . from there into the subconscious or automatic-conscious. He who has the necessary faith will be healed by this method.

I have never heard of Yogananda being at Lourdes or Fatima or any other visionary shrine, and I do not imagine he was. Yet his method is the one which is practised there. The crowds of people assemble in big squares, singing chorales in loud voices, saying the rosary or other devout prayers. The closer they get to the miraculous spot, the lower the volume of the droning chorus. Their attention and concentration is directed at the goal. What they wish for is forced 'from the aural sense into consciousness'. From then on they only speak in whispers and hymns are merely hummed. 'Faith' is wide-awake and concentrated.

In most cases this *faith in the effect* of the method of healing satisfies faith in miracles at visionary sites. In fact, the subconscious (or 'automatic conscious') introduces electrochemical functions into the brain. 'When the nerve impulses . . . enter the brain, they set off various chemical reactions' (Campbell).

Clinical tests of new drugs have proved time and again that belief in the efficacy of a medicine can effect a cure. People are split into two control groups. One is given the new drug, the other a placebo (a harmless imitation of the new medicine, generally 'scented' sugar-coated pills of the same size and colour). Leslie M. LeCron describes the result: 'It is observed that a large part of the control group given the placebo reacts in exactly the same way as the group which has taken the real drug. This effect is attributable to suggestion.'

That which Yogananda Paramahamsa calls faith, will-power and concentration in connection with the healing effect, the doctor calls exactly what it is: suggestion. Yogi and doctor are far away from the highfalutin Christian talk about miracles but they know how 'miracles' happen.

* * *

It is the obstinacy, the partial blindness, I cannot understand. Theologians have still not clearly stated facts about 'miracles' that have been known for over 450 years.

Theophratus Bombastus von Hohenheim (1494-1541), known as Paracelsus, was the founder of a new science of healing. He emphasized the primacy of the 'soul' (today we would use the word 'psyche') in normal life and illness, and was the first to recognize the previously overlooked pathological connections and new types of illness, such as neuroses and psychoses. In the centre he placed man as microcosm. Healing to Paracelsus was the work of the life force and the will to live. Quotations from his treatise on *Imaginatio*[33] shows how modern his views were:

Man is subject to imagination, and the imagination although

invisible and inconceivable works corporeally in a substance.

The imagination can cause disease, terrible disease, and it can cause happiness and health.

Hence it follows that the imagination is more than nature and governs it. It removes innate qualities so that it knows neither heaven nor earthly nature.

Hence it follows that a great deal is impossible for the doctor, and the more powerful the imagination, the weaker the effect of the doctor.

Consequently many people get well through the belief of the imagination, but many people get sick also.

By such imagining (arises) belief both in the miracles of the saints and in the medicine . . . that makes them well and is attributed by them to saints and miracles . . . although it is all the result of belief in the imagination.

Whether the belief is right or wrong, depends solely on the strength of the imagination.

And even if a false prophet manages to influence people, who consider him blessed or saintly, and credit him with results, because their love and hope is concentrated on their faith, these miracles will happen not through his power, but through the power of those who believe so strongly.

The sum total of the advances of scholars such as Aristotle, John Locke, David Hume and Carl Jung provides the explanation of all that was supposed inexplicable. Even if we are not familiar with these pioneers and their pupils, their insights have become part of our everyday existence.

* * *

One 'miracle' was explained to me by the roadside. One spring, while I was driving along the shores of the Bodensee, through the breathtakingly lovely trees in bloom, I remembered my visit to 'Mama Rosa' in San Damiano in March, and the miracle performed by the 'beautiful lady' of making a pear tree flower in October 1964. I parked by the roadside, explained the facts briefly to a fruit-farmer and asked if he had any experience of such a state of affairs – fruit and blossoms on the tree simultaneously. He nodded and said they called it a 'magic bloom', but did not know how it occurred. Nevertheless I had learnt that the flowering of Mama Rosa's tree in October was not unique, and could not be 'breaking the laws of nature' in the sense of an ecclesiastically acceptable miracle.

I sought information from botanist friends.

Pear trees and indeed plum trees belong to the family of Rosaceae. The pear tree is one of the deepest rooted species: it needs warm soil, into which the roots penetrate up to a depth of nine feet. The subsoil water should not rise above this height, as pear trees are sensitive to subsoil water. Plum trees flourish best on medium damp soil, but need a warm climate, like the related pear tree. An annual rainfall of about 600 mm is enough for both trees. In such conditions the fruit ripens with the steady passage of the seasons. It does especially well in a climate like that south-west of Milan.

This rhythm is sensibly disturbed if an unseasonable cold spell occurs, with unusually high rainfall and subsequent warm spells, like the Italian autumn, say. Owing to the cold shock and the rain – both happened in the Milan region in September 1964! – the trees behave as if it were spring: owing to the cold and the damp soil the biochemical processess of metabolism begin and flower hormones are formed. If the trees are then subjected to autumn solar warmth again, we have the botanical and physiological 'miracle' of an autumn bloom on the tree simultaneously with fruit. The blossoms 'suddenly' stop and fall equally quickly; they bear no fruit because the bees have long since disappeared.

If the coupling of enzymes and hormones in the growth of plants is still a mystery, Mama Rosa's flowering pear and plum trees are certainly not a divine miracle, but a clearly explicable process, which the Bodensee farmer simply called 'magic bloom'.

Miracles fall to the ground from the tree of knowledge just as quickly as that!

* * *

'The sick man is God's gift to us, a direct favour and must be accepted by us as such. He (the sick man!) is an example of God's special favour because he enables us to put into practice that candour of heart called compassion . . .'[34]. So says Ladislaus

Boros, a Jesuit instructor in divinity at Innsbruck. Anyone who is not yet sick is bound to be made ill by such theological tripe. But this kind of dubious 'soul massage' is inflicted on us from childhood. The unreal concept of 'original sin' is on the heels of every Christian, shadowing his every action. It requires tremendous courage for anyone who has been brought up in this doctrine to liberate himself inwardly from all these threats.

One should also mention the theme of the sexual repression of Christians. Obviously getting rid of it also forms part of the act of self-liberation, but it is not the key to the door to personal freedom and self-responsibility vis-à-vis moral laws. Sigmund Freud's once revolutionary thesis that everyone and everything was intelligible in terms of the instinctual life has long been overtaken by new scientific insights.

2,000 years of Christian tradition with the refinement of its dogmas lie deep in the subconscious. The moving Jesus legend with the suffering Mary, the suffering Apostles, and the suffering saints is also stored in the brain-cells of non-practising Christians.

But for the practising Christian this brain programming implies a lasting readiness to believe in miracles and miraculous cures as proof of God's grace. Before a religious 'Lazarus' has taken part in a pilgrimage to a visionary shrine, he had been brain-washed. His family, friends and priests have made it abundantly clear to him why the pilgrimage is the 'last resort'. Day and night the pain-racked sufferer is preoccupied with the hope of the miracle that has been suggested to him. If the children of Fatima or little Bernadette at Lourdes have helped others, why not me, too? On the sickbed – effective pious therapy – hymns to Mary are sung, the Rosary is recited. The sufferer has no idea that perhaps a self-healing process has already begun, that he himself has set the healing mechanism (Bio Feedback) in motion.

The skilful preparatory work done in the sickroom is enhanced at the visionary shrine by the feelings shared by the anonymous masses who also believe in miracles. One is much more likely to 'perceive' Jesus, Mary and the saints at the goal of the journey than in Christian everyday life or in one's home church. From time to time, cures take place for motivations that we know, just as they do in other countries with quite different conditions and religions.

There are several thousand 'faith healers' in America, Europe and Asia. Among the dozens of such people I met, I found helpful, often shy, always modest people who followed their calling without religious rites or pretentious ceremonials. Naturally they accept a fee for their work: they are not saints and cannot live on air and love. I was sceptical about the undefined physical and medicinal powers employed by them. So I arranged to meet the dynamic young faith-healer Marcus Brogler, who is well-known in Switzerland, my home country, at a restaurant in Aarau. I teased him and asked if he really believed in his magic. Marcus got up and stood behind me. 'Sit still I am not going to touch you.' I drank my beer. In less than a minute I felt as if someone was ironing my spine with a red-hot iron. I turned round. Marcus returned to his seat, ordered another round and asked sarcastically: 'Did you feel the magic?'

Alas, we live in a maze of magic and miracles. Like bread fresh from the oven, some of it baked and some of it half-baked, books pour off the presses, books dealing with the mysteriously working powers of telekinesis and telepathy and trying to explain how the miracles are done, books that tell us about the work of faith-surgeons on the Philippines and till the vast field of parapsychology. It would be carrying coals to Newcastle if I were to make a further contribution to these fields. So I am going to stick to the territory I have prescribed for myself – visions.

*   *   *

Yogananda Paramahamsa, who made such intelligent remarks about suggestive healing, died in Los Angeles on 7 March 1952. It is said that after three weeks his body showed no signs of decomposition – as is often supposed to be the case after the death of a saintly man. Harry T. Rowe, Director of Forest Lawn Memorial Park, Los Angeles, said in an official report[35]: 'The absence of any signs of decomposition on Paramahamsa's body is the most extraordinary case in all our experience. . . . Even twenty days after his death no trace of corporeal decay could be observed. . . . No smell of decomposition could be noticed throughout this period. . . .'

The stuff of which saints are made!

Inge Santner writes in *Die Weltwoche*[36], Zurich, about a lecture given to the Viennese Catholic Academy by the Viennese psychiatrist and neurologist, Dr Gerhard Kaiser, Lecturer in Forensic Medicine at Salzburg University.

Dr Kaiser tackled the question of why the bodies of saints retain their shape decades or centuries after their death. Kurt Tucholsky[37] gives a wonderful account of Lourdes in his *Book of the Pyrenees:*

> They have recently exhumed her (Bernadette Soubirous) for her canonization next year. Her body was well preserved, her left eye, which was directed at the vision, is reputed to have remained open and her tomb to have smelt so strongly of flowers that letters which lay there smelt, too, so it was said at Lourdes. . . .

(Bernadette was not a saint at the time; she did not become one till 1933.)

In the opinion of the Viennese scientist it does not need a miracle to preserve the fleshly envelope so that it survives the decades or centuries without visible signs of decomposition. Dr Kaiser examined such cases as these:

Francis of Sales, who died in 1622, was found 'as if he was alive' when exhumed in 1632. His body did not turn to dust until 1656 when it emitted an 'extraordinarily sweet smell'.

Francis Caracciola died in 1608. His flesh and sinews were unchanged when he was exhumed in 1628. When an incision was made, blood flowed from it.

Carlos Borromaus, died 1584, proved 'unnaturally supple' after medical examination in 1608. His corpse still looked exactly the same 250 years later, in 1880.

St John of the Cross, who died in 1591, was found covered with pinkish skin when he was dug up in 1859 (!), sweet smelling fluid kept his body moist.

Maria Magdelena de Pazzi, died 1607, did exhibit a blackened face when she was exhumed in 1663, but she still had an 'exceptionally mild expression'.

Bernadette Soubirous, who died in 1879, seemed to be merely sleeping when she was exhumed; her face was only slightly browned and even her clothing had survived the ravages of time undamaged.

Astounding, uncanny, miraculous facts? Dr Gerhard Kaiser says: 'Wherever the course of events can be reconstructed, signs of miraculous activity must be almost certainly excluded.'

These are the scientific facts:

Bodily reactions are not uncommon after death. Cessation of heart beat does not influence all cells simultaneously. Whole groups of cells survive it for several hours. Spermatozoa continue mobile for at least twenty-eight hours after the death of the organism. A well-known phenomenon are the (uncanny) sighs given by dead people when they are dressed for their last journey and moved in the process. Survivors are often horrified when they observe changes in position caused by heat. Suspended animation? When a pregnant woman dies, the foetus can be expelled from the body by putrefying gases in the coffin. Suspended animation? No, a chemical and physical process.

Normally the process of decomposition begins very soon after the definite signs of death (coldness of the corpse; *rigor mortis,* cessation of heart beat and breathing, reddish blue spots on the skin, a negative curve on the instruments). A bubble-like raising of the skin and formation of gas – often with considerable pressure in the corporeal orifices – soon ensues.

The process of putrefaction is mainly caused by air. It carries *bacteria,* and *oxygen* sets the chemical conversion process in motion. *Moisture* and *warmth* accelerate the decomposition and finally, under ground, worms and insects complete the work of destruction. Ants can lay a skeleton bare in three days! Generally the abdomen dissolves in three or four years, fat in the bones much later. Brain cells and skin on the head last for decades. The protein in the bones lasts for a hundred years or more. Ultimately all that survives of a dead person buried in a *normal grave* is the skeleton.

Saintly men who have already demonstrated their singularity in their lifetime by spectacular deeds, are obviously not buried in normal graves or tombs. That is the vital premise from which Dr Kaiser comes to his convincing conclusions.

The most important prerequisite for the preservation of a corpse is keeping bacteria away. If their presence can be stopped or lessened, the process of putrefaction is slowed down considerably. But how can the environment be influenced to decrease or prevent the access of destructive bacteria?

Dry air and constant strong draughts produce a natural mummification which preserves parts of the body with little flesh on them (ears, nose, fingers, toes).

Cold water flowing in the vicinity of the corpse keeps the temperature down and drives flies and insects away.

This preservative bacteria-reducing cold can be increased by ice. (Bodies have been recovered from glaciers completely undamaged after many years.)

Forensic medicine has histories of corpses found in pitch lakes that were discoloured, but perfectly preserved.

Also well known are bog corpses which are preserved by humus acids resistant to putrefaction. Carbon dioxide prevents the coagulation of the blood. In cases of carbon dioxide poisoning blood can flow from cuts long after death.

Metal coffins cause the formation of metallic salts, which slow down decomposition for as much as ten years. Salts in the earth (arsenic from the iron sources), or sea salts in combination with the dry climate accounted for the hundreds of skulls buried during the Inca period which were found with undamaged flesh and all their hair during excavations in the Lima region. The preservation of bodies by treating them with natron, asphalt and cedar products was known in Egypt from the third century BC. (Today it is simpler. We mummify with formalin, a germ-killing medium. In many American Memorial Parks relatives can pull their beautifully made-up dead out of compartments and contemplate them in all their living beauty. . . . Death in Hollywood!)

Dr Kaiser has no doubt that the majority of incorruptible saints were buried in such conditions.

The survival of Rose of Lima's flesh was unquestionably due to salts. (The nun, who remained undamaged for eighteen months, lay in the same salt-bearing earth in which the Inca skulls were found.)

St Clara of Monte Falco was mummified by dry air and found with an 'exceptionally beautiful face'. Her shorn hair hung above her as a relic 'apparently dried out and showing the face of the crucified Christ'.

The 'smoked Parson of St Thomas' in lower Austria was rendered incorruptible by chemicals – tar products.

Was it pure chance that saintly people found their burial place in surroundings so favourable to their preservation? There is evidence that suitable methods were used to help preserve the bodies of saints 'in the flesh'. Capuchins in Italy and Moravians laid out the burial chambers of their monasteries in such a way that a constant draught of dry air swept through them. Dr Kaiser's supposition that the bodies of many saints were not only embalmed with essences, sweet-smelling oils, salves and aromas to drive away the smell of death, but also because the preservative effect of 'cosmetics' was known, can be accepted as a certainty.

When the bodies of illustrious ecclesiastics turned to dust after being exposed to profane human eyes, it was definitely not a 'sign from God', according to Dr Kaiser. Once the grave was opened, the conditions restraining decomposition created at the time of interment were interrupted and ended. For example, St Vincent de Paul crumbled to bits as the result of a sudden influx of air when his coffin was opened twenty-five years after his burial. 'Rediscovered tombs of ordinary Etruscans, to whom no one attributed particular saintliness, showed the same phenomenon. The corpses which rested undamaged on their stone beds, turned into dust during the exploration of the catacombs. A sweet-smelling golden haze is supposed to have filled the room.'

If the wealthy Catholic Church, which is so worried about the inviolability and divine exaltation of its saints, were to set up a research foundation to examine the post-mortem remains of holy bodies on a broader basis, I should think it an excellent idea and a brave gesture.

Then perhaps we should have an answer some day to the Viennese scholar's tricky question: 'Why should God preserve the bodies of precisely those men whose souls he took to himself by the shortest way?'

*   *   *

Even Jesus, the Master, did not believe in miracles . . . but he knew the effect of suggestion!

Mark (5, 23 *et seq.*) tells us that a woman who lay at the point of death came to him. Jesus' fame as a miraculous healer preceded him and prepared the ground for his direct suggestions. He was asked to lay his hands on her so that she could be cured, for she had suffered from an 'issue of blood' for twelve years. She had spent a lot of money on doctors who had been unable to help her. As usual the crowd surrounded the master expectantly.

They *wanted* to *see* a miracle! And the sick woman *wanted* to experience a *miraculous cure!*

'For she said, If I may but touch his clothes, I shall be whole' (28).

The prerequisite of her readiness to be healed miraculously existed.

'And straight away the fountain of her blood was dried up; and she felt in her body that she was healed of that plague.'

Jesus knew exactly whence the effect attributed to him came, for he asked who had touched his clothes.

'And he looked around to see her that had done this thing' (32).

Then the miraculous healer explained the mystery of the cure in a very modern and relevant way!

'Daughter, thy faith hath made thee whole; go in peace and be whole of the plague.'

The Nazarene *knew* nothing about the mechanism of auto, or heterosuggestion, but he had a good idea of their miraculous effects. If present-day faith-healers take the Bible as a text-book, they can find many good hints in it. 'No one really likes suffering. If he does, he is not really suffering but submissively enjoying his pain. Enjoying the blows as absolutely necessary for his psychic expansion. The martyred look of suffering appears to be calm and even shows a sneaking feeling of gratitude,' says Ernest Bloch[38] and his assertions tally with my observations.

* * *

When I am urged to show more respect for religions, I can assure people with conviction and from the heart that I respect *every* religion *which also respects its followers*.

But where the ignorance of church members is despised and shamelessly exploited, where hocus-pocus goes on with miracles that are not miracles, where jingling coins are struck from manipulated faith, where religions coerce adherents in this world by threats of punishment in the world to come, in all such cases I cannot respect religions, whatever their nature. I strive to be sincere and would like to help those who, like me, were caught from childhood in the power of a religious doctrine from which there was apparently no escape — except at the cost of eternal damnation.

Liberation from the confessional shackles by no means implies abandonment of faith in a god as the moving principle behind all being.

No! 'Miraculous cures' are no proof of the authenticity of a vision. In order to throw light on the darkness surrounding the mystery of supposed miracles, we must try to get on the trail of the visionary phenomena that are supposed to cause them.

Chapter 4

VISIONS DO EXIST –
MY EXPLANATION

This they begin to do: and now nothing will be
restrained from them, which they have imagined to do.

Genesis 11, 6

VISIONS ARE real – they do exist.

Visions originate in intelligent brains.

Every intelligent brain has the prerequisites for creating visions.

The impulse for producing visions is of extraterrestrial origin.

Religious visions originate through an ideal that the visionary
has within him and is suggested by his religious environment.

Do these theses of mine conceal a mass of contradictions?
It might appear so at first sight. But in order to provide proofs
for my theses, I must build on the basis of my theory.

Present-day astrophysics puts forward three theories of the
origin of the universe[1]: the Big Bang theory, the Steady State
theory and the Oscillation theory. None of these three (or other)
theories on the origin of the world explains where the mysterious
original matter of the whole universe comes from and what was
present *before* it came into being. *Nothing* originates from
nothing.

Just as it does not matter for my thesis which of these theories
may ultimately turn out to be valid, it is also unimportant to
me whether the origin of the universe dates back five, ten or
twenty milliard years, or whether matter is finite or infinite, or
whether it constantly renews itself. My question is: *what* did
original matter originate *from?*

In public discussions I have made use of a graphic image to
explain my views on this question in simple terms. I suggested
that my hearers imagine a computer with a hundred milliard
thought-units (bits in computer jargon), a computer that can
think, i.e. has a 'personal consciousness' (Professor Michie, Edin-
burgh University). This consciousness is attached to milliards of
circuits: it would be destroyed if the computer exploded. Our
computer is highly intelligent and capable of ultra-rapid combina-
tions. There is nothing it does not know.

In spite of its consciousness and omniscience the thinking computer is not 'happy', for in spite of its tremendous performance there is something it cannot think out, reckon out or work out, namely experience. But it wants to amass experience. As it has no rival of anything like the same calibre to obtain experience from, it decides to send the hundred milliard bits of its central body out to get information by exploding itself, knowing perfectly well that it would definitely lose its personal consciousness by so doing . . . if it had not in its insuperable cleverness programmed the future *after* its self-destruction long *beforehand*.

Before the bits are catapulted on their long journey to gain experience, the clever computer has programmed magnetic impulses inside them with the order to reassemble at x place at y time. When this hour strikes, the milliards of bits obediently return to the complicated machinery with its 'personal consciousness' and bring home *experiences*, like bees bringing honey to the hive.

From the moment of the explosion to the moment of the return no bit 'knew' that it was and would now be again a minute part of a larger consciousness. If a single bit with its minimal capacity for thought could ask the question: 'What is the purpose of my breakneck journey?' or 'Who created me, where do I come from?', there would be no answer. Thus the tremendous journey was the beginning and end of an act, a kind of 'creation' of consciousness multiplied by the factor EXPERIENCE.

This bold comparison from the arsenal of science-fiction is meant as an aid in tracking down the phenomenon which existed *before* original matter. *Terrible simplificateur!* I beg your pardon, but it gets us a little further.

All human traditions assure us that 'spirit' (or the comprehensive synonym 'God') was 'there' *before* any beginning, i.e. before the origin of matter. The (original) spirit then decided to become matter, to transform itself. (. . . and the word was made flesh . . .) 'Spirit' is not tangible or measurable with instruments. How are we to imagine it? In a gaseous state? This is scarcely possible, gas molecules are already matter. Nevertheless, it is conceivable that 'spirit', that mysterious unknown IT, transformed itself into a gaseous aggregation during the first stage of its materialization.

This assumption no longer smacks of science-fiction, for *every* astrophysical theory of the origin of the universe begins with the gaseous state of original matter – with gas molecules, which slowly and steadily combine to form lumps of matter. But if a gaseous state was the proven original state[2] of all matter *and* the original spirit, that simply means that all existing matter was permeated by the original spirit, a claim that is manifest in all theosophical and esoteric religions. Then, to put it crudely, matter would be crystallized sublimated spirit.

It makes no difference which kind of matter one thinks of – lava, rock, plants, animals or men – they ultimately all come from the same original state. It even makes no difference whether we postulate matter from our planet, Jupiter, Alpha Centauri or the Andromeda Nebule. Matter is creation *per se* and itself the product of creation.

Matter has transversed a millionfold paths of evolution. A stone, product of the same origin and the same original state, can ask itself no questions. But *life* clearly develops from 'dead' matter, there is no longer the slightest academic doubt about that. *Living* matter, say a cell, develops over millions of years into complicated organisms. Development and reactions by organisms are governed by brains with their grey mass of milliardfold cells: they produce 'personal consciousness' by chemical and electrical conversions of matter. Intelligence does not appear until after the existence of personal consciousness which can ask questions. (Descartes: '*Cogito, ergo sum*' – I think, therefore I am.)

So according to the history of evolution, intelligence is superior to any matter below its state of consciousness. Matter is dominated by it. Intelligence is more closely related to the original spirit than dead matter – intelligences can communicate with one another, they can ask questions at a high level: 'Who created me? What is the purpose and meaning of existence?' Pursuing my explanatory image: with their brains bits seek contact with the original consciousness, without understanding that they themselves are components of that consciousness. They may seek for the 'spirit', for the IT, synonym for creator or god, but they do not 'realize' that what they seek is around them and in them.

A fanciful idea?

I leave it to the scientists to answer that question.

* * *

Sir Arthur Eddington (1882-1944), English Astronomer and physicist, Director of the Cambridge Observatory[3,] discovered the pulsation theory of the Cephids. Eddington championed a 'selective subjectivism', of natural laws, in that he assumed that the basic physical laws are essentially determined by the structure of the process of knowledge and asserted that the matter of the world is the matter of the spirit.

The natural philosopher Bernhard Bavink (1879-1947), who strove to close the gap between natural science and religion, held the following view[4]:

The material organization of the world appears to us today as perhaps the transient manifestation of an entirely spiritual concept.

Max Planck (1858-1947), who opened up new paths to physics with his quantum theory and won the Nobel Prize for physics in 1918, admitted:

As a physicist, i.e. as a man who has devoted his life to the most matter of fact branch of science, namely, the investigation of matter, I am surely free of any suspicion of fanaticism. And so after my research into the atom I say this to you: there is no such thing as matter *per se!* All matter originates from and consists of a force which sets the atomic particles in oscillation and concentrates them into the minute solar system of the atom. But as there is neither an intelligence nor an internal force in the whole universe, we must assume a conscious intelligent spirit behind this force. This spirit is the basic principle of all matter. . . .

Sir James Hopwood Jeans (1877-1946), English mathematician, physicist and astronomer, who was mainly a pioneer in the fields of thermodynamics, stellar dynamics and cosmogony, was especially famous for his theory of the origin of the planets[5]. Sir James wrote:

Today scholars are fairly unanimous and physicists almost completely unanimous in saying that the whole current of knowledge is moving in the direction of a non-mechanical kind of reality. The Universe gradually looks more like a great thought than a great machine.

If matter is a product of 'spirit' and vice-versa spirit a product of matter, are spirit and matter of the same nature only in a different state of aggregation? Fifty years ago people used to ask if energy could be converted into matter. Einstein's formula $E = mc^2$ gave the world-shattering answer. The hydrogen bomb was a proof that could not be overlooked or unheard. Might we ask today if 'crystallized' spirit can be set free? The analogical conclusion is obvious. Matter is just as much a form of energy as 'crystallized' spirit. Consequently spirit is simultaneously energy and energy simultaneously spirit. Consciousness, defined as undoubtedly related to the 'spirit', *must* be another (if as yet unknown) form of energy.

The Dutch physicist and mathematician Christiaan Huygens (1629-1695) is considered as the founder of the 'energy principle', according to which all the energy in the universe is constant and *all forms of energy are convertible into each other.*

Hermann von Helmholtz (1821-1894) and Albert Einstein (1879-1955) amplified this basic principle. If we accept consciousness as a form of energy (and all current research supports this conclusion), then the proven energy principle can be applied to it, too. As the totality of all energy must remain constant, this (to me) conclusive line of proof means no more and no less than that consciousness is immortal! Energy is never lost, cannot disappear, cannot die and cannot dissolve into the void – it is always converted into another form of energy.

Converted energy is not what it was before. In death consciousness loses its original energetic activity, is no longer 'consciousness', but converted energy. (Steam is another state of ice and ice is another state of water. Steam, ice and water are easily changed into one of the other forms, yet their effects are quite different from each other).

Is the *ultima ratio,* the last logical consequence, that ALL is one and ONE is ALL? If that is so – and what contradicts this logic? – must it not be possible for the *conscious* intelligent form of energy to affect the *unconscious?* It is happening all round us at every minute with the help of technology and mechanics. When the lumberjack fells a tree, he applies his conscious intelligent energy to make the immovable tree fall. Through his conscious intelligent energy the smith uses other forms of energy (fire, hammer, anvil) to force the iron into a new shape.

Conscious intelligent energy uses all the appropriate known ways of converting energy for the specific case. If mechanics and technology complete conversion processes as a matter of course without conscious intelligence, surely a conscious intelligent form of energy must be capable of causing the desired reactions in other forms of energy?

The above question is really superfluous because such reactions have been constantly produced in the history of humanity and still are today. There have always been men who tracked down the secrets which 'the energy-beast-brain' concealed and then, consciously or unconsciously, astonished their fellowmen by new knowledge and power which they used to help and advance them. But when such knowledge and power are used today to create new religions and 'freshen up' old ones, I call it the most infamous kind of modern gangsterism, because a ruthless game is being played with ignorant people.

*   *   *

Dr Albert Freiherr von Schrenck-Notzing (1862-1929) is considered to be the founder of parapsychology, which is so popular today. He knew perfectly well the attacks he was exposing himself to when he published his account of apparitions, which developed in the presence of a medium in the form of a cloud-like mass (tele- or ectoplast). Dr Schrenck-Notzing had himself co-operated in Rome and Paris in the exposure of charlatans, who feigned materializations by using concealed aids. He knew all the tricks which self-styled mediums used to lead séance audiences up the garden path.

Eva C was the doctor's subject for observation. In 1909 séances were held in the Paris home of the dramatist Alexander Bisson (1848-1912). Several people patricipated, including doctors, as they did later in Munich and London. Eva C's clothing, as well as the lighting, door locks, composition of the walls etc., were constantly checked. Before they began Eva C showed herself in the nude. Madame Bisson gave her a gynaecological examination; her perineum and anus were explored. 'Before each séance the author examined the hair, nostrils (air was blown through them), the external ear channels, the oral orifices, teeth, armpits, feet, the state of hands and fingernails . . . the objection that the medium could have small rolled up pellets somewhere on her person seems to be unfounded.'

After these extremely detailed searches the wretched Eva C was sewn into the dark robe that she had never touched before. 'If one takes into account the fact that the medium had nothing white on her body (neither blouse nor handkerchief) the grey and white materializations against the black background are convincing.'

Schrenck-Notzing made use of a technical innovation of the time: flash photographs with pulverized magnesium. These sometimes nauseating photographs are shown as proof in his book *Materializations-Phänonemene*[6].

What actually happened at these mediumistic séances?

Some examples from the records:

17 May 1910 . . . To the accompaniment of deep respirations and convulsive muscular efforts a large, streaked, flocculent substance formed directly before my eyes and seemed to flow from her mouth, getting bigger and thicker. The substance may have been five to eight centimetres wide and forty to fifty centimetres long. I moved my head about fifteen to twenty centimetres nearer to observe more clearly and saw this sluggish moving mass, like a heap of the finest striped grey veils, slowly sink down. It followed every movement that the medium made with her head and yet seemed to separate itself from it. . . . To our astonishment we could no longer make out any facial features, for the whole head was enveloped in a big veil-like cloud from which light-coloured tatters and strips hung down over her breasts and down to the knee. This image vanished before our eyes, as when a cloud dissolves, and her face was clearly visible again. . . .

1 June 1910 . . . During the next apparition the light-coloured materialization first came out of her lap and right hip. . . . Her mouth had no connection with the substance; I convinced myself of this by putting my finger in her mouth. . . .

2 September 1910 . . . Madame Bisson held a séance during which Eva C wore nothing but a nightdress. . . . Madame Bisson got the hypnotized medium to undo it and I had my first opportunity to observe teleplasma emanation from a naked body . . . it mainly flowed from the bodily orifices, mouth, nipples and genitals . . . the emanation had a smoke-like

character and formed clouds from which veil-like material substances and all kinds of shapes resembling human limbs arose. . . .

Professor Charles Richet (1850-1935) was present at the séance of 5 November 1910. This French doctor recognized the protective action of the blood in infected experimental animals and discovered anaphylaxy.* He won the Nobel Prize for this in 1913.

Today the séance began at once with the phenomena. . . . In the place where the mass of grey matter had thickened most, we saw a white gleam shot with pink, looking like white chiffon or veiling.

At nearly all the Paris séances doctors from every conceivable faculty were present, and also scientists such as Professor Fontenay, who checked the physical data. During the séances in Munich Dr von Schrenck invited lecturers at the University such as Dr Specht and Dr Kafka.

During the years Eva C produced outlines of figures and clearly recognizable photographically recorded faces. Sceptical Paris and London doctors examined the medium thoroughly, even looking under her skin. They also checked her immediate surroundings, but the phenomena were repeated no matter what the conditions.

Eva C came from a comfortable home; she had no money problems. She never accepted payment and appeared willingly before all kinds of doctors, and even journalists. On the list of séances figure such names as Professor Eck Dumoir van Twick, Society for Psychic Studies, The Hague; Professor Courtier, Director of the Physiological Laboratory of the Sorbonne and even Sir William Crookes (1832-1919), Member of the English Society for Psychic Research. Crookes discovered thallium in 1861 and invented the radiometer in 1874. The British Committee invited Eva C to its house at 20 Hanover Square, London. Séances were held there under the strictest scientific conditions.

At the séances of 10 May 1920, four cameras were used, including a stereoscopic camera. One exposure showed 'a small hand on the left shoulder', another 'a flickering mass of light'.

---

* Hypersensitivity of the body to foreign protein which is not accepted through the intestinal canal.

On 28 May Eva's head was sewn up in a veil and the audience 'realized that the object was forced out of her mouth through the veil'.

There were doubters and sceptics, but even they could not say how the phenomena connected with Eva C could be explained. The English Society published accounts of them, both in its periodical and in special reports.

In Paris Professor H. Clararède, Geneva, and Professor de Fontenay of the Sorbonne, as well as leading doctors from Paris hospitals attended Eva's demonstrations. Dr Bourbon, who took the notes, writes:

> Everything that I saw at numerous séances was more than enough to convince me that we were faced with apparitions which originate from an as yet quite unknown field of biology. . . .

The Nobel Prizewinner Charles Richet wrote to Dr von Schrenck-Notzing:

> As far as my former experiments are concerned, I do not wish to retract a word. And I refer to that great and noble scholar William Crookes, who only recently said: 'I take nothing of what I have said back.' Criticism must be exercised, that is a condition of science. In due course the truth will come to light in all its beauty, but it will not be brought to light by incompetents and ignoramuses, who have seen nothing, checked nothing, examined nothing, indeed have not even read the record carefully, but rather by the scholars who have really worked and experimented without cease, who prefer truth to probability. . . . It is surely not our fault if the metaphysical field offers so many improbabilities and contradictions. . . .

To the extent that the documentation of Eva C's case is available, it can be objectively stated that the theory of cheating is not tenable, that Eva C complied with the requirements of the scientific boards, that well over a hundred people observed and confirmed the materializations. One of Dr Schenck-Notzing's arguments seems convincing to me. Why should Eva C have exposed herself to the gruesome tests described without getting any material benefits from them? There are large numbers of cases of materialization for which validity is claimed, but Eva C's case has kept its special position to the present day, because none of the others was so painstakingly recorded and documented. For that reason it constantly reappears as an example in the scientific literature of parapsychology.

There remains the final comment on Eva C's case by Professor Mikuska, University of Genoa:

So it is reserved for an occult biology of the future to research into the mystery of life, the connection between spirit and matter, soul and body, the living and the lifeless. Already today we are shown that the *spirit,* the *idea,* the *will* is the driving agent behind teleplastic manifestations and we hope that in the not too distant future it will bring us closer to the great mystery of how *the universe in its totality, and cosmic processes in the infinity of their development and perfection, originate through creative acts of will by the universal spirit.*

* * *

Materializations of the kind so common with Eva C have nothing to do with spiritualism* and very little to do with the occult†, for the phenomenal apparitions were visible, tangible *and* could be photographed. What happened and was checked in the case described is certainly not a unique case. I do not doubt the documentary reports of Dr von Schrenck-Notzing and his fellow-scientists. Instead I ask a question which was not yet topical at that time: what form of energy was involved? Eva C was in a hypnotic trance during the séances, i.e. in a state of consciousness that precludes the use of free will. The subconscious as a form of energy (for the production of materializations) is conceivable, even though not yet proved. But could converted forms of the energy of dead people perhaps be involved? That supposition is not so absurd as it may seem; if anything it is a logical continuation of the 'energy principle' into virtually virgin territory. If all forms of energy are convertible into one another — one of the few completely accepted and indisputable laws of nature! — the conscious energies of dead people must also be convertible.

* Spiritualism says that reported phenomena are traceable to the intervention of the spirit world in this world.

† Latin, *occultum,* the hidden. The doctrine that there are natural and psychic facts which cannot be incorporated into the existing scheme of science. Today attempts are made to investigate occult apparitions by scientific methods.

For thousands of years we knew nothing about what happened to consciousness after death, apart from vague philosophical and religious speculations. (The 'soul' goes up to heaven. Thus immortality was already ascribed to the consciousness = soul!) Modern research is on the point of carefully removing the dark cloths which were spread over a supposedly inexplicable mystery, and what it has already brought to light appears to show that the consciousness (ergo, conscious energy) of the dead is by no means 'dead'! Might the conscious energies of dead people have been active during the 'host miracle' at Carabandal on the night of 18 July 1962, when a host-like object materialized on the tongue of the girl Conchita? What stage has the exploitation of these phenomena reached today?

Suspended animation occurs when the breath stops owing to paralysis of the breathing centre (asphyxia), in myocardial infarctions, in injuries resulting from accidents (traumas), in poisoning and after convulsions, etc. As Jean-Baptiste Dalacourt[7] says, everyone who recovers from suspended animation testifies that during their temporary stay in 'the other world' they retained consciousness of a quite different kind from their 'living' consciousness. The other world is perceived as timeless, as a world of oscillations, harmonies and colours, as a world in which countless consciousnesses communicate with each other, carry on conversations with each other and, although incorporeal and without sensory organs, can see other people and swap memories with them. Everyone who has come back from the 'other side' has found their abrupt return to the harsh cold facts of mortal life burdensome and repugnant. Everything was so infinitely more beautiful 'over there'.

Doctors say that such descriptions by resuscitated persons are irrelevant and worthless as statements about 'another world', because levels of consciousness continue to function in the brains of those in suspended animation and dredge up into their consciousness illusory pictures of a fairy-tale world from the deeper brain levels.

If the doctors are right, I find it a terrifying idea. There am I down below in my wooden box; insects and worms are thriving on my flesh and my deeper brain levels are still active. How unpleasant! Who knows how long they stay active? Until the moment when conscious energies have been converted? Thank heaven that would happen more quickly with a genuine death than in cases of suspended animation.

But what about the conscious energies of people who have been dead for many long years?

*   *   *

In 1964 the Swede Friedrich Jürgenson[8] claimed that he had succeeded in capturing the voices of people long dead with the help of microphones and tapes.

This phenomenon fascinated the critical parapsychologist Dr Constantin Raudive, born in Latvia in 1909, who left his home as a young man and studied in Paris and Madrid, where his meeting with Ortega y Gasset (1883-1955) became a decisive experience in his life. (Ortega advocated the anthropological theory that the 'spirit' forms the core of personality.)

Raudive spent four years checking Jürgenson's claims. He had an absolutely sound-proof recording studio built and worked with magnetised records which even cut out the minimal background noise of microphones and cartridges. In 1968 Raudive[9] published the results of his experiments, which had all taken place under scientifically controlled conditions. Hundreds of observers confirmed the accuracy of his methods, among them figures such as Professor Hans Bender, Director of the Institut für Grenzwissenschaften, Freiburg, the physicist Dr G. Rönicke, Julian Blieber, PhD, Dr Arnold Reincke, Dr Hans Naegeli, President of the Swiss Parapsychological Society, Professor Atis Teichmanis, Professor Werner Brunner, a surgeon from Zurich, Professor Alex Schneider, St Gall, Professor Walter H. Uphoff, Boulder, USA, Dr Jule Eisenbund, Denver, USA, Dr Wilhelmine C. Hennequin, specialist in anaesthesia, Dr R. Fatzer, Wädenswill, Switzerland, etc., etc.

Constantin Raudive recorded 72,000 voices! Alex Schneider, Professor of Physics at the Eidgenössischen Technischen Hochschule, Switzerland, said on the subject:

Provisionally physics has no objections to make to the voice phenomena. At all events we shall be waiting tensely for the result of further investigations, as they will enlarge our knowledge of electromagnetic radiation.

Anyone can hunt down voices in his own home without great expense. This is the rough recipe. You choose a time and a room with as little external noise as possible. Alone or with others you pick up the microphone and call on dead persons (or 'spirits') to announce themselves. The tape should be running. You wait and repeat your appeal to those on the other side in half a minute. You wait again. You should not keep this up for more than half an hour.

You rewind the tape and if you have made contact, you hear hastily spoken words in different languages. The scraps of language received are babbled so fast that at first you have to take a good deal of trouble to pick words and sentences out of the confused mixture of your own voice, room noises and inter-ference. Sounds, words and fragments of sentences are often hissed and sometimes only whispered. They are spoken by different voices.

You should write down what you pick up, because only then can you recognize languages, dialects and logograms. You get the best results if you play identified voices on to a second tape and cut out waiting periods, background noise, etc. in the process. I should like to destroy the hope that you can understand com-munications from the voices *en clair*, as it were. There is a lot of turbulence in the ether! Aunt Emma's great-great-grandfather follows close on the heels of Nietzsche, and soon after that comes the voice of Caruso or a dead friend. A characteristic feature is that no one voice lets another finish what it is saying. They must be a garrulous lot in the other world, too.

The following is a practical method of receiving voices. You connect the microphone cable of the tape recorder to the radio and choose a setting between two transmitters. The procedure has the disadvantage that voices are overlaid by atmospheric dis-turbances, but also the advantage that any conceivable influencing of the microphone by those present is excluded. It has been proved that voices from the ether can be captured above all atmospheric noise[10].

* * *

There were no noises during Dr Raudive's studio experiments. The academic participants did not say a word. The voices of dead friends and relations were recognized. If a supra- or subconscious form of energy released the phenomena it would have happened *unconsciously*, but it makes no difference, for that, too, would be a proof of the conversion of conscious energy into the energy form of the technical medium's tape!

It is estimated that some 100,000 tape recordings of voices from the other world have been stored away in different parts of the globe. So there is plenty of evidence. The open question is how to interpret it. The crux is that so far it cannot be said with scientific certainty that the transcendental voices really belong to the dead. It is conceivable that the conscious energy of living persons (including sub- and supra-consciousness) may directly affect electronic apparatus. It may even be enough for someone somewhere who is taking absolutely no part in the experiment to release unconscious energy which is converted into electro-magnetic oscillations which get recorded on the tape. From *my* point of view it makes little difference whether the voices of the dead or conscious scraps of conversation by contemporaries are taken down magnetically. In either case there is proof of con-scious energies which produce effects without having caused them *consciously*.

The hunt for voices from the spirit world continues. In May 1974 Dr Constantin Raudive[11] wrote:

For the first time in the history of *post-mortem* examination we have at our disposal an object which exhibits the charac-teristic of 'repeatability' which is to be considered a conclusive proof of the existence of this object. Thus we have the possi-bility of systematic intensive research in this field. From the results of this investigation it can be inferred whether this or that recording is true or false. Facts are the true language of science.

* * *

Obviously the virulent discussion of and research into forms of consciousness after death are far from exhausted by questioning people who have experienced suspended animation or the hunt for transcendental voices. Hypnotists use suggestion to send human 'guinea-pigs' not only back to their youth, but also way past their intrauterine existence into a life before birth.

Thorwald Dethlefsen[12], a young hypnotist from Munich, possesses accurate records of séances in which the hypnotized subject is first returned to the age of a babe in arms and later asked about his existence *before* birth. This hypnotic retrospective covers two or three previous births! When asked the 'guinea-pigs' assured him that they had lived *before* their subjective birth under other names, in other places and often with a different sex. They named names and birthdays from these previous lives and, although they did not know them, spoke in the languages of the countries in which they had lived two or three births ago. And to give the reader cold shivers, on more than one occasion they described their own deaths. That makes research really spooky.

Morey Bernstein[13] used hypnosis to send Mrs Ruth Simmons back to the ages of four, three, two and one years. Bernstein forced Mrs Simmons to think even further back — before her birth. Suddenly she began to talk under a different name, as Bridey Murphy, from another life in Ireland about the middle of the nineteenth century. Everything Ruth Simmons said was recorded on tape, transcribed and checked up on the spot in Ireland by linguistic comparisons (Gaelic), examination of church registers and village records. The descriptions of places and people by Ruth Simmons alias Bridey Murphy tallies exactly with the information gleaned on the spot. Naturally the hypnotized guinea-pig Ruth Simmons had never seen the old records, nor could she have known of them by telepathy, because no one who could have acted as a 'transmittee' had shown any interest in the dust-covered documents.

Did Ruth Simmons experience all the things described in her trance in an 'incarnation' in the last century? It seems inadmissible to accept that, because it would be overstretching our imagination and demanding too much of our realistic way of looking at things. Yet: 'What everyone considers settled is what is most worth investigating,' as the physicist George Christoph Lichtenberg (1742-1799) said.

It is the old, old story. People who take a great interest in the explanation of such phenomena do not waste their time convincing materialists who find the only metaphysical reality in material things and reject as nonsense everything that cannot be described by their formulae, masses and weights. Incidentally I feel that materialists are the very people who ought to agree with 'my' Trinity of spirit-matter-energy — after all it concerns the centre of their world picture. I want to keep my hobby-horse on a

F

loose rein and not ride it to death, especially as it is given un-equivocal support by a man like Werner von Braun[14]:

'Science has established that nothing can vanish without a trace. There is no destruction in nature, only transformation.'

In contrast to the religious interpretation (the 'soul' is im-mortal) I consider it very probable in the physical sense that the conscious energy of dead people can make itself felt in our four-dimensional world by conversion into another form of energy. If energies from the 'other world' can make themselves perceptible among us, the reverse path – from the earth to the 'other world' – must also be practicable. *Our* state of consciousness is bound to the fourth dimension, the unfolding of time, an attachment that is possibly not applicable in the 'other world'.

* * *

The world-famous French clairvoyant Belline, aged 50, lost his only son, aged 20, in a car accident in 1969. For twenty months Belline vainly tried to establish contact with Michel through his telepathic abilities. But suddenly he sensed an 'in-visible nearness', which he described as a 'third ear' or 'light-hearing'. Belline was afraid he was the victim of an illusion con-jured up by his suffering. He began to tape the conversations he had with Michel: in 1973 they appeared in a book[15] with a foreword by Gabriel Marcel of the Institut de France, as well as the opinions of 90 personalities in the world of art and science about the experiment.

The timelessness of the fourth dimension in the other world became clear from the records.

8th April 1971, 8 a.m.

Belline: Michel, what is it like 'over there'?

Michel: It is another world, a dream which cannot be ex-pressed in words. Movement, transparency, thoughts. Here neither earthly good nor earthly evil exists. It is a kind of home-lessness, a kind of dream in countless dimensions and vi-brations. . . . Here, time, as you conceive of it at this moment, becomes a caricature. That's all I can say.

If it ever becomes possible to direct conscious energies from here to the 'other world', we should be able to ask those who live there for data about past *and* future. The reason: the 'otherworlders' exist in a timeless dimension; their state does not seem to be shackled to the passage of time.

In terms of physics this possibility is quite feasible. Variable states of energy – say elementary particles which can transform themselves into each other: a neutron into a proton, an electron into a neutrino – have quite different 'life spans'. Many of them have such short life spans that they really ought not to exist. The life of a positron or sigma particle lasts for a trillionth of a second. How can we really conceive of that? A million times a million times a million = a '10' with 18 noughts! A neutral pion 'lives' exactly 10^{-15} (i.e. ten to the minus fifteenth) seconds and the luckless neutrino has no life span at all in a state of rest (rest mass = 0). But if such a neutrino is accelerated it 'lives' again.

In spite of their absurdly minute life spans, elementary particles conceal up to 10^{22} electron volts. They shoot out of the universe through suns and planets, later to transform themselves into myons and neutrinos – in 100/1,000th of a second.

Forty years ago physicists were convinced that they had discovered the smallest particle in the atom. Today they know that there is a subatomic world which is tinier than the atomic nucleus and contains much more energy than anything that we can so far conceive of as 'nascent energy'.

The concept of time breaks down in this *miraculous world*. Physicists no longer know where or how they should classify the electron, that building stone and atomic envelope. With mathematically proven particles which travel faster than light – say, the tachyons, tradyons and luxyons calculated by Gerald Feinberg – all concepts of time collapse definitively. They behave in exactly the opposite way to our 'normal' elementary particles.

Instead of exhibiting infinite mass and with it infinite energy when they reach the speed of light – as Einstein reckoned they would – these particles *lose* mass and energy the faster they travel. What is really inconceivable is that the speed of light is the lowest limit of their velocity – above it they can reach a trillionfold the speed of light. If our concepts of time have already become hazy owing to the prospect of interstellar space travel, they fall into a state of total confusion when they tackle particles that move faster than light. Every normal person is convinced – and justifiably so until now – that *before* an effect exists there must be a cause. But here everything is upside down. With particles travelling faster than light, the effect can come *first* and the cause *later*. Something is going on, but we do not really know what.

Thus, just as physicists in general recognize the existence of antimatter,* we can also postulate in the distant future an 'anti-time' in which a 'counter-time' unfolds opposite to all 'normal time'. Then there would be – how can I make it intelligible? – no past, present or future. Memories of the future are taking place now, today, at this very moment! The concept of time becomes the subjective unfolding of states of consciousness. If we can still speak of consciousness in such a context. . . .

In so far as the conscious energy of the dead exists outside all ties of time, and terrestrial conscious energy can make contact with it, the mystery of prophesy would be solved. What is still hypothesis could in future not only be proved by the conclusions of technical research, but also realized in practice. Hypotheses in the sense of 'accepted suppositions' are the prerequisites for *all* development. We only need a little courage to bring them into the conversation. I've got that courage.

Let us assume that for one reason or another an *otherworldly* consciousness is interested in influencing the behaviour of one or several people or a group (peoples, countries, religions, kingdoms). It leaves its timeless state, and makes contact with a *terrestrial* consciousness. The reverse process is also conceivable. The conscious energy of an earthly person (who else could it be but a prophet?) could in specific situations communicate with the timeless conscious energy of someone from the other world. From the dead colleague and his intact conscious energy (don't give me that old stuff about the 'soul'!) it could learn what is going to happen *in the future*. From historical experience the person knows that the event communicated by energy cannot have taken place yet, and therefore is announced ('prophesied') for the future.

The paradox is that the event prophesied can *never* be held up or prevented. No visionary saint is *that* holy.

A man dies. His consciousness (in the form of energy) reaches a 'timeless state'. In this version he 'sees' his home town swallowed up by the floods. As this event has not happened in his

---

* Matter from atoms which consist exclusively of antiparticles, incapable of existence in the presence of normal matter.

lifetime, it *must* take place in the future. A consciousness that
becomes *timeless* after death cannot know *when* the future has
laid down the deadline for the catastrophe. Otherworldly consciousnesses (in spite of their energies) still have links with living
children, relatives and friends. They strive to win influence over
the conscious energies of the people on the old earth with whom
they have ties, for they want to warn them of the catastrophe
which is pending at some unknown time in the future.

The inhabitants of the earth, tied to the daily round, have not
trained the cerebral functions that could perceive such phenomena
– the impulses radiated from the other world by the conversion
of energy (the energy principle) do not reach them. The otherworlders have to make their impact through a medium (who has
trained the faculties that are capable of reception). In a trance
(the state which develops paranormal faculties) the medium 'sees',
by the action of conscious energy, a town swallowed up by the
floods, but he does not know *when* it will happen – this is plausible for the otherworlders themselves do not know it in their
timeless state. So if a medium (prophet, priest, seer) preaches:
'Pray! Pray fervently, otherwise your town will be swallowed up
by floods!' it may be a plausible summons, but its contents are a
lie, for the town will disappear *at some time or other* in any case.
If it were not so, the timeless otherworlders would not have been
able to announce the catastrophe.

* * *

Let us consider a different case. By energy conversion a terrestrial prophet sends his (trained) mental antennae into the other
world. He 'sees' events that can *only occur in the future*, because
they have not happened in past history (as known or experienced
by the prophet). In other words, the mediumistic visionary does
not learn what day is to be ticked off in red on the calendar. He
has only *one* chance of giving a more precise 'message', namely if
he has 'seen' the event in such detail that he can work out the
approximate deadline for it. But there is one thing that even the
cleverest and best trained prophet cannot do: prevent the event
he has 'seen'! If it were not programmed for the indefinable
future, an otherworldly conscious energy could not have transmitted it and a terrestrial energy could not have 'seen' it. It

would be old hat if events which have been in the history books for years were communicated.

Does not this physical and metaphysical hypothesis explain quite plausibly why messages received in 'visions' proclaim and warn of coming events, but can never prevent them? Does not that also clarify why prophetic and visionary messages are often so obscure, 'mysterious' and ambiguous? With their present conscious energy, seers and prophets *do* perceive future events, but they cannot 'evaluate' them – except in the form of obscure predictions and unverifiable prophecies.

The last book in the New Testament is The Revelation of St John the Divine. It is the book of a visionary. The prophet sees images of environmental pollution, aircraft, helicopters, nuclear explosions, etc. He uses his own words to reproduce these visions as he received them in communications from conscious energies:

. . . and there followed hail and fire mingled with blood, and they were cast upon the earth: and the third part of trees was burnt up, and all green grass was burnt up . . . and as it were a great mountain burning with fire was cast into the sea . . . and the third part of the waters became wormwood (radioactive?) . . . and the third part of the creatures which were in the sea, and had life, died; and the third part of the ships were destroyed . . . (Chap. 8).

And they (the locusts) had breastplates, as it were breastplates of iron; and the sound of their wings was as the sound of chariots of many horses running to battle. . . . And they had tails like scorpions, and there were stings in their tails. . . . And . . . I saw the horses . . . and them that sat on them, having breastplates of fire, and of jacinth, and brimstone; and the heads of the horses were as the heads of lions; and out of their mouths issued fire and smoke and brimstone . . .' (Chap. 9).

Is it not crystal clear why John wrote his very accurate descriptions in *his* own words using *his* world of ideas? He did not know our modern technical vocabulary. It is stimulating to learn that the atomic physicist Bernhard Philberth[16] has written a modern interpretation of Revelation. The only disturbing thing about his technological exegesis is that he always appeals to God in a highly personal fashion for all the prophetic-cum-apocalyptic explanations. That brushes me up the wrong way. I just don't like it when people offer God, the last and highest instance of being, as an explanation for everything, when the goal can also be reached using reason.

*   *   *

It is much the same with the explanation of somnambulist phenomena: the time when they were interpreted plays an important part.

The poet Justinus Kerner (1786-1862) was the centre of the Swabian School of Poets. Many of his poems figured in schoolbooks for generations, many of them achieved the popularity of folk songs. Justinus Kerner, a doctor, devoted himself to a special field of research, the supernatural. He kept a diary of his observations with scientific precision. For many years his special subject was Friederike Hauffe, the wife of a tradesman. He recorded her somnambulist phenomena in the two-volumed work *Die Seherin von Prevorst*. I possess the first edition of 1829, and so do not have to refer to extracts from Kerner's work in scientific publications, which often quote him.

Friederike Hauffe came from the village of Prevorst near the Wurttemberg town of Löwenstein, in a mountainous district, whose inhabitants, says Kerner, were open to sidereal and magnetic influences. Father Hauffe was a gamekeeper. Friederike was brought up 'simply and naturally'. Never spoiled, she grew up to be a 'blooming, vivacious' child. Whereas her brothers and sisters were bothered by apparitions this peculiarity was not found in Friederike, but she did develop a power of foretelling the future that was announced to her in dreams. She became the 'wife of a tradesman', had children and led a bourgeois existence, but her emotional life became so intense that 'she heard and felt everything over the greatest distances'. She could no longer bear the light. Once when an ecclesiastical relative opened the window shutters at midday, she fell into a cramp that lasted for three days.

About this time, she felt that a spirit only visible to her magnetized her at seven o'clock every evening for seven days in succession. It happened with three fingers which the spirit spread out like rays.

(Presumably preparation by and first traces of otherworldly conscious energies.)

Put into a deep sleep by this spiritual magnetism, she stated that 'she could only be kept alive through magnetization'. In this state, Kerner relates, she saw behind every person who came near her another person, 'also with a human figure, but floating as in ecstasy'. (A phenomenon that many visionaries describe in the same way.)

'I must confess,' writes the doctor, 'that at the time I still shared the views of the world and their lies about her, so that I advised her not to pay any attention to her long lasting sleep-waking state.' On 25 November 1826, Kerner took Mrs Hauffe into his house 'completely wasted away . . . and incapable of lying down'. He told her that he did not take any notice of what she said in her sleep, and that the somnambulistic state which had lasted so long to the despair of her relatives must finally come to a stop.

After many weeks of medical and psychic treatment Kerner asked her while she was in deep sleep whether she felt

that a repeated and controlled magnetic treatment could still save her. She replied she could not give an answer to that until she had received seven magnetic strokes at seven o'clock the next evening . . . . (Had another worldly conscious energy notified her?). . . . The seven magnetic strokes she received had the result that the next morning to her great surprise, for she herself did not know how it happened, she could sit up easily in bed and felt far stronger than after all the remedies tried hitherto.

Kerner introduced a regular magnetic treatment* by strokes from the temples down to the epigastrium.

Mrs H was in such a deep somnambulistic life owing to my magnetic treatment that she was never in the waking state even when she seemed to be so. Admittedly she was more awake than other men, for it is strange not to call this state, which is actually the most vivid wakefulness, awake, but she was in the state of inwardness.

There are no dates in the relevant literature about the visionary's inner state. Friederike Hauffe put on record:

It often seems to me as if I am outside myself, I float above my body and then I also think above my body. But it is by no

---

* The slightest electric current creates a magnetic field. In a straight conductor (hand!) the lines of force form concentric circles.

means an unpleasant feeling because I am still conscious of my body. If only my soul was more closely attached to the 'nerve spirit' (!), then it would also bind itself closer to the nerves, but the bones of my nerve spirit becomes looser and looser.

Mrs Hauffe could also see parts of the body in magnetic sleep:

Once . . . apparently in the waking state Mrs H's eyes closed and she could not open them. She said she saw a sun moving slowly in the region of the stomach and she only wished she could open her eyes so as not to see the sun any longer. She had this vision of a sun slowly moving in the region of the solar plexus quite often later. Mrs H said about it: I've already said that I see the point *like a small sun from which small rays emerge*, yet the more I concentrate on it the more wakeful I become. . . .

For years Kerner noted down many examples of clairvoyance and seeing the future; they related to a large circle of people both known and unknown. Every statement was checked with the many doctors whom Kerner consulted, 'All the experiments and phenomena in connection with Mrs H speak of a nerve spirit that was present in her in great intensity and became free. . . .'

I know of no earlier medical-cum-scientific documentation of a 'case' like the one Dr Justinus Kerner described in the two volumes which are now nearly 150 years old. As doctor and scientist he first examined the phenomena of Friederike Hauffe as a clinical picture of illness: he went into her childhood and origins, living conditions and habits. He wanted to get to the heart of the matter. The final conclusion he came to after all these efforts was that the state of magnetic sleep released special visionary abilities. He examined every case of precognition, which to him verged on the miraculous, with an accuracy and persistence that would do credit to Scotland Yard. Out of dozens of examples I shall describe one of the cases Kerner recorded:

On 25 November 1826, Friederike Hauffe entered Kerner's house in Weinsperg. She did not know the town and had no acquaintances there. The house was on the same level as and not far from the Law Courts. A certain K, who had died in the house some years previously, had managed the affairs of a Mr F very badly, so that the 'business had gone bankrupt'. Mrs Hauffe said, in a magnetic sleep:

That man F is there again, disturbing me . . . what is he showing me? A page, not quite as long as a folio, covered with figures. The upper right-hand corner is folded slightly, in the left-hand corner there is a figure. . . . This page lies underneath a lot of documents; no one takes any notice of it. He wants me to tell my doctor and through him to issue a warning. . . . This page lies in a building that stands sixty paces from my bed. In it is a large, then a small, room. In the latter a tall man sits working at a table. He goes out and now he is returning. Beyond this room there is an even larger one with longish chests in it. I see a cupboard that stands at the entrance and its door is somewhat open. . . . Above on the table there is something made of wood . . . and on it lie papers; I see them lying in three piles. . . . In the right-hand pile there is nothing of this man's, but in the other two I feel from him, to be precise in the centre one, a little below half-way down, that page which torments him so.

Kerner recognized the high court from the building she described, but took her vision for a dream image. Mostly to pacify his patient, for she was constantly plagued by the story, he went to the judge, who was staggered because at the moment described he had actually gone into another room and then returned to his place.

The apparition returned; the data became more and more precise. Kerner and the judge examined the 'pile of files' which Mrs Hauffe had described so vividly. They got the sort of surprise a police inspector would not hope for in his wildest dreams. 'We found in an envelope a page just as the visionary had described it with figures and words in the hand of that man . . . (whom Mrs Hauffe had 'seen'). . . . This page contained a proof, the only one, that K had kept a secret book, which was not found after his death, in which he had apparently entered a great deal that never came to light. . . .'

In a sleep-waking state Friederike Hauffe dictated a letter to the dead man F's wife telling her she was innocent and could face the bankruptcy confidently. The judge prepared a conclusive official statement of the whole business. Frau Hauffe seemed to be revivified after the longdrawn out affair.

On 5 August 1829, the visionary of Prevorst died in exactly the way she had predicted in a magnetic sleep on 2 May.

How could that outstanding doctor Justinus Kerner sense or know about the conclusions of modern psi research 150 years ago? What could he know about the conversion of energy/time? For what else appeared to the visionary but the conscious energy of the dead Mr F, who wanted to help his wife in her imminent bankruptcy? Who else besides Mr F knew about the bundle of files and the letter which played a decisive part in the proceedings?

The case described by Kerner is more than clairvoyance: it is exact knowledge of an event. We can understand why Kerner's account still keeps on appearing in modern scientific literature. It established standards for carrying out experiments and evaluating results. The visionary's message that she received all her impressions and visions from a 'nerve spirit' runs like a *leitmotiv* through all the accounts. I should like to posit boldly that Kerner supplied the first 'proof' of my theory that conscious energies seek the media appropriate to them – and find them!

*   *   *

Mankind cannot complain about a shortage of prophets and their frightening communications. We must have hindsight to understand why the prophecies which every now and then have exploded like thunder in history always announced disaster. For why should otherworldly conscious energies make contact with terrestrial ones simply to spread happiness and joy? 'Children, it's a wonderful age! Rejoice! Taxes are going to be reduced! In twenty years' time you will still own what you do today! Love each other, for no shadow will fall on your lives! Disarm, there will never be any more idiotic wars!' The energetic news apparatus would hardly be set in motion for cheerful messages like that.

The 'spirits above' still exclusively transmit, as they have always done, descriptions of imminent catastrophes, world destruction, misery and famine. A wretched job for a messenger, but who warns anyone about happiness?

What does even a brief glance at the annals of visionaries 'reveal'?

The itinerant Greek priest Peregrinus Proteus at first preached the doctrine of Christianity; then he had doubts and changed his philosophy. He became a cynic, one of those philosophers who cultivated the ideal of frugality to the point of folly. The convert was not happy. He 'saw' – and as a preacher naturally told everybody – that mankind was on 'the brink of annihilation'. As he did not want to take part in this mass disaster, he logically burnt himself to death during the Olympic games in 165.

The Phrygian prophet Montanus (156) belonged to an early Christian sect which aroused among people a brief-lived hope of the imminent return of Jesus. In order to be well prepared, the prophet exhorted his followers to practise rigorous asceticism, for otherwise 'the end of the world was at hand'.

In 140 the Roman apostolic father Hermas in his book 'The Shepherd' (which formed part of the New Testament for a time) called on Christians to do penance as the ultimate salvation 'from the imminent Last Judgment'.

Over 400 years ago (1568) the Provençal plague doctor Michael Nostradamus (1503-1566) posthumously published his book *Les Prophéties*[17]. His prophecies, extending down to modern times, which in the opinion of scholars tally strikingly with recorded facts, consist of a non-stop list of wars, pestilences and disasters. The fact that most of the events are supposed to have taken place according to plan is small consolation.

If we made ourselves a present of a collected volume of prophecies it would be as thick as a New York telephone directory, and poring over disasters is no fun – especially if we've got them at home! But it is fun to meet and talk to a living prophetess.

*   *   *

Jeane Dixon is an American from the wealthy middle-class. She lives in a white-brick terrace house in Washington, D.C., is happily married to her husband Jimmy, a smart businessman. She loves her cat Mike, dresses fashionably and is Secretary-Treasurer of James I. Dixon & Co., a real estate firm. Ater ten hours at the office, she writes columns for 200 American dailies, receives an average of 3,000 letters a week and gives lectures, in addition to her social activities as a company representative. She has calculated that she works 217 days more than her fellow-citizens: 52 Saturdays, 52 Sundays, 9 holidays (except Christmas), 14 days' holiday (which she does not take) and 90 days' overtime. Jeane Dixon has a sense of humour and is deeply religious.

She has, and still does, hit the headlines in the press all over the world.

In 1944 she predicted that China would turn Communist. (It happened in 1949.)

In the summer of 1947 she announced that Mahatma Ghandi would be assassinated within the next six months. (He was shot by a fanatical Hindu on 30.1.1948.)

In 1961 she prophesied Marilyn Monroe's suicide. (Marilyn died on 5.8.1962 of an overdose of sleeping tablets.)

At the beginning of September 1961 she 'saw' the death of her friend Bill Rowallo, private bodyguard to the UN Secretary-General Dag Hammerskjöld (Hammerskjöld and his suite died on 18 September 1961 in an unexplained air crash near Ndola, Rhodesia).

René Noorbergen[18] describes the 'dramatic prediction of the death of President John F. Kennedy' which Jeane Dixon made eleven (!) years before the assassination on 12.11.1963.

She used every conceivable channel to try to stop Kennedy from going to Dallas. Jeane Dixon claims that she has a special affinity with the Kennedy family. She announced at a big convention in January 1968 that Robert Kennedy would not become President of the USA because he would be the victim of an assassin in California in June of that year. On 5 June Bishara Sirhan shot the senator in the Ambassador Hotel, Los Angeles. Jeane Dixon even described the scene of the event.

René Noorbergen spoke to Dr Clyde Backster, the lie-detector specialist and director of a scientific research institute about the phenomenon of Jeane Dixon. Backster took the view that Jeane Dixon had advanced into the range of frequencies established 'for communication in the universe'. To quote Backster: 'I do not doubt that this means of communication has always existed. We have blocked our extrasensory perceptions through our prejudices. We tell ourselves and science and our environment tell us that an extra sense is nonsense. . . . Jeane Dixon seems to have full access to a faculty which once was used quite extensively. . . .'

On Sunday 5 May 1947 I met the grand old lady for a discussion at her Washington home.

Mrs Dixon, what happens when you experience your prophecies? What do you feel? Do you have a revelation, do you see a vision or an apparition?

It is a wonderful thing when I see the future. It does not take the form of an apparition, for that would only be a kind of ghost. Nor is it a revelation, for revelations are signs of the will of God. What I see is the destiny that God has predetermined for you or anyone else, and you cannot alter that destiny. Incidentally, I told Richard Nixon that as early as 1959.

What happens to you at such moments? What goes on in your brain?

It is a higher state of grace. Usually I am prepared for it. My condition changes, so does my attitude to my environment, and my ability to think logically, even my state of health. Suddenly one morning I know that a period of inspiration is coming. The length of this period cannot be compared to normal time.

I have read that you are very religious. Do you practise your religion?

Yes, I went to Church at seven o'clock this morning.

What do the Church and the present cardinal say about your prophecies?

You should read what some priests write about me! The best thing is not to worry about them and pray for them.

Have you really been seriously attacked?

Naturally I have been seriously attacked and from quite high places. One is always attacked by those who do not understand or those who act as if they understand everything. Lazy people always shout the loudest.

Why are you attacked by the Church? After all you've never said anything against Christianity.

And I never will say anything against Christianity. I have actually had visions of Jesus, but they are not comparable with the state of prophecy.

I have just read in the papers that you are convinced of the existence of UFOs. Can you tell me something about that?

I can tell you that there's nothing new in my life. I've known about UFOs for many years. People ask me when I first knew anything about them. That's a question I can't answer; as I've known about UFOs since I could walk. Have you ever thought about why and when you consciously knew you could walk?

So UFOs actually exist, in your opinion. Where do these objects come from?

We shall soon find out that they come from an undiscovered

planet in our solar system. We shall make official contact with the crews and learn from them how existing sources of energy can be better and more simply exploited.

The conditions of gravity in our solar system have been calculated. So there is no room for an unknown planet. Besides, space probes have traversed the space 'behind the sun' and no new planet has been recorded.

That makes no difference. We shall soon discover an unknown planet which is in the vicinity of Jupiter.

Jupiter is very far from our sun. That giant planet no longer forms part of the life zone of our solar system. How is intelligence supposed to originate in such intense cold?

Just wait and see! By the way, UFOs are piloted by women.

How do we know that?

I can feel the vibrations and they're feminine.

Mrs Dixon, you know my books. What do you think about my theories?

You're absolutely right about many things.

Do you think that we shall be revisited by extraterrestrial beings?

Of course I do. We were visited in the past, as you claim. . . . Give me your hand for a few minutes. Look, here in your fingertips I can feel the energy of your supra-supra-consciousness. Look, Herr von Däniken, the next important section of your life. . . .

At this point Jeane Dixon forbade further tape-recordings for two hours and also prohibited publication of that part of the conversation. Our talk ended as follows:

Do you ever drink alcohol?

I've never touched a drop in my life! I don't drink coffee or tea, either. Do you remember when you were nineteen and the great turning point in your life came? *You* didn't cause the turning point. It came over you, as it were. During the rest of your life you will have very powerful enemies, but they will be outnumbered by guiding powers who will help you. Do not misuse your talent. Make sure that you report this interview properly! If you misrepresent the things we have just spent such a long time discussing I'll never give another interview again.

'Something' vibrates from our levels of energy, 'something'

sees images of future events, 'something' vibrates in our brains from alien otherworldly levels of energy and produces visions. Does that mean that *everything* that Jeane Dixon and others prophesied came true?

Of course not, but who would be surprised? If you realize that the world beyond the (hitherto) physically conceivable is 'timeless', radiated energies could naturally be picked up by 'receivers', but could scarcely or only with difficulty be given a date in time — lucky bull's eyes!

The forms of consciousness of *otherworlders* who seek to make contact with us are either emotional or alogical (because they are outside the terrestrial experience and laws of time) or both. Otherwise they would not warn against ostensible *coming* events, which have already happened in the 'timeless state', for there would be nothing they could do to change them.

Or:

Forms of consciousness of *people in this world* penetrate into the 'other world' and *hope* to be able to avert a 'seen' event. But that would be a one-sided attempt at communication by terrestrial beings. In that case the otherworlders would have no connection with warnings of imminent future disasters.

I much prefer the second assumption; it would obviate the need to involve people from the other world. For then conscious energies produced by our brains would be capable at certain intervals of time of communicating with the 'time-reversed' world (tachyons!) and tap otherworldly consciousnesses for prophecies.

*　　*　　*

I extracted a lot of information from Mythology when working on my theory about visits to our globe by extraterrestrial beings. I was fascinated by the knowledge of the old chroniclers, because it handed down to mankind factual information the importance and scope of which the writers did not appreciate in their own days. As far as contacts between the other world and this one are concerned, mythology is an equally valuable source of information. Here are some examples.

The Indo-Germanic Celts were driven across the Rhine by the Germans and later occupied the British Isles. These insular Celts of the first post-Christian centuries were on familiar terms with fairies, beautiful, magic-working, daemonic beings, nature spirits, who constantly went back and forth between the natural and the supernatural world. They astonished the island Celts by their knowledge of the future and when they visited the earth they inspired great respect because they enticed chosen vessels into their 'kingdom' and then let them return to earth again.

The North Germans were firmly convinced of the existence of a 'second I', which they called Fylgja. It accompanied people like an invisible shadow. Fylgja belonged to the personal consciousness, but could also become free from it and appear elsewhere. The Scandinavians looked on Fylgja as a familiar guardian spirit, who, when needed, but especially when danger threatened, could speed into the other world and return with a wealth of information to help earth-dwellers out of their trouble.

The Druids, the ancient pagan priests of the Celts, would only recognize as their prophet the man who could produce the Druid's cauldron, an exquisite and miraculous vessel, which was made out of the 'spirit of the other world'. Not even Uri Geller could cook up all the prophecies the Druidic seers brewed in their cauldrons.

In the phantom-ridden night of the Samhuin (a phenomenon from the ancient Indian Vedas), even the boundaries between this world and the next are supposed to have fallen. Spooky figures of all kinds are supposed to have materialized from the void.

The 'astral body' plays a great part in the occult literature of all ages. This remarkable phenomenon is supposed to be a 'delicate envelope' for the body and soul. The gnostic religion, which makes man's salvation dependent on his knowledge of the secrets of the world, asserts that the astral body penetrates the human body and forms something like a connecting link between the earthly and the 'higher' body.

One cannot mention astral bodies without mentioning auras. Aura means air or breath in Greek. Not only has it been a topic of conversation since ancient times, but it is reputed to have existed always. And precisely today this generally invisible envelope which surrounds human beings is the subject of parapsychological research. (Indeed we say that such-and-such a poet, scholar and even politician has a 'certain aura' in the sense of charisma!)

I do not intend to quote all the periods in which the undefined aura is supposed to have been definitively discovered. But as a proof that serious scholars were interested in this problem, I must mention the scientist and chemist Carl-Ludwig Freiherr von Reichenbach (1788-1869), who discovered paraffin-wax and creosote in wood-tar. Reichenbach was convinced of the existence of this invisible original force (which could be made visible), which he called 'Od force' (from the Germanic 'od' = original) – so convinced that he devoted two whole decades of his working life to its discovery. Like Franz Anton Mesmer, Reichenbach believed that the Od force could be transferred from one person to another. Yet this remarkable phenomenon, astral body, aura or Od force, was first confirmed technically by chance in our own day.

In the second half of the forties, the Russian engineer Semyonov Davidovich Kirlian from Krasnodar on the Kuban noticed that discharges appeared between the body of a patient and the electrodes in the high frequency range of an apparatus for electrotherapeutic treatment. Kirlian was keen to know whether this state, which was visible to the eye, could also be photographed. He and his wife Valentina undertook the difficult job of developing these photographs.

Kirlian photography, which is used everywhere today, exhibits the so-called Kirlian effect. In high frequency alternating current fields which are harmless to man, animals and plants, bodies acquire a luminescence that can be photographed, but are not caused by high temperature. It is also known as 'cold luminescence'.

As a passing example of the phenomenon which Kirlian photography can make visible, I should mention photos that show a fresh flower with many blossoms and the same flower with some blossoms cut off. In the place where the blossoms were their outline still showed up in a photograph taken seconds after the cut was made and they were no longer there. Countless exposures have been taken all over the world using the Kirlian effect. They show radiations around men's bodies that are not visible to the naked eye.

For example, there is a photo taken after a hand was amputated: the outlines of the amputated hand appear on the photographic plate. And most remarkable of all, a man lay down on a sofa, then stood up and went away, and a photo taken of the sofa just afterwards shows the outline of the man lying there! Here an unknown force obviously causes a physical phenomenon. When the technique is developed further, mankind will have a brand new principle, for at the moment the photographed aura – or whatever it is – varies considerably in quality, i.e. clarity.

I am always shaken to observe how almost daily unintelligible passages from myths and holy scriptures turn out to be realities. People used to talk about the aura that surrounded certain people – and it exists! It can be photographed. The way in which the Kirlian effect works has been explained in principle. It is not denied by physicists that every body 'radiates' to a greater or lesser degree. Kirlian discovered how to photograph the radiations. But how do we answer the 'phenomenal' question of how a no-longer existent object (cut blossom, amputated hand, man who has left the room) continues to radiate for a brief period, i.e. can still be 'active' in its former position? When all is said and done scholars claim that the bodies are the *cause* of the radiations. Could it possibly be the other way round? Whither was the energy radiated?

In the physical sense every radiation is 'material'. This applies to light radiation (quanta) and all kinds of corpuscle radiations (particle radiations). Radiation energy disintegrates. Disintegrates into what? According to the energy principle nothing can vanish into the VOID. That is the point at which even nuclear physics is baffled. It is impossible to prove the existence of certain atomic particles after their conversion into energy. A physicist at the European Council for Nuclear Research at Geneva told me (with a plea not to mention him by name):

Supernatural states begin for us here. We record certain effects, we try to establish their working according to laws. But when it comes to the reason for these effects we are overwhelmed with questions. This is really where the spirit world begins.

*　　*　　*

Was Dr Leonid L. Vassilev, Professor of Psychology at Lenigrad University, holder of the Order of Lenin, trying to resign? or was he expressing a hope when he said:

'The discovery of ESP* energy will be just as important as the discovery of atomic energy.'

*   *   *

This apparent detour via parapsychological phenomena to get to apparitions is not a detour. Visions and apparitions *are* parapsychological phenomena. There is energy behind every vision. Where does it come from? What causes several milliard atoms to make themselves visible at a *specified* time in a *specified* place and demonstrate intelligent behaviour by this action? Why are visions always perceived only by a few people? Why do hundreds and thousands of people who are present notice nothing? Why do visions appear to the visionaries for preference at the same place? Are they incapable of changing the venue, once it is established? The visionary is always asked to be at a prescribed place on a certain day at a certain time. Are ('divine') visions incapable of appearing exactly where and when it suits them?

It can be proved from the small selection of visions I have described that in several cases the visionaries did not 'see' the complete apparition spontaneously or suddenly: if anything they were confronted with a 'hazy, indefinable greyish-white mass'. They only perceived the visionary image in this 'mass' after an intensive effort (autosuggestion!). The Heroldsbacher girls 'saw' only a 'white gleam' during the vision of 12 October 1949 – not until later did it assume the form of 'a white lady', and then it was visible only to the boys. Mama Rosa of San Damiano also said that at first she saw only a 'hazy figure' which later 'solidified' into the Mother of God. (Let me remind you of the Jesuit Athanasius Kircher who considered 'mists and vapours' helpful when water-divining in likely spots.)

The official records of the visions seen by the children at Fatima entitle us to conclude that physical events were concerned. The visions always announced themselves with 'lightning', whose electric discharges were accompanied by roaring and cracking noises. The little Lucia said that whenever a vision disappeared she heard a noise as if a 'firework rocket had exploded in the

* ESP = Extrasensory Perception.

distance'. When the Fatima children had their fifth vision on 13 September 1917, several thousand spectators clearly saw a ball of light floating slowly and majestically heavenwards. On 13 May 1924 pilgrims observed a 'strange white cloud' above the oak tree where the visions always appeared. They said that objects like snow-flakes fell from it that dissolved into nothing just above ground-level. Lucia wrote later that the vision of the Blessed Virgin had always approached slowly in 'the reflection of a light', and that the children had always seen the Madonna for the first time when the point of light stopped still above the oak. When Lucia was asked at the official enquiry why she frequently lowered her eyes during the visions, instead of looking the Blessed Virgin straight in the face, she answered: 'Because she often blinded me[19].'

In the case of Lourdes the idea of the *materialization of an alien form of energy* is literally served up on a silver platter! In the first as yet unembellished accounts, Bernadette Soubirous explained that originally she had seen only something indefinite . . . something 'like a fluttering white cloth or a flour-sack[20]'; in addition she had heard a muffled noise 'like a gust of wind' in front of the grotto. (Record by Doctors Lacrampe, Balencia and Peyrus, dated 27.3.1858.) Bernadette also gave these details to other personalities[21].

Three possibilities occur to me:

1.   A vision does not appear suddenly; it must first arrange its atoms into a visible 'image'. (The frequent occurrence of the word 'suddenly' in the records is explained by the indifference of the visionary's examiners to the 'preliminary play' [haze, veil, white cloths, etc.]. By insistent questioning they push forward to the goal, the description of the vision. *That* is how visions 'suddenly' come into being − at least in the official records!)

2.   An electromagnetic, probably highly ionized, field comes into being during the appearance of the vision. Air is compressed very rapidly. This causes sound vibrations of varying volume and strength like a 'dull roaring wind'. Air is sucked out of the grotto as if through an exhaust and compressed.

3. If the apparition collapses, air rushes into the vacuum which is burst open by the spontaneously dissolving magnetic field. That is why even passive spectators hear a 'bang' at many visionary shrines.

Even this brief resumé allows us to conclude that physical laws lie at the root of the unknown causes of visions. Would Almighty God, if he were informed of these phenomena by trusty messengers, simply bow down to these lapidary laws?

The psychiatrist's couch is the place for explaining and curing accounts of ostensible visions feigned by charlatans, would-be visionaries and religious cranks, or cooked up in the brains of hysterics ripe for the asylum. The causes of visionary phenomena that we can take seriously must lie outside human reason and the functions of the human brain. Ionized air, loud bangs, ball lightning etc., offer such hard fact that you can break your teeth on them. Who is the great Manitu, the mighty 'spirit' who gaily produces the phenomena? Am I daring to claim that genuine visions exist?

Yes, I am.

The thousands who heard an explosion, saw lightning or observed the solar miracle were *not* out of their senses. When the visionaries were followed to the scene of their visions by other people, they were not exclusively a flock of dyed-in-the-wool religious bigots. They often included sceptical scientists, generally critical journalists and always a number of unbelievers who had not been inoculated with the religious virus.

But it is always the devout, the undisputed faithful, who insinuate themselves into the mass suggestion of 'holy events' – in a way described by Jacques Hochmann[22], psychiatrist and psychologist at the University Clinic in Lyons, France, in connection with the psychodrama performance:

There is the theoretical model of a 'sociometry' at the centre of which is the social atom. This atom is to be understood as the nucleus which is formed by the attracting and repelling relations in an individual environment. These relations consist of a network of interrelational* chains, which are aroused by affective currents.

But a homogeneous society of 'social atoms' is only formed

* From relationalism. The doctrine that relations have an objective existence.

at places of pilgrimage such as Lourdes, where the pilgrims are definitely bound to each other by 'affective currents'. It does not exist at places where curiosity and the human mass hope for miracles are thrown together.

Apparitions announce themselves to 'visionaries' when the latter are in a state of hypnotic compulsion and what I can only call helplessness. The apparition always safeguards itself by specifying time and place.

'I want you to come here on the 13th of next month,' the vision ordered the three Fatima children. And the Madonna appeared punctually at the promised spot. On 13 July 1917, 2.30 p.m. was exactly astronomic noon for the geographical position of Fatima. (Why?) Again the beautiful lady summoned the children to a meeting on the 13th of the following month at the same place. The flow of information from the vision (transmitter) to the visionaries (receivers) had been set in motion.

So far, so good. But why are visions tied to time and place? I can only suggest a fantastic possibility which admittedly does not fit in very well with the so-called known facts. But I think it is better to put forward a theory than to lurk in the underground like a coward. In doing so I am quite conscious of the warning that the historian Egon Friedell (1878-1938) wrote in the albums of all those who were too bold:

These are the real miracles. We take hold of a taboo and burn not only our fingers but also our tongues, and we must not be surprised if we unexpectedly find ourselves on fire.

How could people of the other world get in touch with people of this world, or vice-versa, over many light-years* of distance? With radio waves? By light signals or radar? *All* electromagnetic waves are tied to the speed of light. Radio or radar communication would take hundreds and thousands of generations.

The waves carrying television images are decimetre waves,† which move only in a straight line, like light rays. If we were to put television pictures on a ray of light via a bridge of relay stations in order to reach the star Arcturus in the constellation

---

* A light year is the distance travelled by light in a year, about 6,000,000,000,000 miles.

† Electromagnetic waves between 10 and 100^{cm} wavelengths (3×10^9 and 3×10^8 Hz).

Bootes, we could expect an answer in 82 years at the earliest, for Arcturus is 41 light-years from the earth. Even for the present-day postal service that's a bit too long to wait!

The stars Riegel and Canopus, to name two more addresses, are 900 light-years away. If we were to take the trouble 'to transmit', we should not even know whether our two stellar 'comrades' still existed. 'Their' light which hits us today is already 900 years old. Meanwhile a great deal can (and will) have happened on those stars! Why should we call them up? Even if they are still in the best of health and possess an adequate technical civilization, an echo could not reach us for 1,800 years. Who would be interested in that? New different systems of interstellar communications must be invented, for even higher frequency astronomy which sends and receives with gigantic parabolic reflectors to observe celestial objects is unsuitable. So far no one knows the right wave-length! In that case is any form of communication possible between such widely separated intelligences?

Yes, through visions.

The first intelligence was formed sometime and somewhere in our galaxy. Astrophysicists know that solar systems incomparably older than ours exist and therefore presumably much older intelligent beings, too. The earliest intelligences began to ask questions in order to extend their knowledge. Before these intelligent extraterrestial beings planned space travel, they engaged in astrophysical and astronomical research (as our own experts did before they sent the first rockets into the atmosphere). When they began to build spaceships their mathematicians and ballistic experts got together and calculated that, given the high velocity of the spaceship, time was different for the launching planet and the crew of the spaceship.

Inconceivable?

It has long been scientifically proved that different times hold good on interstellar flights at high speed. Time dilation, as this time shift is called, was first 'discovered' in our day, but it is an 'eternal' law, which was equally valid for the first space-travelling intelligences. What am I to do, says Zeus? was the question Friedrich Schiller asked in his poem 'Dividing the Earth'. What are we to do? was also the question the extraterrestrial beings asked themselves. How were they to realize the goal of their expedition, namely increasing their knowledge, if millennia would have passed when they returned from their journey into space? If there was no one left alive at home who could evaluate and benefit from the fruits of their voyage?

Time and space could only be conquered, said the extra-terrestrial academics, if they arranged for descendants at various times in as many places in the cosmos as possible – naturally 'in their own image'! So the astronauts were trained and given the mission during the long journey to make for all the planets apparently similar to their home planet and land on them. Having thoroughly explored a planet they had to separate the most advanced form of life and make it intelligent by a deliberate *artificial* mutation.* After what pattern? Obviously 'in their own image'.

Thus time was overcome by a fairly simple trick. From then on intelligent groups of their 'kind' – formed in their 'image' – existed at various times on various planets like their home star. The chronological building up of the planned breeding made it possible to hand on acquired experience and knowledge in a quasi-endless relay race, despite the time shift. The expedition's goal of increasing knowledge was assured.

It would be absurd to claim that human intelligence is unique and alone in the cosmos. There may be millions and millions of forms of intelligence in the universe, but envoys with a different form of intelligence from that to which we owe our development have not sought out our planet. What business would a Jupiter intelligence have on Mercury, if conditions similar to his own did not exist? We can find the extraterrestrials' recipe in Homer's *Odyssey*:

It's always the same,
A god keeps company with his peers!

Intelligence similar to ours exists in our galaxy because the extraterrestrials carried out their mission and performed artificial mutations on existing life at several strategic points. Even though we do not yet know it, there are other intelligences in our galaxy that think, act and feel like ourselves. These cosmic families, that are closely related to us, have brains that function *like*

---

* Lat. 'change'. Discontinuous variation or sudden inheritable divergence from ancestral type.

ours; after all they have the same origin, being built in the 'image' of the alien cosmonauts. These brains produce the same reactions to external stimuli as our much underworked thinking apparatuses. Do *they* ignite the first spark of visions?

Why, someone will ask, has the 'lord of Creation' not become intelligent through Darwinian natural selection, evolution* and mutations, as the anthropologists say? Because the whole of the remaining monkey family (our forefathers!) still live in the jungle! Because they had exactly the same period of time at their disposal in which to evolve. Because the number and shape of their chromosomes† is not identical with ours!

Our forefathers, the hominids, had 48 Y chromosomes; *we* have 46 XY chromosomes. I beseech some geneticist to explain to me (and the anthropologists!) how 48 Y chromosomes turned into 46 XY chromosomes and how products of the coupling of different numbers and shapes could multiply successfully? I expect I shall be told that two Y chomosomes grew up together by chance and produced an X chromosome. Why not? There is an obvious snag. The being to which this genetic defect happened, whether male or female, could never mate again with any other hominid because of the disparate chromosome numbers.

In order to accept this quite illogical explanation I would have to swallow the mathematical impossibility of this purely chance chromosome defect repeating itself at approximately the same time, and of this second 'spontaneous mutation' also having met up with the first one by chance! A pair has two parts. If it wants to reproduce itself, both parts must be of the same nature. It is asking too much to offer such a 'solution' to the problem. If you are in the habit of asking awkward questions like this, you often get answers of the same quality.

With regard to the subject of becoming intelligent, the British geneticist Francis Harry Crick, who won the Nobel Prize in 1962 for research into the chemical bases of heredity (DNA), published in the periodical *Icarus*[23] his conviction that life on our earth had become active by extraterrestrial genes. As I have been

---

* The doctrine according to which higher forms of life have gradually arisen out of lower.

† Rod-like portions of the chromatin of a cell-nucleus, performing an important part in mitotic cell-division and in the transmission of hereditary characters. Each species has its own particular number and shape of chromosomes.

attacked from many quarters because of this very hypothesis. I must admit that this article by such a world-famous geneticist made me very happy.

*   *   *

Before I continue outlining my hypothesis that the extra-terrestrial origin of our intelligence is the explanation of genuine visions, I must get rid of the most important objection to my cosmonaut theory.

Eminent astronauts and exobiologists such as Professor Carl Sagan, New York, say that the concept of an extraterrestrial visit to our planet is impossible because, given the vast number of potential planets, the extra-terrestrial beings could not have predetermined the Now, the point when man became intelligent, out of the whole history of human evolution. So if the earth had been visited by extraterrestrial beings say three million years ago, accounts of the event could not have been incorporated into mythology as I claimed in my books. The extraterrestrial beings could not a) have known that our planet was a worthwhile goal, nor b) that hominids had just achieved intelligence on their evolutionary path.

Homo Sapiens only became intelligent *after* the visit by extraterrestrial beings. If the earth was visited three million years ago, then intelligence has existed exactly since that visit. And if we were first to be visited five hundred thousand years in the future, the point now would first exist then. The temporal assumptions are unreal. Whenever the point Now is fixed, it is in any case identical with the visit of extraterrestrial beings to our planet regardless of where NOW is set in the line of time.

We need a great deal more than is available in our present-day state of technology to practise interstellar space travel. The extraterrestrial beings who made us intelligent by artificial mutations were not only centuries ahead of us technically, but also must have had incomparably greater knowledge of the subatomic worlds *and* the *real* faculties of the brain.

If we add to the phenomena of the human brain, as far as we have understood them the faculties of a far superior intelligence, we can form a very rough idea of the IQs of the creators of our consciousness. There is *nothing new* about any form of the extrasensory perception which is the object of so much research today. What we rediscover with great effort and considerable material expense and then try to use and dominate has been programmed in the human brain since that planned prehistoric artificial mutation.

It has long been common knowledge that only 1/10 of our brain is active. What does the dominating remainder of 9/10 do, the remainder which we *could* have at our disposal? Why did natural selection, evolution and mutation produce a brain with a weight of 1,300 to 1,800 grammes if mankind scarcely uses it? Furthermore, the 'beast brain' is capable of incalculably more than is demanded of it in everyday life. Mediums, clairvoyants, telepathists, telekinetists . . . and prophets prove it.

When they 'grafted' their own genetic characteristics on to hominids – a method adopted on a minor scale in plant cultivation and the breeding of domestic animals – the extraterrestrial cosmonauts also transferred their highly developed faculties of extrasensory perception – in 'their own image'. They did not take the trouble to ennoble (= humanize) hominids out of pure altruism, love or as a gracious gift from the vast coffers of their omnipotence, as religions claim.

It was a technical business for the aliens. They had acquired knowledge they wanted to preserve. Knowing that the inhabitants of their home planet would have 'come to dust' long before their return, they set up 'knowledge depots'. These depots became communications centres for all the children they had fabricated in their image.

Next, transmitting and receiving stations were installed in many places. But how were the communications to be established? Electromagnetic waves diverge at great distances, because of the resultant inevitable interference, but there are no obstacles to thought transference. Present-day researchers have proved this clearly in telepathic experiments when they have sent thought waves from transmitting mediums to receivers through several hundred metres of sea. Researchers have also shut up receivers in Faradaic cages protected against all kinds of waves by lead plates. The telepathic signals came through unobstructed.

Nevertheless language was an insuperable obstacle to telepathic news transfers of this kind. The bright cosmonaut mutation specialists had foreseen the development of different languages. Made exactly after their pattern, in 'their image', they knew that the new race with its various species would have enemies and wage wars. So the development of different languages as a kind of secret code in the nascent family of races was unavoidable – as a safeguard against their enemies. But different moral and ethical concepts would also take shape along with different languages, and scientific and technical knowledge would be expressed in different ways. The news radiated by transmitter X would not be understood by receiver Y because of the language barrier. The only way left was that of emotional and visual telepathy! Feelings such as love, trust, hate, danger etc. would be understood everywhere, just as *pictures* would be understood by commonsense.

In fact every genuine vision begins with the receipt of soothing news. 'Peace be with you.' 'Do not be afraid.' Such emotional telepathy is possible and effective between intelligent beings. Words like 'love' and 'peace' were not transmitted in any one language: they would not have been universally understood. (Esperanto, which aspires to be a universal language remains in the ghetto of the language laboratory.) So *feelings* of love and peace were sent out. The emotional transmission was strengthened and consolidated by pictures and *symbols*. Pictures are international and intercosmic. The Mona Lisa's smile gives pleasure in both Paris and Tokyo.

Music was used as a third frequency. Vibrations and shock harmonies that clash with one another excite the neurons of the brain and release oscillations, conversions of energy.

The elderly are often completely disconcerted by modern music. A new consciousness of the strange oscillations has appeared among present-day youth. The electronically produced cosmic oscillations of the music get right under their skin, just as sub- or supraconscious cerebral layers are activated by the influence of drugs. We should not forget that on the LPs preferred by young people, organs and synthesizers with their echo vibrations are always used as stimuli for expanded consciousness. It is strange that such new 'worlds' appear simultaneously everywhere and are not tied to national or regional taste.

What is the force that *suddenly* makes a composer in Korea hit on the same kind of music as his colleagues in London,

Paris, New York or Berlin? What is the reason for the sudden dominance in painting of surrealism or abstraction? Where do these recognizable limited impulses come from? Because the new kind of music or painting is 'in demand' and modern? Why is something suddenly in demand and modern? The waltz was once modern and fashionable in the western world, though it did not animate Hindus and Indians. Did it not penetrate into the layers of consciousness in which a *common* feeling is programmed?

In spite of the existing gaps in the chain of evidence, I take it as accepted fact that the human brain can register finer and more sensitive oscillations than the most delicate apparatus. No measuring apparatus has ever recorded 'love'. But since brilliant scientists have also been smitten by it, they cannot deny that love exists. The conversion of elements is fully accepted in physics and chemistry. Are other principles meant to be valid for the human brain?

Professor George Ungar[24] of Baylor Medicine College, Houston, Texas, has proved by thousands of animal experiments that brain cells are activated by electrical impulses and form a new matter — memory molecules. He says: 'whether we like it or not, we must take as our starting point today the fact that in the long run our brain is a storehouse for millions of memory molecules and also an apparatus for "playing" them.'

Thought molecules in the brain are circuits by which programmed knowledge can be summoned up. They are material. Once made to oscillate, they influence the micro-parts of the antimaterial world. Emotions cause the same effect in the brain, as the physicist achieves in his syncroton (accelerator for imparting high energies to elementary particles) by electron volts. Each of us carries such energy converters inside him in the form of hate, love, joy, sadness, sympathy, envy. In the normal states emotions release normal reactions. The trance, a state reached by suggestive or hypnotic means, raises para-normal faculties to a higher power. That much is *proved*, even if the forces that bring it about have not yet been confirmed.

The English physicist and chemist, Sir William Crookes, who was already well known, experimented in his laboratory with the medium Daniel Douglas Home. Sir William believed that there was a force which made contact with the body by unknown means. During the experiments the medium D. D. Home —

lifted by invisible forces — rose several feet above the ground. Sir William wrote:

This fantastic event . . . did not take place once or twice in bad light, but was repeated hundreds of times in every conceivable condition. . . . Once Home even floated out of one window at a height of 70 feet and floated in through another. Such distinguished gentlemen as Lord Dunraven, Lord Lindsay and Captain Wynne, who were eyewitnesses, were prepared to confirm this fact on oath[25].

A similar event took place in 1938 before 300 spectators with the English medium Colin Evans as protagonist. This levitation* was photographed at various stages. People have speculated and will continue to speculate about the nature of the forces which cause these phenomena. I should not like to put any chips down on a roulette wheel which spurts out this kind of energy: there are too many possibilities and too few chances of winning. Isn't it enough to know that the forces are there and can be recorded and proved? The mere fact of their existence is quite enough to give us a good idea why figures in visions float in the air and seem to be weightless. Was a statue from Lourdes seen in a garden at Beauraing a case of levitation? Were not similar objects levitated by means of psychokinetic phenomena at other sites where visions were seen? Such open questions should be included in present-day research programmes.

*   *   *

Let us stick to the premises. Extraterrestrial beings visited other solar systems, too, and left behind scions in their image on suitable planets. Some groups of their descendants have an advantage over us. They tamed, developed and trained the 'beast brain' earlier than we did. (As they were visited by the alien astronauts before us in time, they could have an advantage over us of several millennia, owing to time displacement.) These ultramature intelligences are transmitting energetic thought impulses intended to stimulate and extend consciousness in us their brothers and sisters of the same origin. I am firmly convinced

---

* The floating of the human body in the air, attributed solely to saints, fakirs and mediums. In psychokinesis the levitation of objects is also known.

that *this* also explains the failure of all temporal and ecclesiastical dictators to restrict human consciousness and direct it in one particular direction for any length of time.

I am prepared for the question: why did the super-intelligent extraterrestrials leave no apparatus with which they could establish communications with those left behind simply by pressing a button?

Well, astronauts do not normally take heavy apparatus with them on long journeys, unless they are necessary for the navigation, steering etc. of the spaceship. But in this case, they would have to cram in hundreds of transmitting and receiving sets, because they were playing a game of creating intelligence at many many places in the cosmos. With all their technical abilities, they obviously did not consider *us* as their exclusive masterpiece, the unique crown of their creation.

The next question, then, is why did they not build communication centres themselves? But the 'second' in the world process at which they made us intelligent 'in their image' by mutation, found us hominids unprepared. A vast technological infrastructure would have been needed for such a complicated undertaking as the building of interstellar communication centres – factories that could print integrated circuits and produce chemical semi-conductors, etc. None of that existed at hour 'O' of the birth of our intelligence.

Even on the hypothetical assumption that the alien visitors had brought a suitable transmitting and receiving station with them, they could scarcely have deposited it on the planet earth, which was faced with earthquakes, floods and wars – after all, they weren't stupid! The passage of time alone, together with climatic changes, would have destroyed it. The cables and apparatuses the American astronauts left on the moon have already disintegrated, even though the moon has no atmosphere. The extremes of heat and cold alone were enough to do the damage.

The extraterrestrial visitors had made no mistakes in their planning! They *knew* that all mechanically produced and radiated transmissions were tied to the speed of light – they *knew* that electromagnetic waves could not reach the receiving sets over vast interstellar distances. So what was the point of a lot of senseless and useless machinery?

The visions of genuine visionaries advance mankind along the path of its development with giant strides. It is always surprising to find out the fields in which the advances are made: the spectrum of their potentialities is broad. In this connection I think it is important to realize that *every* brain is able to receive visions in so far as it is trained and ready to receive definite impulses through specific fixed points in the environment which influences it – in other words if it is open to communication with extraterrestrial fields of energy.

When I say that all persons trained along egocentric paths are predisposed to visions, there are the (rare) extraordinary cases where the extraterrestrial beings find the 'receivers of the millennium', the geniuses, whose brains seem to be waiting for the impulses with their grey cells vibrating. Leonardo da Vinci was one of these 'receivers of the millennium'! Born 1452, died 1519, he is generally known as a painter, architect and sculptor. Few people know that he was equally gifted as a natural scientist and technician. Da Vinci scholars have made fantastic discoveries about him in the last few years. As a painter he marked the zenith of the classical style; but as a scientist his works belong to our own age.

He was the first technologist in the history of mankind. In his book of patterns of mechanical elements he described problems of hydraulics, dynamics and statics.

He was the first inspector of fortresses under Cesare Borgia: he drew maps which are the earliest examples of modern cartography.

He was asked for advice as 'war engineer' and produced plans for diverting the Arno in order to deprive Pisa, which was waging war with Florence, with its main artery of communication.

He dissected corpses and wrote a treatise on human anatomy.

He investigated the flight of birds and the laws governing air currents, and drew plans for constructing an aircraft.

His sketches contain a doctrine of the original mechanical forces in nature, a whole cosmology.

Through geological observations, he was led to investigate the origin of fossils. His biological studies made him the first scientific illustrator.

He realized that there would never be a *perpetuum mobile* because of the laws of gravity.

G

For Sultan Bayazid II he conceived a bridge over the Bosphorus – '12,000 ft over the sea, 600 over the land'. Such a bridge has been in service – since 1973.

He invented a two-stage rocket which could fly 'more than three miles'.

He devised a machine-tool for cutting cylindrical bore holes, of the kind that has long been indispensable for manufacturing ball-bearings.

He developed a gyroscopic system, like the one invented for blind flying by Sperry Rand, but not until 1920.

The multi-barrelled machine gun in modern jet-fighters can be found on da Vinci's drawing paper.

Leonardo da Vinci.

He lived to the age of 67.

He was painter, sculptor and architect. Brilliantly endowed. My notes on his fields of study are far from complete.

Each individual branch of knowledge he mastered would normally have needed years of study; each individual result would have been the issue of a whole lifetime's work.

Surely an enormous, almost inconceivable amount of knowledge, must have been stored in Leonardo's brain? After all, his artistic production and his scientific researches and plans are worlds apart!

Genius is not just diligence or the intelligent use of reason. I suspect that genius is mainly the ability to open a highly trained brain to extraterrestrial energies. The extraterrestrial beings *know* what primordial knowledge is stored in the grey cells. If they did not know it, they could not make the fuel of genius spark.

That's it.

The communication medium was and is the 'beast-brain'. From the conveyor belt of modern research flow scientific proofs that man possesses parapsychological faculties which are against 'natural' laws. Only now, on the threshold of the third millennium, are we mentally capable of discovering the brain's unknown potentialities and perhaps of using them usefully and sensibly in future. We are taking our first hesitant steps towards mutual communication.

A few 'initiates' – I am not speaking of religious figures – have always had access to the wonderful unconscious, from which they summoned up great discoveries in *visionary* form. The Danish physicist Niels Bohr (1885-1962), who laid down the foundations of atomic theory, has described how he finally hit on the idea of his atomic model after years of vain research[26].

Niels Bohr dreamt he was sitting on a sun of burning gas. Hissing, spitting planets rushed by him and they all seemed to be attached to the sun they were circling by fine threads. Suddenly gas, sun and planets contracted and solidified. At this moment, said Niels Bohr, he awoke. He knew at once that what he had seen in his dream was the atom model.

Niels Bohr was canonized for this vision in 1922 – I beg your pardon – awarded the Nobel Prize for Physics!

To me this 'dream' has the value of a vision. Hissing and spitting before the event, gas which solidifies and forms an image . . . I have heard all that before in another connection. Physicists have *their* world: they live daily and hourly with their formulae, diagrams and plans. Those are *visual signals*, which accompany them everywhere they go. Dialogues and discussions with colleagues, assistants and students revolve round their physical problems – *acoustic signals* which are ever present. The stress of their work causes a 'psycho-feedback' which they cannot escape. Consequently physicists can only have visions of images from their working world, like Niels Bohr who had been fixated on the search for 'his' atom model for years. It appeared to him in a vision. We know whence religious enthusiasts draw their visual and acoustic signals.

In my opinion the physicist's 'dream' was caused by extra-terrestrial impulses. They recalled the 'image' programmed in the unconscious – owing to psycho-feedback the atom model was present. Bohr's brain was trained for this exceptional case! We must liberate ourselves from the absurd idea that visions are a religious privilege. That is only true if we accept religion's claim to exclusiveness. The great men of the intellectual world are not clever enough to make capital out of their visions. They suddenly had an idea . . . they suddenly 'saw' the solution of a long-posed question clearly before their eyes . . . the unconscious whispered something to them and it was an 'inner voice' which spoke to them. They describe the syndrome of many visions simply as a 'brilliant idea'. What sort of a saint would an ecclesiastical organization have made out of Albert Einstein if he had his brilliant ideas suddenly and by inspiration as one of their sheep!

The great Niels Bohr was not the only scientist who frankly admitted that ideas that changed the world came to him in dreams.

For example, there was the chemist Professor August Kekulé von Stradowitz (1829-1896) – and what would the world be without his flash of genius? – who made vitally important advances in the theoretical bases of organic chemistry in the nineteenth century. Kekulé discovered the quadrivalence of carbon and said that the truly revolutionary image of the 'closed-chain' structure of benzene (1865) had appeared to him suddenly as if in a dream. This visionary image became the basis of what is now the most important basic material for chemical manufacturing.

There was also, to name just one example from our own day, the physiologist and pharmacologist Professor Otto Loewi (1873-1961), who taught at Graz and emigrated to New York. His fields of research were the physiology of the metabolism and the physiology and pharmacology of the vegetative nervous system. Once again we must ask what would have become of mankind without the visionary dream that helped Loewi to become the first man to demonstrate the chemical transference of nervous impulses in the nervous system (previously scholars had assumed that the transference was electrical). In 1936 Otto Loewi was awarded the Nobel Prize for Medicine (for his dream). Just imagine our stress-ridden world without a single tranquillizer or any of the neuropsychological medicaments, and you will realize the epoch-making significance of Loewi's vision. When he 'received' it, he was ready for the impulses which, so I believe, extraterrestrial beings transmit when they think X day has come.

There is one more comment I want to make.

In 1968 I was spellbound and absorbed by *The Double Helix*, unquestionably a unique book in its description of a scientific discovery that took place gradually. The book was (and is) all the more stimulating because the author, Harvard Professor James D. Watson, and his colleagues Francis H. C. Crick and Maurice H. F. Wilkins, solved one of the greatest mysteries of life: the make-up of the DNA molecule which contains all the hereditary information and cell-building plans of a living creature. In 1962 the team received the Nobel Prize for Medicine.

I share the opinion of *Nature*'s critic, who said that if Watson had not already been awarded the Nobel Prize for Medicine he should have got the prize for literature. What I had read in 1968 left me with the unforgettable impression of having been within an ace of participating in the growth of a discovery myself. Because it all stayed so fresh in my mind, I picked up the book seven years later and read it again when my years of investigation had spurred me on to track down the phenomenon of visions. Now the sequence of signals that drove the researchers on appeared to me in a new light. Watson related how lightning-like and often phantasmagoric hints at possible solutions kept on cropping up, whether he was playing tennis, flirting or spending a pleasant weekend. Unannounced and unwanted (because he was amusing himself), a signal relating to the subject of his research would appear in his brain quite unexpectedly, in situations that were worlds apart from his university laboratory. . . . 'I huddled as close to the chimney as possible and dreamed of several DNA chains folded up in attractive and scientifically productive ways. . . . Soon after it had struck midnight, I was much happier. How often had Francis and I worried that the DNA stucture might turn out to be quite boring in the end. . . . But now, to my surprise and delight, the solution proved to be extremely interesting. I lay awake for more than two hours, sleepless but happy, and saw a pair of adenin remains whirling round before my eyes. Only for brief moments was I afraid that such a good idea could be wrong. . . .'

These two quotations from Watson's book were not specially chosen by me: these flashes of summer lightning on the way to the goal form the excitement of the book. From the point of view of my theory of visions, Watson's detailed account indicates how he and his highly trained intellectual team were dominated by a series of encouraging impulses and finally by the idea that solved the problem, all of which came from an intelligent energy-emitting force. These men, who thought in formulae and codes, who thought the structures of molecules in images, who speculated in discussion, were suddenly 'ripe' for the summoning up of the discovery from their unconscious by extraterrestrials. Obviously this is still a speculation, but I am firmly convinced that from time immemorial, namely from the day on which *homo sapiens* was made intelligent by artificial mutation, knowledge stored in the brains of selected people has been summoned up. Always on X day.

Such impulses, such dreams, have the value of visions for me. Physicists and doctors have *their own* world, they live daily with their *images*, their formulae diagrams, X-rays of organs and nerve structures and with the reactions of sick and healthy people. Those are their *visual* signals, which follow them everywhere. Dialogues and discussions circle round their specific problems – acoustic signals which are always present. The continuing stress of their research work produces a 'psycho-feedback' which they cannot escape. Consequently *these* men can only have visions (=dreams) from their own world. They call the inspirations ideas, and if they are not afraid of their colleagues they sometimes speak openly of the dreams they have had.

In my view, dreams, as I have proved by certain examples, are released by extraterrestrial impulses. 'Images' programmed in the unconscious are summoned up from it, because the brains were trained for this exceptional case. We know where religious zealots draw their visual and acoustic signals from.

The situation seems clear to me. *Extraterrestrial impulses* cause the brain to produce visions. The vision itself is *not* extraterrestrial; it 'reveals' the image desired by the visionary. An Arabic visionary 'sees' Mohammed or his youngest daughter Fatima, a Hindu 'sees' Brahma, Vishnu or Shiva, a Red Indian 'sees' Manitu . . . and a Catholic 'sees' Jesus, the Blessed Virgin, angels and saints. Every recipient of a vision reproduces the religious world of ideas familiar to him.

If the news of a Christian vision becomes public and is mysterious and attractive enough, it is accepted by the Church (provided it fits into the traditional system); or it is cast out root and branch, if the visionary rejects the version which is built up by suitable questioning.

At the moment the visionary comes into the sphere of an extraterrestrial impulse field – as I should like to call it – he becomes a medium. He cannot avoid the impulses which reach his brain. The brain begins to produce figures which are only visible to him. Visions may be immaterial or material (ectoplasmic materializations), but they are always *real to the visionary*. Even though outside 'courts' presume to do so, it is impertinent to decide and judge which visions are genuine and which are not. It is *not* the Blessed Virgin who gives the order to say the Rosary. This order is inspired by the religious trappings with which the Christian visionary's inner life is decorated. That is also where he gets the images of the beautiful ladies, archangels and saints which become the objects of his visions.

What happens in the brains of the numerous child visionaries?

'Something' flashes in the brain (radiated by extraterrestrial impulses). It is repeated. The child feels frightened. He seeks a refuge. A feeling of peace and security comes over him unawares. He 'sees' mist, fine undulating veils, the air seems to shimmer, somewhere a light shines. These unreal illusory images, in which the child *would like* to recognize the familiar portraits of Lord Jesus or Mary, suddenly take shape. Finally he sees the familiar figures in the puzzle picture. He enjoys hearing messages of love and peace from them. A feeling of joy overcomes the child, he would like to nestle against them.

A hint is necessary.

Children are not specially selected by the extraterrestrials. They do not know which receivers are in the energy field of their impulses. Strictly speaking the fact that children so frequently have visions would be pure chance, were they not ideally prepared for the supernatural by their intensive religious upbringing, by their introverted life concentrated on the figures of the church. The childish brain is full of naïve belief, crammed full of Christian images, sayings, stories and hymns. When extraterrestrial energies penetrate into minds thus prepared they produce *exclusively* religious visions. In other words, children are predisposed by their religious environment. The extraterrestrials do not create the conditions.

In fact, faster than light communications produced oscillations in the sub- or supraconsciousness, and communication with extraterrestrial beings was established. The impulses simply produced graphic (mute) representations of peace, love and security, which the childish brain then transferred to the figures of the Holy Family.

This takes the following form in the official records of investigations of visions:

I know with absolute certainty that I had a vision.

I know that the vision disturbed me at first (fear) and then calmed me (love, peace).

I felt that the vision was strong and powerful; it was greater and more beautiful than anything I ever saw before.

The vision did not actually say anything, but I sensed its wish and desire to spread peace. (If visions took place in time of war, these feelings of the visionary would always become an appeal for peace − an expression of the general subconscious!)

I mean that all men would become one with the vision. (Symbol of the extraterrestrial; we were a unity originally.)

Visionaries do not realize how their visions take place. This realization is deliberately withheld from them, because the extraterrestrial impulse field could be destroyed by their defensive reactions. For the visionary faced with the phenomenon, the only alternatives are GOOD and BAD. If it is good, it can only have been a manifestation of God − transformed into figures such as Jesus, Mary, Buddha, Shiva, Mohammed etc. If it is bad the vision can only have been from the devil and he has hundreds of terrifying masks and lots of evil words on his lips. In cases where the religious visionary is still sceptical about identifying the figures he has seen, the Church takes very good care to see that he is left in no doubt.

Why do the visionary figures so often want to have a pilgrimage church built on the site where they appear? There may be two reasons. The visionary was once very happy at the scene of the vision and experienced the most wonderful moments of his life there. Confused by the sensation, he manages to give such a wonderful description of what he saw that everybody who would like to share in the promises and future miracles wants to erect a church. And no Church refuses buildings offered by those with money to burn.

It is a wonderful experience for the visionary. He keeps on returning to the place where he was so happy . . . like lovers who always seek out their own bench in the park to recapture their former bliss. Hypothetically we can assume that the extraterrestrial contact partners had picked out the place as particularly favourable and wanted to make sure that mutual contact was possible there. Is that why visions appear exclusively in places where there is no interference? It would not occur to anyone to set up radio-astronomic aerials in terrain occupied by heavy industry.

* * *

I am going to be the advocate of my own devil.

Why must or should visions have anything at all to do with extraterrestrial beings? Are not visions purely the figments of psychopathic imaginations? Are not even genuine (photographed) visions caused by unknown powers of the human brain? So why bring in extraterrestrial superbeings?

As soon as contact exists between visionary and vision, *every* vision spontaneously announces that it is 'extraterrestrial'.

In the Christian vocabulary it goes like this:

'I am the mother of the universe.'

'I am the queen of heaven (Cosmos).'

'I am the immaculate conception.' (Highflown description of the original artificial mutation?)

The visionary describes transmitted groups of symbols in the words at his disposal, using analogous images.

The claim made by visions to be of extraterrestrial origin would not be sufficient by itself. For example, when an angel appears to the eighteen-year-old Joseph Smith, the founder of the Mormon Religion, and says he knows the secret place where tablets with the history of mankind are hidden, and if it then turns out that the tablets are found exactly at the spot described, this means to me that extraterrestrial beings have given Joseph Smith information that could only be known to them. (Because they prepared the hiding place on our planet thousands of years ago!) What was later made out of the vision phenomenon (it was Jesus!), belongs to the fairy-tale factory in which religions are manufactured. 'Belief, not disbelief, is what is dangerous in our society'[27].

However much these interesting details may arouse our interest, we must not lose sight of a central phenomenon, the solar miracle! Whether at San Damiano, Fatima or Heroldsbach, tens of thousands observed – and put it on record – a gigantic flying wheel with spokes, revolving furiously in the sky. Sometimes this wheel slowed down its revolutions; it moved in front of the sun and past it. Who is not reminded of the grandiose space-station in the film *2001* by such descriptions? Space-stations are like gigantic wheels which turn slowly on a central axis. This creates in the external rooms round their 'equator' the artificial gravity that is necessary for interstellar journeys. In the centre, at the hub of the wheel, are the energy stations from which the propulsive forces are led to the actual 'wheel' down spokelike communication shafts.

Is that *also* a possible explanation of solar miracles? I do not think it is out of the question. The tens of thousands who witnessed the phenomena are no fools and their descriptions of what they saw tally to such an extent that some 'object' must have existed for them to see.

Space journeys over interstellar distances last for thousands of years, according to our terrestrial chronology. I consider it plausible that extraterrestrial brains akin to ours order 'visionaries' through apparitions to lead large groups of people to a place named by them on a day and at an hour also named by them. At this point of time X the space-station, travelling somewhere among the stars, uses its concentrated energy to transmit the *picture of the station*. Result: tens of thousands of receivers on our planet *see* a gigantic gleaming wheel, flashing all colours of the rainbow, that sails majestically past the sun. Then why is this phenomenon not visible from all places illuminated by the sun? Well, the extraterrestrials, by fixing the specific place and specific time, had also chosen the angle from which their signals would be perceivable (via visions).

The question remains why the extraterrestrials started such a manoeuvre. To me it is conceivable that they wanted to give a clear sign. 'Here we are: we live in a great space-station and you puny men must understand that your intelligence originates from us who are capable of staging such a spectacle.'

We earthworms crippled by our upbringing do not realize this, but turn the message into a religious miracle. I'll wear sackcloth and ashes if I'm wrong, but I can't see miracles in physical events.

Genuine visions have been vitally concerned in opening up the consciousness of mankind. All founders of religions, who went among men inspired by these phenomena, announced that it was not they themselves who were speaking, but that 'that which is in me and above me' was speaking through them. *De facto* they often told mankind about new things which were far above the state of knowledge and experience of their time.

But, thank heaven, founders of religions and adepts were not the only recipients of visions. There are also the great brains which got their ideas from contacts with extraterrestrial beings. We talk of geniuses. They are the chosen few, those ripe for contact, who are able to convert extraterrestrial impulses into thought molecules. The scientifically trained and investigating brain, which grasps symbols and transforms them into knowledge, does not talk about visions. At some point in the biographies of the great men in human history moments occur in which visions, illuminations or inspirations caused the great turning point or the decisive earth-shattering realization (the idea). The justification of the visions of great men is their contribution to mankind.

Religions, especially their founders, use visions like 'crumbs which fall from their masters' table' (Matthew, 15, 27). The visions that are useless from the religious point of view, the visions and illuminations which great men get from the supernatural, are the ones which bring progress.

They are the ones I believe in.

A CALENDAR OF VISIONS

No one knows the countless number of visions that have been received since men were able to think. In order to give a rough idea of the extraordinary gamut of visions (with visions of Mary predominant in the Christian era), I have prepared a calendar composed *solely of those cases* I came across during the writing of this book. If investigators collaborated in listing all known visions in the world and the results were compiled at a central research centre, the result would certainly be a work with many more volumes than the *Encyclopaedia Britannica*.

The following is a very brief resumé:

Mythology: The Slavic Fates, the Sudenica, who appeared after the birth of a child, frequently showed themselves in threes at midnight.

Borovit, the Slavic wood spirit, appeared as shepherd or wolf.

A tall, green 'Water Man', bedecked with aquatic plants, frequently appeared to Croats, Slovenes and White Russians.

Csodasiuszarvas, a kind of flying stag, appeared to the ancient Hungarians, surrounded by radiant light.

Bodb, Irish goddess of battles, sometimes appeared in the form of a crow.

The Irish Mother Goddess Macha appeared to various heroic figures in hideous guise. If the heroes did not do what Macha wanted, she turned them into beautiful maidens.

The Roman god of war, Mars, appeared to Numa Pompilius (715-672 BC), second King of Rome.

Valkyries appeared on wild flying horses and intervened in battles.

The Celts believed that the hero Finn could turn himself into the stag Mongan by twisting his cape, and appear anywhere he wished in this new transformation.

In addition to many other gods, the god Huracan constantly appeared to the Maya and gave them instruction.

Angels and archangels often appeared to our ancestors, Adam and Eve, and so did gigantic revolving flying wheels.

c.5,000 BC   The divine sister Inanna appeared to Enme-Kar, the ruler Uruk, and advised him how to overthrow the city of Aratta.

c.4,000 BC   Various divinities appeared to Gilgamesh, King of Uruk, and gave him wise counsel.

c.3,500 BC   The Sumerian gardener Shukallituda saw the goddess Inanna resting in his garden.

c.1,500 BC   After Manu had survived the Flood on the peak of the Himalayas, the God of the Universe Brahma appeared to him and transmitted the 'Laws of Manu'.

727-722 BC   Tobias, hero of the apocryphal Book of Tobit, who lived in the time of the Assyrian King Salmanazar, had a vision in Mesopotamia of the Archangel Raphael.

c.500 BC   Buddha, the Enlightened One, received his wisdom from the 'Universal Spirit' in visions.

204 BC   Ptolemy IV decided to have all the Egyptian Jews killed. Two radiant angels of terrifying aspect appeared and paralysed the attacking army.

c.287   In the open country two angels watched over the corpse of St Vicentius of Valencia, Spain.

c.300   Angels, who liberated him from prison, appeared several times to St Erasmus, Bishop of Antioch.

c.300   The cross of Christ and a dove which promised her the heavenly martyr's crown appeared to St Regina in the prison at Alice-St-Reine, France.

c.303   The devil appeared to St Juliana of Ismir, Asia Minor, in the form of an angel.

c.303   Christ appeared to St George of Lydda (now Ludd, near Jaffa, Palestine), when he was in prison, and consoled and fortified him.

c.303   Sts Cosmas and Damian were saved from the sea at Aegea, Asia Minor, by an angel.

c.303   St Timothy of Rome was consoled by angels, saw the heavens open and Christ holding out the martyr's crown to him.

c. 304   St Dorothy of Caesarea in Cappadocia had a vision of a golden-haired boy in star-studded raiment with a little basket full of roses and apples.

c.304   When St Vitus was in prison in Sicily, angels illuminated the darkness of his cell.

c.307   When St Margaret of Antioch, Asia Minor, was in prison,

Satan, the tempter, appeared to her in the guise of an enormous dragon.

c.311 A white dove brought food to St Katherine of Alexandria, Egypt, in prison and an angel consoled her. Katherine and the Empress saw angels, who applied ointment to their wounds.

311 St Adrian appeared to his wife after his death.

c.312 The body of St Katherine of Alexandria was carried to Mount Sinai by angels.

c.334 Christ, wearing the remnants of his clothing, appeared at night to St Martin of Amiens, France.

7.5.351 At eight in the morning, in broad daylight, a radiant cross appeared to the inhabitants of Jerusalem.

356 When disciples were burying St Anthony of Heraklea, Egypt, angels were seen standing round him.

c.356 Peter appeared to St Servatius of Tongern, Belgium, and handed him a silver key.

30.8.357 St Cyprian saw God the Father floating above the clouds.

c.398 On several occasions an angel gave St Onuphrius communion at Goreme, Cappadocia.

452 In Mantua, Italy, Attila, King of the Huns, saw Peter and Paul with drawn swords standing next to St Leo.

c.458 Peter appeared to St Leo I, the Pope, at Rome and handed him the pallium (a white woollen papal vestment).

5th cent. When on her deathbed, St Tharsilla saw Jesus descend and cry: Go back, go back! Jesus comes!

547 The Benedictine monks of Montecassino, Italy, saw St Benedict carried up to heaven by angels on roads that shone brightly and were covered with carpets. St Benedict himself saw the soul of St Scholastica flying up to heaven as a white dove.

589 Gregory the Great, Saint and Pope, hid in a cave, but was discovered by a pillar of light on which angels ascended and descended.

610 The angels of Allah appeared to Mohammed, the founder of Islam.

627 St Heraklius, Emperor of Byzantium, saw an angel, who opened the city gates of Jerusalem to him.

c.648 Christ, in the guise of a beggar, appeared thrice to St Jodokus, St Josse-sur-Mer, France.

651 Cuthbert, saint of the Anglo-Saxon and Celtic church, saw a great light in the sky one night in Ireland and angels ascending heavenwards, carrying a soul with them.

735 The inscription on the grave of the Venerable Bede of the Monastery of Yarrow, England, was found one morning already carved by angelic hands.

c.750 The infant Jesus appeared to St Alto, Italy, during Mass.

814 Christ appeared to St Anskar, the great missionary of the north, on the night of Whit-Sunday.

819 St Cecilia of Rome appeared to Pope Paschalis I, when he was looking for her tomb.

970 St Othmar appeared to Wolfgang of Regensburg at Einsiedeln, Switzerland.

973 Two angels with chalice and paten appeared to St Ulric at Augsburg, Germany, when he was dangerously ill. The hand of God raised in blessing and emerging from golden rays became visible to him.

c.981 A wolf appeared to St Wolfgang while he was praying in church at Regensburg, Germany, and the devil disappeared in a rage.

1008 Churchgoers at Valenciennes, France, saw visions of the Blessed Virgin during a time of pestilence.

c.1020 An angel is supposed to have brought a reliquary to St Bernhard of Hildesheim, Germany.

August, 1060 Jesus and the Queen of Heaven appeared to St Albert in the village of Espain, France.

16.1-17.4.1095 The 'Queen of the Universe' appeared in the clouds to all the inhabitants of the town of Arras, France.

c.1100 St Anselm of Canterbury, England, saw Mary many times.

1110 The Madonna and angels appeared to St Bernard of Clairvaux, France.

c.1114 While St Isidore of Madrid, Spain, was praying, two white oxen, driven by an angel, were seen ploughing.

1117 At Cremona, Italy, a one-year-old baby suddenly spoke and described a very beautiful, non-existent lady.

1155 When St Dominic of Spain was baptized, his nurse saw a golden star on the child's brow.

1186 A swan with a chalice out of which the infant Jesus climbed is supposed to have appeared during Mass to St Hugh of Lincoln, England.

1170-1221   St Dominic of Spain saw himself face to face with Christ, who had drawn three spears against the evil of the world. Peter and Paul also appeared to him and gave him a staff and a book with his mission to preach. The saint's mother saw a black and white dog, which lit up the whole world with the torch in its mouth. Mary gave St Dominic a rosary and explained its laws to him.

c.1180   A stag with a blue and red cross on its antlers appeared to Sts Felix of Valois (1127-1212) and John of Matha.

2.8.1218   The Blessed Virgin appeared to St Peter Nolasco at Barcelona, Spain, and persuaded him to found the Order of our Lady of Ransom to rescue captives from the Moors.

1219   The 'Queen of Heaven', accompanied by two beautiful maidens, appeared to Dean Reginald of Orléans.

c.1221   Mary and the infant Jesus appeared to St Anthony of Padua, Italy.

7.10.1224   Our first ancestor, Adam, and seven very beautiful maidens appeared above Schloss Bardenbourg to the wife of Theobald, Count of Luxembourg.

September 1224   Jesus conferred the five wounds he received at the crucifixion (the stigmata) on St Francis of Assisi at Monte La Verna, Italy.

c.1225   Ludwig of Thüringen, husband of Elisabeth of Thüringen, Germany, saw Christ crucified lying in his bed.

22.12.1226   The Son of God appeared on several occasions to St Aegidius of Assisi, Italy.

c.1228   While St Elizabeth of Thüringen, Germany, was praying, an angel adorned her with jewellery and gleaming light.

c.1232   The Virgin Mary appeared several times to Hermann Joseph, Hoven-in-der-Eifel, Germany, during his night watches.

c.1250   An angel gave communion to St Bonaventure of Pisa, Italy.

1263   During Mass in the church of St Christina of Bolsena, Italy, a drop from the chalice is reputed to have appeared to a German priest as blood on the cloth covering the host.

c.1277   A star appeared above the altar to St Nicholas of Tolentino, Italy; he also saw angels round the altar.

c.1288   Christ often appeared to St Angela of Foligno, Italy, and showed her his wounds.

c.1299 Jesus frequently appeared to St Gertrude of Helfta, Germany, in the Convent of Helfta.

c.1315 The Madonna appeared to St Birgitta of Sweden when she was only a child.

1320 When St Rock of Piacenza, Italy, was sick of the plague, he was healed by an angel.

1328 The Mother of Grace appeared to St Andrew Corsini on the day he celebrated his first Mass. In a later vision Mary is supposed to have warned him of his imminent death.

No date When St Aegidius of St Gilles, France, was praying before the altar, an angel brought him a piece of paper confirming the forgiveness of his sins.

c.1362 Christ gave St Katherine of Siena a wedding-ring while she was praying.

18.8.1370 The stigmata of our Lord appeared on the body of St Katherine, after a visionary experience.

3.10.1399 Christ, accompanied by Dominic and Francis, appeared to the ailing St Vincent Ferrer at Avignon, France, and stroked his cheeks.

c.1413 The Blessed Virgin and her son appeared to St Lidwina at Schiedam, Holland.

c.1424 Joan of Arc, from Domrémy, France, saw the Archangel Michael and other saints.

26.5.1432 Gianetta di Pietro Vacchi saw Mary promising peace at Caravaggio, Italy.

1438 A 'wonderful' lady was seen above the roofs of Bologna, Italy, by the inhabitants.

c.1440 The monogram of Christ (IHS) is reputed to have appeared above the head of St Bernardine of Siena while he was preaching a sermon.

2.3.1440 During the last 23 years of her life, St Frances of Rome constantly saw an angel by her side.

1449 Mary appeared to a woman at Anderlecht, Belgium, and desired to be venerated as 'Dame de grâce'.

c.1450 While St Didacus, a Spanish laybrother, was praying in ecstasy, angels did all the cooking for him in the monastery kitchen.

1463 St Katherine of Bologna, Italy, saw the 'Lord sitting on a gleaming throne'.

3.5.1491 While the smith Dieter Schöre was riding to market in Niedermorschweier, Alsace, Mary appeared to him in a white mantle and veil, holding an icicle in one hand and three ears of corn in the other.

10.8.1519   The Blessed Virgin was seen by the worker Jean de la Baume when she suddenly appeared standing above the hills of Mont Vardaille, France.

1521   When Martin Luther was translating the Bible on the Wartburg near Eisenach, Germany, he had a vision of the devil on the wall of his turret room; he banished it by throwing an inkpot at it.

1550-1561   The Blessed Virgin repeatedly appeared to Sebastian Baraddas at Lisbon, Portugal, and urged him to join the Jesuit Order.

c.1564   Jesus and Peter appeared to St Theresa of Avila, Spain.

16 cent.   The miraculous image of Adlwang, Diocese of Linz, Austria, was torn down and buried by Protestants. It was only rediscovered when mysterious rays of light shone from beneath an ants' nest in the church. It is said that the ants could not be driven out until the image was set up again in its rightful place.

c.1571   Jesus Christ appeared to Anna of St Bartholomew at Avila, Spain, and urged her to fight against the unfaithful.

1582-1591   The chronicler of the Capuchin Order, Zacharias Boverius, recorded that over many years 30 brothers, who were named by name, had seen members of the Holy Family at different times in different places.

30.10.1593   A gigantic motionless eagle with 'gleaming feathers' appeared above Zittau, Germany. Rays shot at the bird from all sides, but were powerless against it. An hour later, the apparition vanished.

1594   Mary is reputed to have appeared to Indians who wanted to leave the new faith in Quito, Ecuador, and kept them in the Church by saving them from famine.

1596   The Capuchin Abrosius of Ziron related that he saw the 'fortunate Mother of our Lord' several times in 1580. She commanded him to honour all orders, but to join the Capuchin Order.

1600   When the Araucani stormed the town of Concepcion, Chile, a miraculous image of the Madonna is supposed to have left the chapel and appeared in a tree, from which it pelted the Indians with clods of earth and put them to flight.

10.9.1602 Christ appeared to Marina of Escobar in the form of a seraph from whose wounds rays were emitted.

6.4.1604 Father Jakob Rem, Ingolstadt, Germany, saw Mary floating above the ground.

1605 The Jesuit Peter d'Anasco was pressed against the breast of a vision of Mary.

1609/10 An image of Mary and the infant Jesus became famous at Chiavari, Italy, owing to two miraculous visions. 'Miraculous events' took place.

15.12.1631 The 'Queen of Heaven' appeared above a corn field near Naples to several Jesuits, to whom she announced the imminent eruption of Vesuvius.

3.11.1637 Mary and the infant Jesus appeared to Frère Fiacre, Paris, in his cell.

1640 Jesus Christ appeared to the Jesuit Brun-Brun, who was awaiting execution in an Ethiopian prison, and told him to have courage.

1654 When he was out hunting, the farmer Dietrich Müufahrt of Aldenhoven near Aachen found in the branches of a tree a miraculous image which he and two friends revered with a miserere every night. It always produced a wonderful light. Today the pilgrimage church stands on the spot.

1647 The Blessed Virgin appeared to a farm girl and a lay-brother in Buenos Aires, Argentine, and ordered them to exhort everyone to do penance.

8.11.1660 A bloody sword that was visible to everybody appeared in the sky at Görlitz, Silesia.

1671 Marguerite Marie Alacocque, France, had already had visions of Mary in her worldly life; after she entered the Salesian Order she had more visions of Christ.

1679 Wonderful luminous apparitions repeatedly appeared over the pilgrimage church at Albendorf, Germany.

c.1682 Our Lord, with his body pierced with wounds, showed himself to Veronica Giulani at Mercatello, Italy.

1696 The bishop of Quito, Ecuador, had a miraculous cure when he was dangerously ill. The miraculous image of Guapulo had been brought for an evening procession. When the Gloria was sung, Mary appeared as Queen of Heaven.

21.9.1823 Joseph Smith, founder of the Mormon religion, had a vision of an angel who disappeared on a shaft of light going up to heaven. Subsequent visions led Smith to a secret place where he found the gold tablets that he translated. That was how the Mormon Bible originated.

1835 In Trinitapoli, Italy, Mary told the six-year-old Joseph Maria Leone, who had fallen into a ditch, to be a good boy and stop playing with his naughty friends.

28.1.1840 In Paris, the nun Justine Bisqueyburu saw Mary with her flaming heart pierced by a sword and wearing a white robe and a blue mantle.

8.5.1840 Jean-Baptist Vianney, the Curé of Ars, and Mme Etienne Durié, saw a vision of Mary in his room. The Madonna was in a white dress dotted with golden roses; her brow was encircled with a crown of stars and diamonds flashed from her hands.

8.9.1840 The nun Justine Bisqueyburu had a further vision at Blangy, Seine-Inférieure, France. It appeared to her in a green scapula.

20.1.1842 Alphonse Ratisbonne, a former Jew, saw the Virgin Mary in a side chapel of the church of St Andreas delle Fratte in Rome. She looked exactly as she did on the medal he had been wearing for some time.

14.8.1842 The nun Maria-Stanislaus frequently saw the Blessed Virgin in the 'Classroom of the Poor' in the Convent of the Visitation at Celles, near Tournai, Belgium.

19.9.1846 The Madonna appeared to the children Maximin Giraud (11) and Melanie Calvat (15) at La Salette, Isère, France. She wore a gleaming white robe and held a conversation with them.

12.5.1848 On the morning and afternoon of the same day, the farm labourer Stichmayer of Obermauerbach, Bavaria, saw Mary in the meadows. She wore a pink dress, with a white veil and a gold crown. She sat there motionless and wept.

23.6.1848 Eleven citizens of the village of Montessé, near Lourdes, France, had repeated visions of Mary.

17.6.1849 Three shepherdesses had several visions of Mary at Dolina, near Poggersdorf-Gurk, Kärnten, Austria.

19.5.1853 Veronica Nucci of Ceretto in Tuscany, Italy, had frequent visions of the Madonna in a blue robe decorated with flowers and wearing a gold crown.

22.7.1856 Marie-Frederike de Bray saw Mary as Queen of the Angels after a miraculous cure at Assisi, Italy.

11.2.1858   St Bernadette Soubirous had several visions of the Blessed Virgin at Lourdes, France, when she called herself the 'Immaculate Conception'.

1860   At Green Bay, USA, Mary appeared to Adele Brisse in a white robe with a yellow belt.

6.9.1860   After experiencing several visions of Our Saviour, the mystically gifted Pauline Périé saw the Madonna in the church at Francoules, France. She looked very young, wore a dress dotted with stars and a gold crown, and carried small white flowers in her hand.

1863   Mary, as Queen of the Angels, showed the Reverend L. E. Cestac, founder of the monastery of N. D. du Réfuge, Anglet, France, how devils destroyed the world.

13.1.1866   Magdalena Kade, 30, of Philippsdorf, Bohemia, Czechoslovakia, was on her deathbed, when Mary appeared to her and cured her.

15.4.1868   In Bois d'Haine, Belgium, the blessed mystic and stigmatic Luise Lateau had visions of Jesus, Mary, angels and saints.

2.12.1870   Mary appeared to the wounded General de Sonis, former commander of the papal Zouaves, on the battlefield near Potay-Loigny, France, and consoled him.

1871   During a vision of Mary, Maria Kalb was shown a cave in the Inntal near Locherboden, Innsbruck, Austria.

17.1.1871   At Pontmain, France, seven children saw the Blessed Virgin in a dark blue robe with pale gold stars, a black veil, gold crown and broad sleeves 'like a lawyer's'.

4.8.1871   Marie-Françoise Décotterd, who had been ailing since her youth, experienced two visions of Mary in her sick-room at Chapelles, near Lausanne, Switzerland.

15.8.1871   After several visions of Mary, Barbara Conrad, 9, was suddenly healed of her illness at Walschbronn, France.

25.8.1871   Mary in a white robe and gold crown of stars appeared to Therese Schaffer, who was dangerously ill, at St Louis, USA.

5.12.1871   In Paris Sister Thérèse Emmanuel de la Mèrede Dieu had a revelation of a future Marianist host which the Virgin would follow as recruiting officer.

7.7.1872   Clementine G., saw the Virgin for a whole hour in the church at L'Hôpital, France. She wore a golden robe, had a ball in her hand and was surrounded by German and French soldiers.

1873   Soon after nocturnal visions of Mary on several occasions, two little girls died near Michelsberg in Rixheim, near Mühlhausen, France.

10.3.1873   Mary, in a blue robe and white veil, appeared to Catherina Filljung near St Avold, France.

17.3.1873   Many persons of all ages had numerous visions over a lengthy period at Wittelsheim, Alsace.

14.4.1873   Several people, but especially Joseph Hoffert, of Walbach, Alsace, France, had visions of Mary, 'Our dear lady on the Rhine'. She urged them to pray and do penance.

7.6.1873   During work in the vineyard at Saint-Bauzille de la Sylvie, Montpellier, France, Mary appeared to August Arnauld and asked him to set up a statue of Mary in the vineyard and organize a procession.

19.2.1876   Estelle Faguette, Pellevoisin, Indres, France, who was dangerously ill, had 15 visions of Mary.

3.7.1876   Three children and some adults experienced visions of numerous angels and a dove above the infant Jesus.

27.6.1877   Four females of different ages in Dietrichswalde, near Allenstein, East Prussia (now Poland) had 160 visions of Mary over a lengthy period. Sometimes she was floating, sometimes sitting, but always surrounded by a radiant cloud and accompanied by angels.

21.8.1879   Cnoc Mhuire, Ireland. 15 visionaries of various ages saw Mary wearing a white dress and a crown. Her hands were raised in prayer and she was silent. On her right was St Joseph, on her left St John the Evangelist, as well as an altar with a sacrificial lamb on it.

2.1.1882   In the hospital at Lyons, France, Anne-Marie Coste saw Mary on a cloud in a magnificent dress and precious diadem. She carried the infant Jesus in her arms, holding a globe with a broken cross.

1884   Maria Lordeau of St Columbin, France, had several classic visions of Mary at the age of nine.

29.11.1886   Marie-Louise Nerbolliers, 27, had a vision of the Madonna at Diémoz, France.

22.3.1888   Two virgins, aged over 30, had a vision of Mary first as Pietá and later as Our Lady of Sorrows in a cave at Castelpetroso, Italy.

8.5.1890   Mary, in a cloud of light, with a long veil held by angels, hands folded and silent, appeared to the children Alfred and Marie Caileaux at Signy, France.

1893   Berthe Petit saw Christ crucified, with Mary and John, during Christmas Mass at Enghien, Belgium. Some years later she saw the Sacred Hearts of Jesus and Mary, pierced by a sword.

1895   'Our Dear Lady with the Infant Jesus' appeared to the ailing Krishnannesti Sankaranarayanam, 12, at Vellangany, India.

18.3.1896   50 schoolchildren at Tilly-sur-Seulles, Bayeux, France, had visions of Mary with angels and saints.

1906   A ball flashing white light and floating above the ground appeared to Professor Charles Richet, Nobel Prize Winner.

1906   During breaks in the classroom of the Jesuit College San Gabriel at Quito, Ecuador, teachers and pupils saw the image of the suffering Madonna open and shut her eyes several times and change her expression.

12.9.1914   A voice told the farmer's wife Eudokia Andrianova at Potschinki that a black icon was hidden at Kolomenskoye, near Moscow. The icon was found there.

13.5.1917   After an unexpected flash of lightning, three shepherd children of Fatima, Portugal, saw Mary in a gleaming white robe, with a brilliant crown of roses, floating above an oaktree.

22.5.1918   Three children had 65 visions of Mary at Muzillac, near Vannes, France.

8.12.1921   Anna-Maria Goebel had numerous visions of Our Saviour at Bickendorf, near Trier, Germany.

10.12.1925   Mary, on a shining cloud with the infant Jesus, appeared to Sister Lucie at Couvent de Tuy, Spain.

July 1926   At Marlemont, France, Maria P, 6, twice saw Mary weeping. Maria P was so moved that she tried to wipe the tears from the floor.

2.3.1928   At Ferdrupt, Vosges, France, children had a vision of the Blessed Virgin, in white (without mantle!), but with rays shooting from her hands.

8.4.1930   Sister Amalia, co-foundress of the Institute of Missionaries of Christ Crucified, had several visions of Mary at Campinas, Brasil.

22.6.1931   At Ezquioga, Spain, many people of all ages (including unbelievers) had a vision of Mary as immaculate, as Our Lady of Sorrows, accompanied by angels and saints.

29.11.1932　At Beauraing, Belgium, the five Degeimbre children saw Mary in a white dress and veil, with a gold crown and often a golden heart.

15.1.1933　The 'Mother of Heaven' showed herself to the twelve-year-old Mariette Beco at Banneux, Belgium.

16.7.1933　Children at Crollon, near Mont-St-Michel, France, saw Mary dressed in white, with a crown of roses.

4.8.1933　Mrs Nieke von den Dijk, ailing mother of 13 children, had many visions of Mary at Onkerzeele, Belgium. On 28.12., she saw a greenish-red revolving sun.

2.10.1933　Jules de Vuyst, 40, saw Mary surrounded by light in his room at Herzele, Belgium.

22.10.1933　At Olsene, Flanders, Belgium, Mary dressed in blue with a wreath of stars appeared to Maurice Vandembroeck.

11.4.1936　Emelda and Adeline Pietcquin of Ham-sur-Sambre, Belgium, saw Mary surounded by angels in a clear blue sky.

1.11.1937　At Heede, Emsland, Germany, four girls aged between 12 and 14 saw Mary in a cemetery, with the infant Jesus and a gold crown.

15.8.1938　At Bochum, Germany, Ursula Hibbeln frequently saw Mary as the 'snow-white lily of the most holy Trinity'.

15.9.1938　'A young lady', magnificently clad in blue, appeared to the farmer's wife Jeanne-Louise Ramonet of Kerizinen, Brittany.

9.12.1939　For a long time the villagers of Kerrytown, Co. Donegal, Ireland, saw the shining figure of Mary above the cliffs.

13.5.1940　The 'Queen of the Rosary' appeared to Bärbel Ruess, 16, at Pfaffenhofen, Germany. Six years later she had more visions.

19.6.1940　Thérèse Coat of Bodennou, near Brest, France, saw Mary and child in dark clouds.

18.6.1940　Mme Jeanette Tochet saw Mary in all the variations of her holy personality at Ortoncourt.

1943　Mr and Mrs Débord, Paris, saw the Pietá watching her child.

8.12.1943　The villagers of Grinkalnes, Lithuania, saw the Virgin one evening in a crown of rays above the church.

13.5.1944   Adele Roncalli had 8 visions of Mary at Bonate, near Bergamo, Italy. She wore a white dress, white cloak and a precious diadem.

27.5.1945   Several visions of the Madonna as Our Lady of Sorrows were seen first by Marcelina Barossa, 10, then by adults, too.

11.6.1946   Adults and children saw Mary, crowned with stars, in a cloud at Pasman, Dalmatia.

22.8.1946   For several years adults and children saw visions of Mary, angels and saints at Espis, near Mossac, France. The visions could be relied on to appear on the 13th of the month.

10.10.1946   At Vilar-Chao, the sick girl Amelia Nahiridade had visions of Mary in the presence of thousands of spectators.

12.4.1947   The Adventist Bruno Cornacchiola, 34, and his three children had several visions of Mary in the grotto of Tre-Fontane, near Rome. She wore a white dress, a pink belt, green veil, and had a little book in her hand.

27.6.1947   The Madonna appeared to the children Anton and Bertus van der Velden at Vorstenbosch, Holland, in a sky-blue dress and golden crown of lilies.

2.7.1947   Mary appeared to Clara Laslone in her house at St Emmerich-Berg, Hungary, and showed her a healing spring for the sick.

4.7.1947   At Tannhausen, Germany, Mrs T. Paula, 48, saw Mary on various occasions in a wreath of gleaming white roses.

16.11.1947   Mary as 'Rosa Mystica' appeared to the nurse Pierina Gilli in the street and later in the church of the Convent of the Sisters of Mercy at Montichiari, Italy.

26.12.1947   Mary appeared to the girls Thérèse Le Cam, Annik and Monique Goasguen from Pleskop, near Vannes, France, as the Immaculate Conception.

19.5.1948   Mary appeared first to four children, then to many inhabitants in a cave at Marta, near Viterbo, Italy.

12.9.1948   Mary often appeared to the novice Teresita at Lipa, Philippines. She wore a white dress, crown of roses, with hands first folded, then outspread.

11.11.1948   Men of Aspang, Austria, saw a cloud stop above the Königsberg, become lighter and split open. From it floated Mary in a blue mantle, with a gold crown, and holding the rosary.

7.12.1948   Louis Mercier, father of a family and a Communist, and eleven other men, saw a silent Madonna at Liart in the Ardennes, France.

18.12.1948   A brief vision of Mary was had by Mme Lucie Manteau, 23, of St Jean-aux-Bois, France.

1.5.1949   During the Civil War, Christians at Zo-se, Shanghai, saw Our Lady of sorrows above the church while Mass was being celebrated.

12.5.1949   Senta Roos saw Mary in a long white dress, gold crown and whitish-yellow rosary, at Fehrbach, near Pirmasens, Germany.

July 1949   A statue of Mary in the cathedral at Lublin, Poland, wept bloody tears for two whole days.

9.10.1949   First four, then seven, little girls and later up to 300 adults in Heroldsbach-Thurn, Bavaria, had many visions of Mary, mostly as queen with ample blue mantle and gold crown.

14.3.1950   Pina Mallia, 12, saw Mary in a white robe with sparkling diadem at Casalicchio, Italy.

7.4.1950   At Casalicchio and Acquaviva, Italy, thousands claimed to have seen a cloud parting and in it a bright star and a shining sun, which revolved and radiated every conceivable colour.

11.9.1950   Mary appeared to the schoolgirl Mary Ellen, 15, on a cloud at Denver, USA. Wrapped in a veil, she wept and crossed her arms over her breast.

30.10.1950   According to an express communication from Cardinal Tedeschini, Pope Pius XII several times saw a rotating sun, like the solar miracle of Fatima, in the Vatican Gardens.

Autumn, 1951   The 'Virgin of the Poor' appeared to Luigia Nova, 39, at Arluno, near Milan, Italy.

19.8.1951   Mary and the infant Jesus appeared to three workers in a chalk works at Dugny, France. She wore a white robe and a blue mantle.

1.7.1952   At Rodalben, Germany, in the presence of some 60 people, Anneliese Wafzig, 26, received a drawing in blood of heart, chalice and host on a white linen cloth during a vision.

10.7.1952   Rosette Colmet, 7, saw Mary at Gerpinnes, Belgium. She wore a white dress decorated with red and blue hearts.

Early 1953   O. Lavoisier, 10, and later 50 adults, saw Mary in a cave at Hydrequent, near Calais, France. Blue robe, white veil.

August 1953   Galileo Sacrestani, a 49-year-old cook, had several visions of the Madonna on Monte Senario, near Bivigliano, Italy.

19.7.1954   Two evangelical housemaids frequently saw Mary in a halo of flashing rays at Pingsdorf, Germany.

Autumn 1954   At Eisenberg, Germany, Anna Lex, 6, saw Mary floating in a gleaming sphere.

1.7.1958   The forester Matousch Laschut, 42, affirms that from 1st July to August 1958, he saw Jesus seven times at Turzovka, Czechoslovakia. Our Saviour was always in an equilateral triangle full of roses. Turzovka became a place of pilgrimage.

18.6.1961   At Carabandal, Spain, four little girls had visions of the Archangel Michael and the Virgin over a period of weeks. Solar miracle.

29.9.1961   Mrs Rosa Quattrini of San Damiano, Italy, had visions of the 'Queen of the Universe' and various figures in the Holy Family.

2.4.1968   In the Cairo suburb of Zeitun, on several consecutive evenings, an apparition consisting of a very bright light appeared above the domes of the Coptic Church. Believers identified it as the Blessed Virgin.

12.4.1974   An 'otherworldly' face appeared on a chalice cloth to all the congregation in the church of Castalnaud-en-Guers, France.

Bibliography

AGRIPPA, H. C., *Magische Werke* (1486), Neudruck, Anton Hain, Meisenheim, undated.

ALFVEN, Hannes, *Worlds – Antiworlds*, London, 1966.

ARAM, K., *Magie und Zauberei in der alten Welt*, Berlin, 1927.

ARNOLD, Frankl., Dr, *Gemeinschaft der Heiligen und Heiligungs-Gemeinschaften*, Lichterfelde-Berlin, 1909.

BAERWALD, RICHARD, *Der Okkultismus in Urkunden (Intellektuelle Phänomene)*, Berlin, 1925.

BARB, A., *Klassische Hexenkunst*, Vienna, 1933.

BEAL & SCHULTZE, *Buddhas Leben und Wirken*, Leipzig, 1894.

BECK, C. H., *Menschenzüchtung*, Munich, 1969.

BENDER, H., *Biologie und Biochemie der Mikroorganismen*, Weinheim, 1970.

BENDER, H., *Parapsychologie*, Bremen, 1970.

BENDER, H., *Unser sechster Sinn*, Stuttgart, 1971.

BENDER, H., *Telepathie, Hellschen und Psychokinese*, Munich, 1972.

BENDER, H., *Verborgene Wirklichkeit*, Olten, 1973.

BENZ, E., *Die Vision, Erfahrungsformen und Bilderwelt*, Stuttgart, 1969.

BLUMRICH, Joseph, *Da tat sich der Himmel auf, Die Raumschiffe des Propheten Ezechiel und ihre Bestätigung durch modernste Technik*, Düsseldorf, 1973.

BÖRNSEN, H., *Naturwissenschaft an der Schwelle (Studien und Versuche*, Vol. 7), Stuttgart, 1964.

BOXBERGERE and GLASENAPP (Translators), *Bhagavad Gita*, 1955.

BRAUNBEK, W., *Korpuskularstrahlen*, Stuttgart, 1952.

BRAUNBEK, W., *Atom-Energie*, Stuttgart, 1953.

BUTTLAR, Joh. von, *Reisen in die Ewigkeit*, Düsseldorf.

CALDER, N., *Das Phänomen der kleinen grauen Zellen*, Düsseldorf, 1972.

CALDER, N., *The Life Game*, London, 1973.

CENTURIO, N. A. Dr, *Nostradamus*, Bietigheim, 1971.

CORDAN, W., *Das Buch des Rates, Mythos und Geschichte der Maya*, Düsseldorf, 1962.

CUMONT, F., *The Mysteries of Mithra*, London, 1903.

DÄNIKEN, E. von., *Chariots of the Gods*, Souvenir Press, London, 1969.

DÄNIKEN, E. von., *Return to the Stars*, Souvenir Press, London, 1970.

DÄNIKEN, E. von., *The Gold of the Gods*, Souvenir Press, London, 1973.

DÄNIKEN, E. von., *The Däniken Picture-Book*, Souvenir Press, London.

DAVID-NEEL, A., *Meister und Schüler, die Geheimnisse der Lamaistischen Weihen*, Leipzig, 1934.

DAVIS, A., *What Your Dreams Mean*, New York, 1969.

DEBON (Translator), *Tao-Te-King, Das heilige Buch vom Weg und von der Tugend*, 1964.

DELACOUR, J.-B., *Stimmen aus dem Jenseits*, Munich, 1973.

DELACOUR, J.-B., *Vom ewigen Leben*, Düsseldorf, 1974.

DELACOUR, J.-B., *Die Kunst des Hellsehens und Gedankenlesens*, Geneva, 1974.

DESCHNER, Karl-H., *Kirche des Unheils, Argumente und Konsequenzen zu ziehen*, Munich, 1974.

DESCHNER, Karl-H., *Der manipulierte Glaube*, Munich, 1971.

DIETERICH, A., *Eine Mythrasliturgie*, Leipzig, 1923.

DOPATKA, Ulrich, *Kontakt und Echo (als Manuskript)*, Solothurn, 1974.

DOYE VON SALES, F., *Heilige und Selige der römisch-katholischen Kirche*, Leipzig, 1929.

DRAKE, W. R., *Gods and Spacemen in the Ancient East*, London, 1973.

DUCROCQ, A., *Atomwissenschaft und Urgeschichte*, Hamburg, 1957.

EBERHARDT, P., *Das Rufen des Zarathustra*, Ludwigsburg, undated.

EGGENSTEIN, K., *Der unbekannte Prophet Jakob Lorcher*, Bietigheim, 1973.

EIBL-EIBESFELD, I., *Der vorprogrammierte Mensch*, Vienna, 1973.

EILERS, W., Dr, 'Die Gesetzsstelle Hammurabis' (In: *Der Alto Orient*), Leipzig, 1932.

EINSTEIN, A., *The Evolution of Physics*, London, 1938.

ELIADE, M., *The Myth of the Eternal Return*, London, 1955.

ERNSTING, Walter, *Wanderer zwischen drei Ewigkeiten*, Düsseldorf, 1959.

ERNSTING, Walter, *Sprung ins Jenseits*, Munich, 1967.

FALKE, Robert, *Buddha, Mohammed, Christus*, Gütersloh, 1908.

FARADAY, A., *Dream Power*, London, 1972.

FIGUIER, G. L., *Histoire du Merveilleux dans les temps modernes*, Paris, 1860.

FORELL, U., *Wunderbegriffe und logische Analyse*, Göttingen, 1967.

FRESE, W., *Die Sache mit der Schöpfung*, Munich, 1973.

FRIEDLÄNDER, Max, *Religionen und Konfessionen*.

FRISCHAUER, P., *Es steht geschrieben. Die grossen Dokumente*, Zurich, 1967.

GAUQUELIN, M., *Die Uhren des Kosmos gehen anders*, Berne, 1973.

GENZMER, F., *Edda, altnordische Dichtung und Prosa* (2 vols.), Düsseldorf, 1963.

GERBER, J., *Der Verkehr mit der Geisterwelt Gottes*, Teaneck, 1970.

GLASSENAPP, H. von., *Die nichtchristliche Religionen*, Frankfurt, 1957.

GLASSENAPP, H. von., *Die grossen Religionen des Ostens* (Sep. Abzug 'Organisator', Zurich), undated.

GRABER, Rudolf, *Die Weltreligionen im Blickpunkt Albert Schweitzers*, Berlin, 1953.

HADAM, K., *Jesus Christus*, Düsseldorf, 1949.

HAUCK, F., *Theologisches Fach- und Fremdwörterbuch*, Munich-Göttingen, 1967.

HAUER, J. W., *Toleranz und Intolaranz in den nichtchristlichen Religionen*, Stuttgart, 1961.

HEBERER, G., *Homo — unsere Ab- und Zukunft*, Stuttgart, 1968.

HEILER, Friedrich, *Die Religionen der Menschheit* (Reclam), 1962.

HEINDEL, Max, *Die Weltenschaung der Rosenkreuzer*, Zurich, undated.

HEISENBERG, W., *Physics and Philosophy*, London, 1959.

HELL, V. and H., *The Great Pilgrimage of the Middle Ages*, London, 1966.

HESSE, P. O., *Der Jüngste Tag*, Bietigheim, 1967.

HILTGART, L. Keller von, *Reclams Lexikon der Heiligen und der biblischen Gestalten*, Stuttgart, 1968.

HOENN, K., *Sumerische und akkadische Hymnen und Gebete*, Zurich, 1953.

HORNEY, K., *Our Inner Conflicts*, London, 1946.

HÜBNER, Paul, *Vom ersten Menschen wird erzählt*, Düsseldorf, 1969.

HUDSON, P., *The Devil's Picture Book*, New York, 1971.

IRANSCHÄR, H. K., *Zarathustra-Worte, Urtext übersetzt und ausgelegt*, Olten, 1968.

JACOBSON, N. O., *Leben nach dem Tod?*, Düsseldorf, 1973.

JEREMIAS, A., Prof., 'Der Sohleier vom Sumer bis heute' (In: *Der alte Orient*), Leipzig, 1932.

JORDAN, Placidus, *The Divine Dimension*, Dublin, 1970.

JUNG-STILLING, *Theorie der Geisterkunde*, Nuremberg, 1808.

KAHL, J., *The Misery of Christianity*, Harmondsworth, 1971.

KARLINS, M. and ANDREWS, L. M. *Biofeedback*, New York, 1972.

KEHL, Robert, Dr, *Sexus und falsche Schuldgefühle*, Zurich, 1965.

KEHL, Robert, Dr, *Jesus, der grösste Betrogene aller Zeiten*. (Schriftreihe 'Stiftung für universelle Religion'), Zurich, undated.

KELLER-GRIMM, M., *In Lichte des Meisters*, Ratingen, 1970.

KERNER, Justinus, *Die somnambulen Tische*, Stuttgart, 1853.

KOCH, H., Dr, *Constantin der Grosse und das Christentum: Ein Vortrag*, Munich, 1913.

KOESTLER, A., *Roots of Coincidence*, London, 1972.

KRASSA, Peter, *Als die gelben Götter kamen*, Munich, 1973.

KRASSA, Peter, *Gott kam von den Sternen*, Freiburg, 1974.

KURTH, H., *So deute ich Träume*, Munich, 1968.

LEHMANN, Johannes, Dr., *Die Jesus GmbH.*, Düsseldorf, 1972.

LEHMANN, Johannes, Dr, *The Jesus Report*, Souvenir Press, London.

LEIPOLDT, J., *Von den Mysterien zur Kirche*, Leipzig, 1961.

LEIPOLDT, J., *Die Religionen in der Umwelt des Urchristentums*, Leipzig, 1826.

LEIPOLDT, J., 'Dionysos', Angelos-Beiheft 3/1931.

LEIPOLDT, J., 'Die Religion des Mithra' (In: Bildatlas von Dr Hass), Leipzig, 1930.

LESTREL, H., *Fabrikation von Menschen*, Munich, 1971.

LINDENBERG, W., *Über die Schwelle*, Munich, 1973.

LINDNER, H., *Physik im Kosmos*, Leipzig-Cologne, 1971.

LINDQUIST, S., *Siddhi und Abhinna, eine Studie über die klassischen Wunder des Yoga*, Uppsala, 1935.

224 Bibliography

Löbsack, Th., *Die unheimlichen Möglichkeiten oder die manipulierte Seele*, Düsseldorf, 1967.

Lovell, Bern., *Signale aus dem Weltall*, Munich, 1970.

Maeder, A., *Selbsterhaltung und Selbstheilung*, Munich, 1947.

Magopholis, *Neue Gallerie des Geheimnisvollen*, Weimar 1860.

Manns, P., *Die Heiligen in ihrer Zeit*, Mainz, 1966.

Mattiessen, E., *Leben und Werke der hiligen Margareta Maria Alcoque*, Heidelberg, 1926.

Mattiessen, E., *Das persönliche Überleben des Todes*, 1936.

Mensching, Gustav, *Die Söhne Gottes*, Wiesbaden, undated.

Monroe, R. A., *Journeys out of the Body*, London, 1972.

Montgomery, R., *A Gift of Prophesy, the Phenomenal Jeane Dixon*, London, 1966.

Osten-Sacken, P. von der, *Die neue Kosmologie, Astronomen auf der Suche nach der Wirklichkeit unsere Welt*, Düsseldorf, 1974.

Pakraduny, T., *Die Welt der geheimen Mächte*, Wiesbaden, undated.

Panaillar, Raimundo, *Religionen und die Religion*, Munich, 1965.

Paul, G., *Die dritte Entdeckung der Erde*, Düsseldorf, 1974.

Paul VI, Pope, *Das Credo des Gottesvolkes, gesprechen zum Abschluss des Glaubenjahres am 30 Juni 1968*, Leutesdorf a. Rh., 1968.

Peek, W., *Fünf Wundergeschichten aus dem Asklepieion von Epidauros*, Berlin, 1963.

Popp/Pleticha, *Wir leben seit fünf Sekunden*, Würzburg, 1970.

Pruyser, P. W., *Die Wurzeln des Glaubens*, Berne, 1968.

Rahner, C., *Visions and Prophecies*, London, 1964.

Rahner, K., *Kleines Konzilskompendium*, Freiburg, 1968.

Rebut, R., *Les messages de la vierge Marie*, Paris, 1968.

Robb, S., *Prophecies on World Events by Nostradamus*, New York, 1972.

Rosenberg, A., *Macht und Wirklichkeit des Bösen*, Munich, 1958.

Rüeegg, W., *Die aegyptische Götterwelt*, Zurich, 1959.

Rüeegg, W., *Zauberei u. Jenseitsglaube im alten Ägypten*, Zurich, 1961.

Sacharow, B. Yogi, *Das Öffnen des dritten Auges*, Munich, 1958.

Saher, P. J., *Eastern Wisdom and Western Thought*, London, 1969.

Saher, P. J., *Happiness and Immortality*, London, 1970.

SAUSSERET, C. P., *Apparitions et Révélations de le très Sainte-Vierge*, Paris, 1854.

SCHIRMBECK, H., *Ihr werdet sein wie die Götter*, Düsseldorf, 1966.

SCHLEMMER, J., *Sind wir allein im Kosmos?*, Munich, 1970.

SCHNAPPER, Edith B., *One in All*, London, 1952

SCHOTT, Albert (trans.), *Das Gilgamesch-Epos* (Reclam), 1958.

SCHRADER, H. L., *Der achte Tag der Schöpfung*, Frankfurt, 1964.

SCHULTZE, H., *Die biologische Zukunft des Menschen*, Frankfurt, 1971.

SCHURÉ, E., *The Great Initiates*, London, 1912.

SHERMAN, W., *How to Make EPS Work for You*, New York, 1964.

SINCLAIR, U., *Mental Radio*, London, 1930.

SPALDING, B., *Life and Teaching of the Masters of the Far East*, 2 vols., San Francisco, 1924-27.

STABELL, Th., Dr, *Lebensbilder der Heiligen*, Schaffhausen, 1865.

STADLER, J., Dr, and HEIM, F. J., *Vollständiges Heiligen-Lexikon*, Augsburg, 1858.

STADLER, W., *Botschaft Jesu*, Freiburg, 1973.

STADTER, E., *Psychoanalyse und Gewissen*, Cologne, 1970.

STANGE, Hans O. H., *Die Weisheit des Konfutse* (Insel), 1964.

STAUFFER, Ethelbert, *Jerusalem und Rom im Zeitalter Jesu Christi*, Berne, 1957.

STAUFFER, Ethelbert, *Jesus and his Story*, London, 1960.

STAUFFER, Ethelbert, *Die Botschaft Jesu damals und heute*, Berne, 1959.

STEARN, J., *The Sleeping Prophet*, London, 1968.

STEARN, J., *The Search for a Soul*, New York, 1973.

STEIGER, Brad, *Mysteries of Time and Place*, Englewood Cliffs, 1974.

STELTER, A., *PSI-Heilung*, Berne, 1973.

STIEFVATER, E. W., Dr, Beiträge zum Problem des Magnetismus.

STOCK'S, *Grosses illustriertes persisch-ägyptisches Traum-Buch*, Vienna, circa 1912.

STUTTERHEIM, W., *Rama-Legenden und Rama-Reliefs in Indonesien*, 2 vols, Munich, 1925.

SULLIVAN, N., *Die Botschaft der Gene*, Frankfurt, 1969.

TAYLOR, J., *Black Holes: The End of the Universe?* London, 1973.

TEILHARD DE CHARDIN, Pierre, *The Future of Man*, Collins, 1964.

TEILHARD DE CHARDIN, Pierre, *Man's Place in Nature*, Collins, 1966.

H

226   *Bibliography*

Teilhard De Chardin, Pierre, *The Phenomenon of Man*, Collins, 1959.

Trede, Th., *Wunderglaube im Heidentum und in der alten Kirche*, Gotha, 1901.

Tucholsky, Kurt, *Schnipsel*, Reinbek, 1973.

Tyrrell, G. N. M., *The Personality of Man*, London, 1946.

Ullmann, L., *Der Koran, das heilige Buch des Islam*, Munich, 1964.

Veith, I., Prof., 'Psychiatric Thought in Chinese Medicine' (*Journal of the History of Medicine and Allied Sciences*) Vol. X, 1955/3.

Vogt, H. H., *Das programmierte Leben*, Rüschlikon, 1969.

Vries, T., de, *Der Mensch im wachsenden Weltall*, Munich, 1968.

Warner, S. J., Dr, *Ein Psychotherapeut berichtet von Selbstzerstörung und Selbstverwirklichung*, Düsseldorf.

Weigert, H., *Kleine Kunstgeschichte der aussereuropäischen Hochkulturen*, Stuttgart, 1954.

Weizsäcker-Gopi Krishna, *Biologische Basis der Glaubenserfahrung*, Weilheim, 1973.

Wetter, G., *Der Sohn Gottes*, Göttingen, 1916.

Widengren, G., *Iranische Geisteswelt von den Anfängen bis zum Islam*, Baden-Baden, 1961.

Wimmer, O., *Handbuch der Namen und Heiligen*, Innsbruck, 1966.

Zehren, E., *Der gehenkte Gott*, Berlin-Grünewald, undated.

Zink, Jörg, *Das alte Testament*, Stuttgart, 1966.

* * *

Das Gupta, K. *Essence of Religions*, New York, 1941.

The Bible of the Cansteinsche Bibel-Anstalt, Halle a.S., 1886.

Newspapers and periodicals

Walter Nigg, 'Verabschiedung des Christentums.' (In: *Reformierte Schweiz*, Zurich, 4/1951.)

Christian Lipp, 'Sind Katholiken dümmer?'. (In: *Die Weltwoche*, 28.12.73.)

Helmut Aichelin, 'Die Jesus Bewegung – was ist aus ihr geworden?'. (In: *Esotera*, 4/1973.)

Friederich Baumgartner, 'Wie von einer unsichtbaren Riesenfaust gehoben.' (In: *Esotera*, 9/1973.)

K. O., Schmidt, Direkte Verbindung von Seele zu Seele.' (In: *Esotera*, 3/1974.)

Erich Wunderli, 'Beweise für die Unsterblichkeit.' (In: *Esotera*, 5/1974.)

Francesco Piccolo, 'Der Nazarener hat gesiegt.' (In: *Esotera*, 6/1974.)

Rudolf Passian, 'Erziehung durch Erinnerung an frühere Leben.' (In: *Esotera*, 7/1974.)

Dr Robert Kehl, 'Der Mensch Kehrt zu Gott zurück.' (From: *Die Religion des modernen Menschen*, No. 1, Zurich.)

Dr Robert Kehl, 'Die Kraft des positiven Denkens und die kritische Religionsverkündigung.' (From: *Die Religion des modernen Menschen*, No. 5.)

Dr Robert Kehl, 'Ein neues Schriftprinzip.' (From: *Die Religion des modernen Menschen*, No. 6.)

Dr Robert Kehl, 'Lanzen für Paulus?'. (From: *Die Religion des modernen Menschen*, No. 7a.)

Dr Robert Kehl, 'Ein Wort wird gestrichen.' (Christ und Christentum.) (From: *Die Religion des modernen Menschen*, No. 11.)

Dr Robert Kehl, 'Wahre Toleranz – eine Voraussetzung auch für den Weltfrieden.' (From: *Die Religion des modernen Menschen*, No. 15.)

Dr Robert Kehl, 'Das Ende der Theologenherrschaft.' (From: *Die Religion des modernen Menschen*, No. 16.)

Dr Robert Kehl, 'Den Alten is gesagt worden – ich aber sage Euch, oder "was würde Jesus heute sagen?".' (From: *Die Religion des modernen Menschen,* No. 19.)

Dr Robert Kehl, 'Ein sonderbarer heiliger Geist.' (From: *Die Religion des modernen Menschen,* series 'Ideologische Grundlagen universeller Religion,' No. 12c.)

REFERENCES

Chapter 1 Visions, Do they exist?

[1] FRANZ TENGG, *Ich bin die geheimnisvolle Rose*, Vienna, 1973.
[2] *Marienerscheinungen in Montichiari und Fontanelle* (Immaculata), Lucerne, 1967.
[3] E. SPEELMANN, *Belgium Marianum*, Paris, 1859.
[4] MARIA HAESELE, *Eucharistische Wunder aus aller Welt*, Zurich, 1968.
[5] J. ACKERMANN, *Der fromme Wallfarhter nach drei Aehren*, Colmar, 1856.
[6] KONRAD ALGERMASSEN (and others), *Lexikon der Marienkunde*, Regensburg, 1957.
[7] *Die heilige Schrift des alten und des neuen Testaments*, Zwingli Bible, Zurich, 1961.
[8] EMIL KAUTZSCH, *Die Apokryphen und Pseudepigraphen des alten Testaments* (2 vols.), Hildesheim, 1962.
[9] GUSTAV MENSCHING, *Die Söhne Gottes aus den heiligen Schriften der Menschheit*, Wiesbaden, undated.
[10] H. J. CAMPBELL, *The Pleasure Zones*, London, 1973.
[11] SANCHEZ-VENTURA Y PASCUAL, *Carabandal*, Paris, undated.
[12] *Ibid.*
[13] *Ibid., Die Ereignisse in Carabandal*, Zurich, undated.
[14] H. U. VON BALTHASAR, *Wahrheit*, Einsiedeln, 1947.
[15] CHRISTEL ALTGOTT, *Heroldsbach, eine mütterliche Mahnung Marias*, Rheydt-Odenkirchen, 1969.
[16] PAUL SCHNEIDER, *Heroldsbach – ein geistiges Bollwerk gegen den Bolschewismus*, Frensdorf, 1954.
[17] CHRISTEL ALTGOTT, *Heroldsbach, eine mütterliche Mahnung Marias*, Rheydt-Odenkirchen, 1969.
[18] CATHERINE OF SIENA, *Politische Briefe*, Einsiedeln, 1944.
[19] JUSTINUS KERNER, *The Seeress of Prevorst*, London, 1845.
[20] HOFFMANN/GRATTAN, *Geschichte der Menschheit*, Hamburg, 1961.

230 References

[21] *Das Buch Mormon, Kirche Jesu Christi der Heiligen der letzten Tage,* 1966.

[22] *Der Stern,* No. 22, Hamburg, 1968.

[23] JEAN GABRIEL, *Présence de la très Sainte Vierge á San Damiano,* Paris, 1968.

Marienbotschaften aus San Damiano (Immaculata), Lucerne, 1967.

JEAN GABRIEL, *San Damiano, Ruf an die Welt,* Bulle (Fribourg), undated.

[24] WALTER NIGG, *Die Heiligen kommen wieder,* Freiburg, 1971.

Chapter 2   Who Really Speaks Through The Bible?

[1] JOACHIM KAHL, *The Misery of Christianity*, Harmondsworth, 1971.
[2] JOHANNES LEHMANN, *The Jesus Report*, Souvenir Press, London, 1972.
[3] FRIEDERICH DELITZSCH, *Die grosse Täuschung*, Stuttgart/Berlin, 1921.
[4] ROBERT KEHL, *Die Religion des modernen Menschen*, No. 6a, Stiftung für universelle Religion, Zurich, undated.
[5] JEAN SCHORER, *Pourquoi je suis devenu un chrétien libéral*, 8 Vorträge, Geneva, 1949.
[6] ROBERT KEHL, *Die Religion des modernen Menschen*, Stiftung für universelle Religion, Zurich, undated.
[7] EDUARD SCHWARTZ, *Kaiser Konstantin und die christliche Kirche*, Berlin, 1936.
[8] JOHANNES LEHMANN, *The Jesus Report*, Souvenir Press, London, 1972.
[9] JOEL CARMICHAEL, *The Death of Jesus*, London, 1963.
[10] RUDOLF AUGSTEIN, *Jesus Menschensohn*, Munich, 1972.
[11] RUDOLF PESCH and GÜNTER STACHEL (Eds.), *Augsteins Jesus*, Einsieldeln, 1973.
[12] *Brockhaus*, 1968.
[13] RUDOLF AUGSTEIN, *Jesus Menschensohn*, Munich, 1972.
[14] Philo JUDAEUS ALEXANDRINUS, *Die Werke Philos . . . in deutscher Übersetzung von Leopold Cohn* (6 vols.), Breslau, 1909.
[15] FLAVIUS JOSEPHUS, *The Jewish War*, transl. G. A. Williamson, Penguin Classics, 1959.
[16] EDUARD LOHSE (Ed.), *Die Texte aus Qumran*, Munich, 1964.
[17] HEINRICH ALEXANDER STOLL, *Die Höhle am Toten Meer*, Hanau/Main, 1962.
[18] ANDRÉ DUPONT-SOMMER, *Die Essenische Schriften vom Toten Meer*, Paris, 1959.
[19] MILLAR BURROWS, *More Light on the Dead Sea Scrolls*, London, 1958.
[20] ALBERT SCHWEITZER, *The Quest of the Historical Jesus*, London, 1910.
[21] EMIL KAUTZSCH, *Die Apokryphen und Pseudepigraphen des alten Testaments, Die Testamente der zwölf Patriarchen* (Vol. 2), Tübingen, 1900.

[22] JOEL CARMICHAEL, *The Death of Jesus*, London, 1963.

[23] *Ibid.*

[24] *Ibid.*

[25] GÜNTHER BORNKAMM, *Jesus of Nazareth*, London, 1960.

[26] NORBERT GREINACHER, Professor für Pastoraltheologie, Katholisch-Theologischer Fachbereich, Tübingen University (for example).

[27] ROBERT KEHL, Dr jur., Stiftung für universelle Religion, Frymannstrasse 82, 8041, Zurich.

[28] ROLAND PUCCETTI, *Ausserirdische Intelligentz in philosophischer und religiöser Sicht*, Düsseldorf, 1970.

[29] E. L. MASCALL, *Christian Theology and Natural Science*, London, 1956.

[30] OSTRANDER, S., and SCHROEDER, L., *PSI: Psychic Discoveries Behind the Iron Curtain*, London, 1973.

Documentation re Dr Robert Kehl
Letters [a] to [i]
At this point I should like to thank Dr Robert Kehl for his valuable co-operation and also for his work 'Das Christentum war nichts Neues', which was published by the Stiftung für universelle Religion, Blumenstrasse 40, 4900, Langenthal, Switzerland.
The following notes refer to the letters in square brackets in the text. The literature is in the General Reading List.

[a] These details are mainly based on the authors Cumont, Deschner, Glasenapp, Heiler, Leipoldt, Mensching and Stauffer.

[b] N.B.: Deschner, Falke (p. 54), Jordan (pp. 150 *et seq.*), Heiler, pp. 45, 183, 353, 383, 499), Mensching (pp. 43 and 126), 'Taoteking' (p. 13).

[c] Cf.: Buddhalehre (pp. 15 *et seq.*), Deschner (literature, p. 38), Falke (p. 133), Heiler (pp. 209 and 323), Jordan (p. 154), Mensching (p. 211) and 'Universelle Religion', Nos 7/8, 1973.

[d] Cf.: Falke (pp. 54, 133 and 135), Heiler (p. 379), Keller (p. 28), Mensching (pp. 24 and 26), Stauffer, 'Jesus . . .', (p. 40).

[e] Cf.: Buddhalehre (pp. 143 *et seq.*), Falke (pp. 54, 130 and 136), Keller (p. 34), Mensching (p. 191), 'Universelle Religion', Nos 7/8, 1973.

[f] Cf.: Trede (pp. 98 and 109 *et seq.*), Keller (pp. 36 *et seq.*).

[g] Cf.: Leipoldt, 'Die Religion des Mithra' and Mensching, 'Dionysos' (p. 24).

[h] Cf.: Falke (p. 54), Jordan (p. 226), Leipoldt, 'Dionysos' (p. 51), Mensching (p. 28), 'Universelle Religion', Nos 7/8, 1973.

[i] Bhagavadgita VII (p. 25).

Chapter 3 When Miracles Do Happen

[1] MICHAEL FALTZ, *Bernadette, die Seherin von Lourdes*, Fribourg, 1954.

[2] ALPHONSE OLIVIERI, DR. *Y-a-t'il encore des miracles à Lourdes?*, Paris, 1969.

[3] ALPHONSE OLIVIERI, *Gibt es noch Wunder in Lourdes?*, Aschaffenburg, 1973.

[4] A. M. FRIARD, *Lourdes und seine Wunder*, Wels (A), 1953.

[5] DR FRANZ L. SCHLEYER, *Die Heilungen von Lourdes, eine kritische Untersuchung*, Bonn, 1949.

[6] RENÉ LAURENTIN, *Les Apparitions de Lourdes*, Paris, 1966.

[7] *Die geweihten Stätten der heilgen Jungfrau von Lourdes* (Ed. 'werk der Höhle'), Lourdes, 1948.

[8] ANDREAS RAVIER, *Bernadette und ihr Rosenkranz*, Nevers, Saint-Gildard Convent, undated.

[9] *Ibid., Lourdes, Land der frohen Botschaft*, Nevers, Saint-Gildard Convent, undated.

[10] APIO GARCIA, *Bodas de ouro de Fatima*, Lisbon, undated.

[11] GILBERT RENAULT, *Fatima, esperanca do mundo*, Paris, 1957.

[12] 'Kinder von Fatima', Mitteilungsblatt über die Seligsprechungsprozesse von Franz und Jacinta, from 1968/2 to 1973/4.

[13] MARIA WINOWSKA, *The True Face of Padre Pio*, London, 1961.

RAOUL VILLEDIEU, *Das Geheimnis des Pater Pio*, Aschaffenburg, 1966.

[14] DR JOSEF HANAUER, *Konnersreuth als Tesfall*, Munich, 1972
JOHANNES STEINER, *Therese Neumann von Konnersreuth, ein Lebensbild nach authentischen Berichten*, Munich, 1967.

[15] PROF. DR MED. O. PROKOP, *Medizinischer Okkultismus*, Jena, 1973.

[16] DR HANS SELYE, *The Stress of Life*, London, 1957.

[17] RICHARD SERJEANT, *Der Schmerz*, Bergisch-Gladbach, 1970.

[18] H. J. CAMPBELL, *The Pleasure Zones*, London, 1973.

[19] LESLIE M. LECRON, *Selbsthypnose*, Geneva, 1973.

[20] DR A. PLOEGER, *Psychodrama-Therapie*, Paderborn, 1970.

[21] PROF. ILZA VEITH, 'Psychiatric Thought in Chinese Medicine' (Journal of the History of Medicine and Allied Sciences, Vol. X, 1955/3).

[22] DR G. A. LEUTZ, *Übertragung, Einführung und Tele im Psychodrama*, Paderborn, 1970.

[23] DR H. J. VON SCHUMANN, 'Antike Inkubation und autogenes Training', Medizinische Monatschrift, 1968/3.

[24] KURT POLLACK, *Wissen und Weisheit der alten Ärzte*, Düsseldorf, 1968.

RUDOLF HERZOG, *Die Wunderheilung von Epidauros, ein Beitrag zur Geschichte der Medizin und Religion*, 1931.

[25] OTTO WEINREICH, 'Eine delphische Mirakelinschrift und die antiken Haarwunder.' Sitzungsbericht der Heidelberger Akademie der Wissenschaften, Heidelberg, 1925.

[26] ADOLF ERMAN, *Ägypten und ägyptisches Leben im Altertum*, Tübingen, 1923.

[27] SAMUEL J. WARNER, *Ein Psychotherapeut berichtet*, Düsseldorf, 1969.

[28] T. P. KLEINHANS, 'Der Karlsruher Ärztekrieg', Merck-Spiegel, 1969/4.

[29] L. MONDEN, *Theologie des Wunders*, Freiburg, 1961.

[30] PROF. D. LANGEN, 'Hypnose und Meditation', Lecture to the Religio-Philosophical Society, Munich, 1965.

[31] DR E. W. STIEFVATER, 'Beiträge zum Problem des Magnetismus,' Erfahrungsheilkunde, 1951.

[32] PARAMAHAMSA YOGANANDA, *Autobiography of a Yogi*, London, 1950.

Ibid., Wissenschaftliche Heilmeditation, Weilheim, 1972.

[33] THEOPRASTUS VON HOHENHEIM (known as 'Paracelsus'), *Sämtliche Werke*, Ed. Karl Südhoff, Section I, Vol. 7, pp. 328-334.

[34] LADISLAUS BOROS, *Pain and Providence*, London, 1966.

[35] PARAMAHAMSA YOGANANDA, *Wissenschaftliche Heilmeditation*, Weilheim, 1972.

[36] INGE SANTNER, 'Als hätte der Tod sie nie berührt', Die Weltwoche, 12 July, 1974.

[37] KURT TUCHOLSKY, *Ein Pyrenäenbuch*, Reinbek, 1962.

[38] ERNST BLOCH, *Atheismus im Christentum*, Reinbek, 1970.

Chapter 4 Visions Do Exist

[1] ERICH VON DÄNIKEN, *The Gold of the Gods*, Souvenir Press, London, 1973.

[2] ERICH VON DÄNIKEN, *Return to the Stars*, Souvenir Press, London, 1970.

[3] A. EDDINGTON, *The Nature of the Psychic World*, Cambridge, 1928.

[4] BERNHARD BAVINK, *Die Naturwissenschaft auf dem Wege zur Religion*, 1946.

[5] J. J. JEANS, *The Universe Around Us*, Cambridge, 1929.

[6] DR A. FREIHERR VON SCHRENCK-NOTZING, *Materializations-Phänomene*, Munich, 1923.

[7] JEAN-BAPTISTE DELACOUR, *Aus dem Jenseits zurück*, Dusseldorf.

[8] FRIEDRICH JÜRGENSON, *Rösterna från Rymden*, Stockholm, 1964.

[9] DR KONSTANTIN RAUDIVE, *Breakthrough*, Gerrards Cross, 1971.

[10] FRANZ SEIDEL, *Phänomen Transzendentalstimmen*, Stuttgart, 1971.

[11] DR KONSTANTIN RAUDIVE, *Erfahrungen mit dem Stimmenphänomen*.

[12] THORWALD DETHLEFSEN, *Das Leben nach dem Leben*, Munich, 1974.

[13] MOREY BERNSTEIN, *Protokoll einer Wiedergeburt*, Berne, 1973.

[14] ARTHUR FORD, *The Life Beyond Death*, London, 1972.

[15] BELLINE, *Das dritte Ohr, ein Dialog mit dem Jenseits*, Bonn, 1973.

[16] BERNHARD PHILBERTH, *Christliche Prophetie und Nuklearenergie*, Wuppertal, 1966.

[17] NOSTRADAMUS, *Prophetische Weltgeschichte*, Bietigheim, 1971.

[18] JEANE DIXON, *My Life and Prophecies* – as told to René Noorbergen, London, 1971.

[19] DR RENÉ LAURENTIN, *Les Apparitions de Lourdes, Récit authentique . . .*, Paris, 1966.

[20] *Ibid.*, Vol. 2, *L'enfance de Bernadette et les premières appar-*

itions, 7 January 1844-18 Feb., 1858, Paris/Lourdes, undated.

[21] *Ibid., Lourdes, Documents authentiques,* Vols I and II, Paris.

[22] JACQUES HOCHMANN, *Thesen zu einer Gemeindepsychiatrie,* Frankfurt, 1973.

[23] FRANCIS CRICK and LESLIE ORGEL, 'Directed Panspermia', Icarus, Vol. 19, p. 341.

[24] ULRICH SCHIPPKE, 'Der Stoff, aus dem Gedanken sind', Stern, No 28/4.7.1974.

[25] WERNER KELLER, *Was gestern noch als Wunder galt,* Munich, 1973.

[26] PAUWELS L. F., and BERGIER, J., *Aufbruch ins dritte Jahrtausend,* Berne, 1962.

[27] G. B. SHAW.